Foreign Fighters

Foreign Fighters

*Transnational Identity
in Civil Conflicts*

DAVID MALET

OXFORD
UNIVERSITY PRESS

OXFORD
UNIVERSITY PRESS

Oxford University Press is a department of the University of Oxford.
It furthers the University's objective of excellence in research, scholarship,
and education by publishing worldwide.

Oxford   New York
Auckland   Cape Town   Dar es Salaam   Hong Kong   Karachi
Kuala Lumpur   Madrid   Melbourne   Mexico City   Nairobi
New Delhi   Shanghai   Taipei   Toronto

With offices in
Argentina   Austria   Brazil   Chile   Czech Republic   France   Greece
Guatemala   Hungary   Italy   Japan   Poland   Portugal   Singapore
South Korea   Switzerland   Thailand   Turkey   Ukraine   Vietnam

Oxford is a registered trademark of Oxford University Press
in the UK and certain other countries.

Published in the United States of America by
Oxford University Press
198 Madison Avenue, New York, NY 10016

Library of Congress Cataloging-in-Publication Data
Malet, David.
Foreign fighters : transnational identity in civil conflicts / David Malet.
pages cm
Includes bibliographical references and index.
ISBN 978-0-19-993945-9 (hardback : alk. paper)
1. Insurgency.   2. Special forces (Military science)   I. Title.
JC328.5.M34 2013
355.3'3–dc23
2012046792

ISBN 978-0-19-993945-9

To Michelle Malet
Thank you for your love, strength, and patience

Contents

Acknowledgments

IT IS DIFFICULT to identify the moment of conception of this work. Apparently, I first pitched the idea to my wife while hiking in the Baga Khentii in Mongolia in July 2005, although I do not remember having had it until months later. Questioning the construct of "the international system" early in my doctoral program had led to an interest in applications of systems theory and social network analysis to contemporary international security issues. But it probably began many years before that with my grandparents, Shum and Alma Malet, who gave me love, support, and a love of learning that made everything possible.

For the realization of this book, my gratitude goes to David McBride and the staff of Oxford University Press for their interest in this project and their investment of patience, as well as the two anonymous reviewers who provided very useful feedback and suggestions. Along the way, a number of mentors and colleagues provided invaluable assistance in developing and refining this study. First and foremost is Martha Finnemore, for serving as my advisor, and without whom this project would never have been begun, still less completed. My gratitude goes out as well to my dissertation committee members James Goldgeier, Marc Lynch, and Deborah Avant, and reviewers Paul D. Williams and James Lebovic.

I received early assistance with research design and implementation from Christopher Deering, James Rosenau, Erik Voeten, Susan Sell, Holger Schmidt, Elizabeth Saunders, Chad Rector, Robert Stoker, Michael Brown, and Matthew O'Gara. I also received useful suggestions and vital support from John Schulz, Bernard Finel, Miriam Anderson, Michael Schroeder, Gallia Lindenstrauss, Jennie Schulze, Jeffrey Hornung, Davy Banks, Aaron Dusso, Maryam Zarnegar Deloffre, Pete Sickle, Enze Han, Christopher Dallas-Feeney, Joseph O'Mahoney, Stephanie Kaplan, and Maria Rublee.

I also received generous assistance in obtaining and reviewing information about the case studies I researched: Thomas Hegghammer, who shared several megabytes of files, and Najib Lafraie were instrumental to the chapter on Afghanistan, and Jared Reene provided information about foreign fighters in Iraq. I am grateful to the Machalniks who answered my surveys on the Israeli War of Independence and particularly for the assistance I received from World MACHAL staff Doreen Bliss, Joe Woolf, and Smoky Simon in Israel; from David Susman, Ute Ben Yosef, and Julie Berman in South Africa; and from Oren Barak, Howard Kohr, and David J. Bercusson for introducing me to the MACHAL story and reviewing my work.

Stephen Hardin, Kevin Klaus of the Texas General Land Office, Bruce Winders, Elaine Davis, and the staff of the Daughters of the Republic of Texas Library were of tremendous help in researching a conflict never covered in the international security literature. And for the Spanish Civil War chapter, I received assistance in searching the largest archives on the subject from Lynda Corey Claassen and the staff of the Mandeville Special Collections Library at the University of California San Diego, from Gail Malmgreen and the staff of the Abraham Lincoln Brigade Archive at the Tamiment Library and Robert F. Wagner Labor Archives of New York University, and from Candace Frost and Russell and Jill Levan for hosting me at each location. My cousin Sophia Levan, then 15 years old, was the only person who ever suggested a historical foreign fighter case (Lord Byron in the Greek War of Independence) that I had not already considered and was able to add to my data set.

In completing the project, I received the support of the Foreign Policy Research Institute, and particularly Michael Noonan, which commissioned me to produce a paper for the Foreign Fighter Problem Conference in July 2009. That material was subsequently reprinted both in the conference report and in the winter 2010 issue of *Orbis, A Journal of World Affairs*, and it appears in this manuscript as well, particularly in the conclusion. Dan Miodownik, Oren Barak, and the Leonard Davis Institute of International Affairs at Hebrew University in Jerusalem hosted me at their May 2009 workshop on the Global Effects and Local Dynamics of Intrastate Conflicts, giving me access to valuable feedback from other participants and the chance to conduct additional research at the World MACHAL office in Tel Aviv.

Mohammed Hafez provided valuable feedback on an earlier version of this manuscript. Clinton Watts has provided current data on foreign fighters, as well as advice and support on multiple occasions. Finally, I thank the United States Special Forces Command staff for their interest in and support of this line of research.

Foreign Fighters

Introduction

Why Foreign Fighters?

IN JUNE 2007, authorities in Lebanon arrested several men of diverse nationalities with ties to the Fatah al-Islam militant group that had just launched attacks against Lebanese military installations. Among them was Ahmed Elomar, the undefeated Australian Super Featherweight boxing champion. Elomar, whose uncle was one of several Lebanese Australians arrested in 2005 for plotting an Islamist terror attack in Sydney, had departed two months earlier without informing his friends of his whereabouts. His trainer told reporters that Elomar was "a great bloke" and "he could have been at the wrong place at the wrong time, that is what I am desperately hoping"[1] (Pandaram and O'Laughlin, 2007).

How did Fatah al-Islam apparently involve an Australian sports celebrity in the civil conflict in Lebanon? Although the group's leadership would be unlikely to acknowledge it, they probably employed the same strategy that a Zionist organization called Haganah used in the late 1940s to recruit a Sephardic Jew of Iraqi descent who grew up in London's Whitechapel slums. The young man's father had abandoned him at an early age, and his mother had arranged for him to cover expenses by finding employment as a hairdresser. She also imparted her identification with antifascist and Zionist political movements to the degree that "the passion that I felt about these issues" led him in 1948 to Palestine to fight for the creation of a Jewish state. After the establishment of Israel, Vidal Sassoon returned to London to resume his career, later using his financial success to found the International Center for the Study of Anti-Semitism at Hebrew University in Jerusalem (Rennie, 2006).

The same practices had been used a decade earlier by the Communist International to recruit the son of a wealthy Paris stockbroker in yet another civil war, and he soon used these methods to become a recruiter himself. Despite a reported affliction with Tourette's syndrome and a conviction for antiquities theft, André Malraux was a noted author when he organized a successful recruitment drive at the Paris Palais du Sport for 100 pilots to join him in flying combat missions for the Loyalist side in the Spanish Civil War (Edwards, 1997). Despite being wounded twice in combat and having violated French neutrality laws, he returned to France to pen a popular novel about the war and later serve in both the French military and the underground resistance movement (Liukonnen, 2007).

Malraux recruited transnational insurgents using the same strategy as an American politician who had risen from a rural Huguenot family to be elected to multiple terms in the U.S. Congress beginning in the 1820s. Despite the national success of his lecture circuit tour, he told voters during his final campaign that, if he lost, "You may all go to Hell, and I will go to Texas." He fulfilled this threat in January 1836, leading a score of followers into the ranks of separatists in Mexico. Within two months, Davy Crockett was killed at the Battle of the Alamo. The following year, the town of Crockett was incorporated in the newly independent Republic of Texas, which would exist as a sovereign state for nearly a decade (Elliot, 1944).

The Communist nephew of Winston Churchill, the baron whose poetry had made him a leading figure in the Romantic movement, the decorated World War II veteran of the Queen's Own Rifles and heir to a chain of Canadian clothing stores, the scion of a Saudi construction and equity group who would become an icon to generations of insurgents—each of these individuals and tens of thousands of other foreigners fighting in modern civil wars were, if not in direct violation of the laws of their own country and the international community, at least acting against commonly accepted norms of military service, under which individuals are presumed to owe allegiance to their own country and to fight on its behalf and not that of an external group.

Just how did various insurgencies, operating across the globe in different decades, recruit outside the conflict zones and draw in individuals who would seem neither to have had a direct stake in the conflict outcome nor to have been likely mercenaries? Despite the historic and rising numbers of foreign fighters, and despite a good number of studies that address how nonstate armed groups are successful in recruiting combatants at the subnational level in civil conflicts, researchers have largely overlooked transnational recruitment until recently. And empirical evidence indicates that foreign fighters do not appear to mobilize for the same reasons that the civil conflict literature assigns to local rebels.

Although the growing body of work on transnational terrorist recruitment provides useful insights, it is focused specifically on contemporary Islamist networks that clearly do not apply to prominent historical cases of foreign fighters. It is apparent from the historical records that Islamism is neither necessary nor sufficient to explain foreign fighters. But given the recent international attention to Islamist foreign fighters, it might initially seem easy to imagine what messages recruiters use and to whom, how, and where they target their appeals. The reality, however, is far more complicated.

Many foreign fighters have been secular; they and others have shared neither ties of ethnic kinship nor homeland with the local insurgents they joined. How, then, did the insurgencies promote their causes abroad? As noted, a number of well-known foreign fighters already possessed significant wealth before becoming combatants. What kinds of appeals motivate foreigners to travel to unfamiliar war zones to engage in high-risk behavior? How do recruiters try to persuade their targets to join rebel groups in distant states instead of fighting for political changes in their own country? Why join groups that are nearly always at a material disadvantage relative to their enemies, confer no legal protection upon their combatants, and usually lose their conflicts, often because they are battling not just fragmented local governments, but their hegemonic benefactors as well?

This study seeks to answer the question of what messages insurgencies use to recruit foreign fighters. The answer is highly consequential because of the overwhelming evidence that insurgent groups are reinforcing their ranks both by dispatching recruiters to distant states and, increasingly, by using the Internet. Journalists and intelligence agencies have recently documented active foreign fighter recruitment programs by insurgents in Iraq (Whitlock, 2007), Afghanistan (Witte and Hussain, 2009), Pakistan (Whitlock, 2009), and Somalia (Elliot, 2009, 2010). If insurgencies actively recruit, there must by definition be some recruitment message, some rationale offered to relatively prosperous Westerners to risk their lives in distant benighted countries (in these cases, for Americans to fight in Somalia or Germans to fight in Afghanistan). If enough individuals were joining spontaneously, then insurgencies would not need to devote resources to recruitment. And while some foreign fighters do join insurgencies under their own volition rather than being brought in by recruiters, they, too, can be observed to have internalized and been motivated by the narrative of the conflict promoted by recruiters.

Although "greed"-based models of civil conflict mobilization suggest that insurgencies draw local participants through the prospect of loot or pay, the empirical evidence indicates that recruiters rarely promise foreign fighters material incentives. Instead, most transnational volunteers receive very limited or no offers of compensation but then still engage in costlier military actions than do local fighters. How, then, do recruiters solicit costly actions made even riskier because they violate international laws and norms of national military service? How can counterinsurgency planners respond to what appears to be a growing wave of transnational violence?

A number of works have attempted to analyze the origins and motives of foreign fighters in the Iraq War,[2] but there have not been cross-case studies determining whether the recruitment mechanisms of transnational insurgents in Iraq were unique to that specific conflict or are comparable to those for foreign fighters in other civil wars. This question is particularly pertinent with the international presence in Iraq concluded and security concerns focusing more on other areas of intrastate conflict that also feature foreign fighters, such as Afghanistan, Yemen, Somalia, and, more recently, Syria, Nigeria, and Mali.

Foreign Fighter Recruitment Messaging

Surprisingly, the evidence from extremely diverse historical cases of foreign fighters indicates a common approach to recruitment messages and mechanisms regardless of the particulars of the conflict: Insurgencies try to recruit foreign fighters by framing distant civil conflicts as posing a dire threat to all members of a transnational community of which both the foreign recruits and local insurgents are members. The precise relationship between the insurgents—shared ethnicity or some other tie such as religion—and the particulars of the conflict are irrelevant to the logic of transnational recruitment, which consistently emphasizes existential threat.

Recruitment occurs when local insurgents, who always begin conflicts as the weaker faction because they do not control the instruments of the state, attempt to broaden the scope of conflict to increase their resources and maximize their chances of victory. However, due precisely to their lack of resources, they typically must motivate outsiders to join them for reasons other than material gain. They therefore frame their victory in the conflict as necessary to the interests of outsiders with whom they share connections and who might be credibly convinced by these claims. Ironically, as U.S. forces engaged with transnational insurgents in Iraq to "fight them over there so we don't have to fight them at home," their opponents offered precisely the same argument.[3]

Recruitment efforts therefore typically follow the same model:

1. Insurgencies, initially the weaker factions in civil conflicts, attempt to strengthen their forces by obtaining outside support, including manpower and specialists.
2. They target outside groups expected to identify with their cause because of some relation to the insurgents. Sometimes they have success in

obtaining aid from foreign governments; in other instances, they find assistance more forthcoming from nonstate groups with whom they have an existing relationship because of shared ties of ethnicity, religion, or ideology.

3. Among these transnational groups, the most receptive members of the audience are individuals who are highly active in the institutions of that community and identify with it closely but who tend to be marginalized within their broader polities, often because they are part of some minority group. Community social structures therefore provide both the rationale and the mechanism for participation.

4. Recruiters tell potential recruits that their common group is under existential threat and that their participation is necessary for the survival of their people and, ultimately, themselves.

Data from across historical cases indicate that recruitment occurs via the social networks of the transnational communities, and potential recruits are generally highly connected to these identity subgroups rather than to their wider national society. Legal restrictions against recruitment tend to force insurgent groups to target selectively rather than advertise to mass audiences. The use of social group networks for recruitment also permits recruiters to employ social pressures to join.

In some instances, there is an obvious tie of ethnicity or other immediate connection between domestic and foreign insurgents. In others, recruiters manipulate identities to make them salient, strategically using messaging to activate a sense of appropriate obligation or duty to the common group. When possible, recruiting organizations engage in displacement, broadening the definition of the involved group to a wider pool of potential recruits, thereby enlarging the scope of conflict and altering the balance of forces. The group identity that enables recruiters to frame the distant war as self-defense is constructed; the messaging of self-defense remains constant.

As one person's freedom fighter is another's terrorist, the validity of the causes that justify fighting, killing, and violating citizenship is subject to debate. But no matter how real or imagined the threat to the recruits, the recruiters engage in operations similar to Madison Avenue advertising executives: identifying a target audience, creating emotive responses over matters that may have previously seemed of little import, and reframing the message when initial approaches do not meet goals.

An example of this strategy was evident in Morocco, where Islamist groups recruiting foreign fighters maintained "watchers" at "radical" mosques and other places where people expressed anger about the occupations of Iraq and Palestine (rather than, notably, Moroccan affairs). The watchers discussed social justice and the duty to intervene on behalf of fellow Muslims with likely prospects and then subjected them to background security checks and psychological assessments for willingness to die for their cause. Those who passed were assigned a handler, who smuggled them out of the country on false passports to a training and indoctrination center abroad prior to entering the conflict (Whitlock, 2007). In a bit of irony that would probably be lost on the watchers, this procedure is nearly identical to the practices used by Communist and Zionist recruiters decades before them.

The Significance of Transnational Insurgency

The impact of this effort in the theater of conflict has been considerable. In 2005, NBC News reported that an investigation of foreign fighters killed in the conflict in Iraq indicated that, while the majority were citizens of Arab states bordering Iraq, there were at least 21 nationalities among the 400 combatants (Myers, 2005). Another report the same year indicated that although transnational insurgents comprised less than 10 percent of the Iraqi resistance, they were responsible for more than 90 percent of suicide bombings and high-lethality attacks (Quinn and Shrader, 2005).

Studies of civil conflicts predict that spillover effects and cross-border activity by insurgents will draw in participants from adjacent territory concerned with their own security or enticed by the prospect of looting. But if insurgents travel from too far away to be explained by regional violence and are engaging in suicide operations, then the prevailing explanations for recruiting rebels do not explain the presence of foreign fighters. And though it might be convenient to dismiss many among the current crop as religious fanatics who are offered paradise, this explanation does not cover the full range of ethnic nationalists and atheist Communists who joined other distant wars. But did these transnational insurgents also behave more aggressively than locals, as contemporary foreign fighters in Iraq have done? If so, what lessons would this provide about conflict recruitment and counterinsurgency planning? If not, what insights might we glean from the differences across cases?

Some observers contend that the Islamic social institutions in these regions do not distinguish secular from religious authority, making state boundaries irrelevant. Abdullah Azzam—regarded as Osama bin Laden's mentor—had in fact called for Muslims to give up their "narrow nationalism" based on "borders drawn by non-believers" and fight for the global Islamic community

(Zeidan, 2001: 44). Certainly, international boundaries drawn by colonial powers have not carried the salience for foreign fighters in the Middle East or South Asia that they have for counterinsurgency and counterterrorism planners.

Rather, it is the violation of the laws and norms of citizenship of the state-centric international system that have made foreign fighters a noteworthy phenomenon to states and their militaries. In particular, the United States developed the policy in late 2001 of differentiating local militants in Afghanistan, who were offered amnesty, from those from elsewhere, who were subject to indefinite detention and enhanced interrogation techniques (Worthington, 2007: 5–11), and focused on the small but deadly contingent of foreign fighters in Iraq as threats to postinvasion nation building.

Beginning with the work of Reuven Paz in 2005, published quantitative analyses of non-Iraqi militants in that conflict indicated something distinctive about those actors but did not directly address whether the foreign fighters examined might not view themselves as foreign. For the purposes of this study, I retain the distinction of foreign fighters primarily because the data show that local insurgents treat volunteers from abroad quite differently than they do native combatants. However, it would be useful for both students of international relations and practitioners of counterinsurgency operations to consider the extent to which citizens of developed countries have been trained to see a world of states while their subjects likely would paint their globes quite differently.

Research Design

The object of this study is to examine what recruitment pitch insurgencies and their agents abroad offer to target audiences and to analyze why they expected them to be effective. I also describe how recruits reported receiving and understanding these messages across disparate civil conflicts, but the data are insufficient to support determinations that particular frames were more successful than others in producing volunteers. Even among well-documented cases, self-reported explanations for joining exist from only dozens of recruits out of thousands in each instance. Additionally, many recruits who did not record their experiences may have had ulterior motives, such as adventure or profits, in addition to the rationale for fighting offered by recruiters. Although we can observe whether the rationales offered by recruiters were absorbed by their target audience, as reflected in recruits' statements about their participation, we cannot verify whether this messaging is actually what prompted their activity.

In fact, it is extremely problematic to collect reliable data about why individuals engage in political behavior of any sort. It is for this reason that public opinion researchers create elaborate experiments designed to reproduce decision-making conditions. Even asking voters to retrospectively identify which candidate they voted for proves to be unreliable. Without valid experiments that mimic transnational recruitment by insurgencies, the problem is far more acute in explaining why individuals choose to go fight for a distant rebel group.

Another limitation on the research, one that makes it problematic to conclude whether certain recruitment efforts were more effective than others, is the lack of available original records. In each of the in-depth case studies I present, there are anecdotes of failed or modified recruitment efforts or of individuals who ultimately decided not to become foreign fighters. But there are not enough data available to justify conclusions about whether particular efforts were more or less effective than others because we do not necessarily know how many potential volunteers recruiters reached or attempted to reach in each instance.

A more approachable question, and perhaps a more interesting one, is why the recruiters select the messages that they do. How do these organizations attempt to sell recruits on engaging in high-cost, high-risk behavior (e.g., attacking the U.S. military from a position of material disadvantage) when their interests would not appear to be at stake? We would reasonably expect that if insurgencies hope to gain volunteers through the promise of loot or excitement that they would advertise opportunities for pillage and the probability of success. Instead, many emphasize adversity and threat. Why do they expect these appeals to be successful, and how do they choose their targets for recruitment? How do they respond to successes and failures, both in recruiting and on the battlefield? What, if any, lessons do they learn from prior recruitment efforts in other conflicts?

This information is available to us in the better documented cases, where the rationales recruiters offered for participation have survived in the form of propaganda pamphlets, broadsides, and recordings. Whether greed, grievance, or some other cause (self-defense, as I argue), the message that the recruiters used can be evaluated, and it is also possible to determine whether these rationales are reflected in the statements of the recruits.

Definitions: What Is a Foreign Fighter?

Although transnational insurgencies have existed for centuries, the fact that political scientists have not perceived them as a singular type of phenomenon is evident from the lack of an existing term in the discipline used to describe the concept. Indeed, prior to studies of foreign mujahidin in post–Saddam Hussein Iraq, it is difficult to locate any studies of the motivations or operations of transnational insurgents as compared with locals or with foreign fighters in other conflicts. This lacuna comes despite successive generations of transnational insurgents attempting to legitimize their activities by directly comparing their actions with those taken by other foreigner rebels in other wars.[4]

When I began research on this project in 2005, I was therefore required to define the parameters of what counted as a foreign fighter and to determine how many instances of them there had been to make any inferences or valid case selections. Without shared meanings, it is impossible for different researchers to analyze the same propositions, and conceptualization and justification of which data are to be included are necessary initial steps of research. Although I find *transnational insurgent* to be more meaningfully descriptive, I use it interchangeably with *foreign fighter* because the latter term has been widely employed in popular media reports (see appendix A for the emergent use of the term in the discourse), and it has been my experience that it generates wider and more immediate recognition of the concept.[5]

In this study, *foreign fighters* are defined as "noncitizens of conflict states who join insurgencies during civil conflicts." This definition does not include belligerents enlisted in a foreign state's military that is ordered into the conflict, such as German and Italian forces in the Spanish Civil War; foreigners who join another state's regular military for pay or citizenship, such as French Foreign Legionnaires; or employees of private security companies (PSCs) under contract in a state where they are not citizens. (See chapter 2 for a discussion of these types of actors.)

Service with state militaries or PSCs does not require individual efforts to, usually illegally, travel to a foreign conflict zone. State-affiliated combatants enjoy legal protections, can reasonably expect to be compensated, and, considering that states usually defeat insurgencies, can expect to survive to enjoy their compensation. Their recruiters can make credible offers of payment and victory in a way that most insurgencies cannot. For the same reason, most insurgencies are not in the position to hire PSCs to fight for them. Likewise, the evidence indicates that foreign fighters in a number of civil conflicts (including the Spanish Civil War, the Israeli War of Independence, and the Iraq War) were told directly during the recruitment process that they could expect only token payments.

It is also important to note that the term *insurgency* holds slightly different meanings for different readers, with some preferring it to describe particular technologies of combat, usually the employment of guerrilla warfare. Rebels who employ guerrilla tactics are certainly following the dictums of notable insurgent leaders, such as Mao Zedong and Ché Guevara, of the need for asymmetric attacks while the insurgency gains its strength against a more powerful adversary. However, this strategy is only the temporary means to the ultimate goal of seizing power. When the Communists finally took Beijing and Havana, they had become the superior conventional forces and no longer needed to rely on hit-and-run attacks and retreat into the bushes. Rebel groups are therefore insurgents against the state regime regardless of whether they are strong enough to confront it conventionally. The recruitment of foreign fighters represents a strategic decision by rebel groups to attempt to leapfrog the need for guerrilla tactics by assembling a conventional force through greater manpower and technical proficiency.

Modelski (in Rosenau, 1964: 14) defines an *insurgency* as a faction in an internal war that does not control the legitimate (i.e., internationally recognized) machinery of the state and is therefore (at least initially) in the weaker position. For the purposes of this study of civil wars, I employ Kalyvas's (2006: 17) definition of an "armed conflict within the boundaries of a recognized sovereign entity between parties subject to a common authority at the outset of hostilities."

Historical Data

Discerning how transnational recruiters for insurgencies attempt to accomplish their objectives requires examining the available information in two stages. First, as there were no existing comparative studies of foreign fighters to draw upon, in stage 1 of the project I used the Correlates of War (COW) Intrastate War 1816–1997 and the Uppsala-PRIO Intrastate Conflict 1946–2005 to create an observation set of civil conflicts over the past 200 years and determine which involved transnational insurgents. The COW and Uppsala-PRIO have coded them as civil wars and identified the government and insurgent forces for each, rendering historical and contemporary cases comparable.

Of the 331 civil conflicts contained in the set, I was able to document the presence of foreign fighters in 70, meaning that foreign fighters have participated in more than one in five civil wars over the past 200 years. I used the data to test the hypothesis that foreign fighters are less likely to appear in ethnic conflicts, an expectation generated by claims in the literature that foreign intervention in civil wars is likelier when more universal values, such as ideology or religion, are at stake than when the object is a question of which individual or group will control a particular government. With the expectation advanced by numerous scholars that globalized communications are building new identity cleavages that mobilize transnational civil society, I also tested the hypothesis that the number of transnational insurgencies has increased over time.

The results contribute to the theoretical literature on civil conflicts and also yield new data that should be of interest in counterinsurgency planning. The data show that transnational insurgencies occur mostly in nonethnic conflicts and that they have been increasing both in absolute numbers and relative to the total number of insurgencies. Additionally, foreign fighters are not more likely to appear in conflicts in the Middle East despite the rise in Islamist mujahidin, and transnational insurgencies win civil conflicts at a rate disproportionate to other insurgencies. They also indicate that, while it may be evolving and is perhaps most prominent today in Muslim societies, transnationalism is a long-standing phenomenon that has also motivated a wide array of individuals in the Western world to participate in contentious politics and armed conflict.

Case Study Selection and Findings

Despite providing useful information, the data in stage 1 do not address the central question of which message or messages were employed in recruitment; stage 2 therefore consists of process tracing in historical examples of recruitment efforts. I use the data coded on transnational insurgencies to establish a typology that delineates between insurgencies based on the relation of the foreign fighters to the locals and the issue of contention of the conflict.

I selected cases from each type, representing each combination of the variables of ethnic conflict and coethnicity of transnational with local fighters: the Texas Revolution (1835–36), the Spanish Civil War (1936–39), the Israeli War of Independence (1947–49), and the Afghanistan War (1978–92). Each of these cases was also significant in leading to the present global ubiquity of foreign fighters. Although some individual participants reported being motivated by other incentives, usually adventure, regardless of the particulars of the conflict, recruiters framed their local insurgencies as defenses against broader threats to transnational communities. These included obvious forms of social organization, such as ethnic or religious groupings, but also purely ideological categories as well. In some conflicts, when the insurgents did not believe that their approach was generating enough transnational recruits, they reframed the conflict as threatening a different group to try to draw a larger potential audience. Although recruiters did provide pay and selective incentives, recruits were typically informed at the outset that these would be minimal and that the likelihood of casualties was high.

Structure of Analysis

To explain why this counterintuitive strategy would be common across highly disparate cases, I examine in chapter 1 competing theoretical claims concerning recruitment and mobilization for civil conflict and military service. If recruiters elect to base their appeals on defensive mobilization and norms of group membership, why should they assume this strategy will be successful? Why might such methods be fruitful in cases like the Spanish Civil War, where the foreigners shared no evident common traits of ethnicity, religion, language, or homeland ties? To construct an explanatory framework, I explore the theoretical contributions of an array of fields concerning mobilizing collective action and social identity formation.

I next turn in chapter 2 to an empirical evaluation of the role of foreign fighters in modern civil conflicts. I begin with a historical overview of participation by nonstate foreign nationals in wartime, as well as an examination of policy responses by states. This is followed by the introduction of the observation set and typology and the data derived from them. Following these conclusions, I present the research design I use to structure the case studies selected from the typology.

Each of the subsequent four chapters offers a detailed case history of how a different type of insurgency recruited transnationally. Chapter 3 examines the evolution of recruitment messaging in the Texas Revolution. What began as a call to defend fellow democrats in Mexico against military dictatorship, financed by border-spanning business interests seeking to roll back Mexican centralism, morphed into a crusade to defend white settlers against rapacious Hispanic soldiers. Chapter 4 moves forward a century to the Spanish Civil War and the creation of a common antifascist identity by the Comintern to aid in the recruitment of the International Brigades, as well as the countereffort on the Fascist side to mobilize Catholics worldwide to defend the church against Communism. Chapter 5 presents the recruitment of Diaspora Jews into MACHAL during the 1948 Israeli War of Independence, as well as the responsive formation of the transnational Arab Liberation Army on the opposing side. Chapter 6 examines the role of the enduring conflict in Afghanistan that resulted in the formation of a transnational corps of mujahidin that decades later continued to operate around the globe.

In the conclusion, I present the most recent large case of foreign fighters, the Iraq War, and compare contemporary foreign fighter activity to historical cases. Finally, I suggest what lessons policy makers might draw for conflict reduction and peace building from the lengthy history of foreign fighters in civil conflicts.

I

Why We Fight (Elsewhere)

I come here not in search of adventures, but to assist the regeneration of a Nation. . . . Firstly because they will sooner listen to a foreigner than one of their own people, out of native jealousies; secondly, because the Turks will sooner treat or capitulate (if such occasion should happen) with a Frank than a Greek; and thirdly, because nobody else seems disposed to take the responsibility. . . .

—GEORGE GORDON BYRON[1]

WHILE LORD BYRON may be revered by lovers of poetry for shaping the ethos of the Romantic era, many scholars of political conflict would not be persuaded by his romantic explanation for joining and recruiting others to join a distant insurgency. Although there are a number of contending explanations for insurgent mobilization in civil wars, many tend to rely on material incentives for rousing belligerents. Foreign participants in the literature on civil wars and terrorism tend to be portrayed either as mercenaries or as martyrdom-seeking Islamic fundamentalists who do not pay heed to secular state borders.

However, these models do not adequately explain the many examples such as Byron's London Greek Committee (with no Greek members), which requested funds from the public, sent recruits to battle against the Ottoman Empire, and brought the survivors home again after their victory without claiming land. With material incentives as a motivator, insurgencies that begin conflicts as the weaker faction would have to be able to make credible promises of victory, or at least plunder, a part of their appeal to draw foreigners who bear the cost and risk of travel to an unfamiliar war zone. Requesting money to fund the war effort from the same target audience, as many transnational insurgencies do, would seem an unlikely strategy for making credible mercenary appeals.

This chapter examines what incentives might be used to persuade individuals to fight and die, seemingly for strangers and when their own interests would not appear to be at stake. I first examine contending explanations for participation in civil conflicts and wars in general. How do insurgencies mobilize, and how might foreign recruits differ from locals? Why do organizers presume individuals join armed groups, and what incentives are offered by states and other forms of organization?

There is very little in the wide array of civil conflict literature to explain foreign combatants, and most works examining transnational insurgencies are limited to ethnic kin relations with sponsoring states (Saideman, 2001) and cross-border safe havens (Salehyan, 2009), although these functions are conducted by the same organizations. Other works have examined Arab foreign fighters in non-Arab territories (Hegghammer, 2010), presenting detailed descriptions of the origins of the jihadi movement but not accounting for the multitude of foreign fighters who are not Islamists. However, there is already a great deal of literature on mobilization and recruitment by transnational networks, including both nonviolent civil society groups (transnational activist networks or TANs) and terrorist groups. Whereas the civil conflict literature has offered few insights into foreign mobilization, the transnational network literature is rife with them, and I draw more heavily on it.

I use it to determine why recruiters might presume they can overcome collective action barriers without offering material incentives. With the data indicating that most insurgencies are too resource-poor to offer guarantees of reward, what alternative reasons might they offer to motivate extreme risk-taking behavior? I examine proffered rationales for military sacrifice and theories of constraints on decision making imposed by normative identity roles in social structures and networks.

Finally, I turn to the question of why there might be more instances of transnational insurgency evident in recent decades. Do cases of recruitment occur independently of each other, or is there a cumulative effect as instances mount? Is there, in fact, anything new about a phenomenon that is observable centuries ago? While globalization is a ready answer for many modern transnational phenomena, I search for specific factors that have influenced the development of other forms of transnational organization, such as activist groups, to determine which conditions may be conducive to the recruitment and mobilization of foreign fighters.

Participation in Civil Conflicts

In international relations theory, the nation-state is considered the primary political unit of the international system, and individuals are typically expected to affiliate with and fight for their own state. With the conclusion of the Cold War and a flare of ethnic conflagrations in the 1990s, attention turned to the influence of substate polities in armed conflicts, often based on the supposedly inexorable pull of blood ties or deeply ingrained civilizations. How, then, to explain fighting for foreign nonstate actors? As the armed forces of some states offer citizenship in exchange for service, and privately held mercenary organizations promise shares of profit, there are readily explicable arguments for how recruiters may persuade individuals to switch service to other political jurisdictions. But these offers of selective incentives do not easily explain how insurgent rebel groups can recruit abroad, persuading foreign fighters to travel to join the weaker side in a civil war, often with no firm promises of significant payment and the obligation to avoid prosecution by their own government before even reaching the theater of conflict.

Greed versus Grievance

Many of the most widely accepted explanations for recruitment and mobilization in civil wars center on appeals to locals to maximize material gains. The formulation, commonly known as "greed and grievance" in the civil conflict literature, proposes that rebellion is produced by some combination of the two, with debate focused on how much of each element is necessary or sufficient. Greed proponents generally support the Collier-Hoeffler model (2004: 563)—abbreviated in the literature as CH—in which "opportunity provides considerably more explanatory power than grievance." Under the CH model, which assumes economic decision making by recruits, the demand for rebel labor is the product of some grievance, and the supply is the result of the expected net positive utility of rebellion. As the net income of the population falls, so, too, does both the opportunity cost of war and the government's ability to pay for deterrent defenses, and civil war becomes more likely (Sambanis, 2001: 264).

The CH model and subsequent work on greed and grievance (including the 2000 edited volume *Greed and Grievance*) indeed claim that mobilization for civil war is a rational, self-interested activity. Kalyvas and Sambanis (2005) argue in this vein that participation by Bosnian civilians in their country's conflict was motivated by the opportunity to obtain looted property from neighbors. Lichbach (1994) claimed that grievance is neither a necessary nor a sufficient condition for rebellion and that rebel leaders prompt collective action through the promise of individual concessions, such as land grants, in addition to the public good achieved through victory. Fearon and Laitin (2003) contend that the main consequence of poverty is that the state apparatus is too weak to prevent incitement to opportunistic rebellion and that identity cleavages such as ethnicity and religion have little impact. Among the exceptions, Sambanis (2001: 260–264) did find that a lack of democracy is a significant predictor of ethnic war, and Gurr (1993) advocated for at least examining the stated cause of rebels in the context of relative economic and political deprivations suffered.

If these greed-based explanations for recruitment into civil conflicts are correct, observing recruitment efforts should readily yield evidence of appeals by insurgencies to foreign volunteers to aid them in exchange for loot or material incentives. Alternatively, if a conflict state is known to be rich in extractable resources, would-be foreign fighters might not require any encouragement and would participate of their own accord without recruitment drives. In either case, we would expect to observe foreign fighters engaged in widespread resource extraction and looting, with Saudis traveling to Afghanistan and Americans to Kosovo in an attempt to return with enough riches to justify the risks. Such foreign fighters would therefore not necessarily have any ties to their local colleagues, and might actually be unlikely to have kinship with the wider population subject to their predations, but would instead simply be mercenaries.

However, the data from diverse cases indicate that recruiters typically explicitly inform volunteers prior to their enlistment that their services will bring minimal, nonguaranteed payments, often in a nonconvertible currency. Even when large land grants were offered as direct payment for paramilitary service, large numbers of victorious foreign fighters have left conflict zones without claiming their bounty, as in the case of the Texas Revolution in the 1830s. While the CH model of participation may apply to local insurgents, evidently recruiters do not necessarily offer foreign fighters the same incentives.

But would local grievances, such as the lack of democracy, be sufficient rationales for outsiders to travel to the war to fight? This would seem unlikely, as foreign recruits would not be affected by the political conditions in the conflict state. If grievances do play some role in the recruitment of transnational combatants, this raises the question of whether recruiters tell foreign fighters that they are fighting for something different than the stated cause of the local fighters. If grievance is the basis for recruitment, examining transnational recruitment requires expanding upon either the nature of the grievance or the definition of which parties are aggrieved.

External Interventions in Civil Conflicts

Rather than rely on the same types of motivators used to prompt local mobilization, transnational recruiters, while sometimes offering payment for service, instead frame the conflict as one that impacts outsiders and requires intervention by individuals because state regimes will not act. There is no single standard for what constitutes an intervention in foreign conflicts (Finnemore, 2003: 7–11), and studies of mobilization either tend to focus on states rather than insurgent groups or simply do not distinguish between types of actors. For example, Pearson (1974) included French regular troops in Algeria, the International Brigades in Spain, and professional mercenaries hired by Biafran separatists in Nigeria as examples of interventions but focused exclusively on state behavior in his analysis.

An exception is the edited volume *International Aspects of Civil Strife* (Rosenau, 1964), which attempts to describe what distinguishes civil conflicts from interstate conflicts and explain why the former nonetheless attract foreign involvement. In civil conflicts, the fission of the state's political system results in the development of parallel political structures on each side. The incumbent side retains the instruments of statehood and therefore has international ties through diplomatic, military, and trade institutions. Insurgents attempt to mirror these external relations in the hope of gaining similar access to outside resources, often through elite-level contacts (examples include the ANC and PLO). Thus it is common for rebel groups to attempt to involve outside parties in the hope of changing the balance of power (Modelski, in Rosenau, 1964: 14–15).

Rosenau argues that foreign states are likelier to participate in a conflict if it will determine not merely which individual or faction will control the mechanisms of power but is waged over the structures of society, such as ideology or religion, so that outside parties see the opportunity to advance their own agenda. In either case, proximity is expected to be a factor in intervention, as the concerns of neighboring states are the most likely to be affected by the conflict (Rosenau, 1964: 45, 51, 63, 66, 292–294). Kaplan (in Rosenau, 1964: 92) further argues that decision makers in external states or "social systems" may seek to intervene in civil conflicts if they believe the victors will emulate them and cites the Comintern-sponsored International Brigades and foreign fascists in the Spanish Civil War as examples. Subsequent works attempting to build on this platform argue that outside intervention occurred as internal conflicts widened to involve a greater scope of contested "universal values" rather than local power arrangements (Sullivan, 1969; Kelley and Miller, 1969).

Why We Fight

Just what are these values that enable mobilization efforts in interventions? Modelski (in Rosenau, 1964: 16–20) notes that political solidarity is often not limited by national political boundaries. Instead, foreign individuals, movements, and corporations all have links to one or both sides in insurgencies through a variety of transnational ties, and many of these foreign entities provide the resources that insurgencies require to match those of the incumbent forces. But Modelski does not specify just what these "ties" might be and what element of "solidarity" might sell self-sacrifice. To attempt to answer that requires first an examination not of foreign fighters, but of recruitment by military forces more generally.

Our contemporary concept of national military service and the obligation of all citizens to their state does not extend back beyond the advent of professional national militaries during the nineteenth century. Instead, in feudal societies, the province of warfare belonged to knights, and peasants could even be punished for presuming to take up arms for their sovereign.[2] Rulers did not want a populace that saw itself capable of an uprising, and large standing armies were expensive and potentially dangerous. But with the rise of the nation-state, armies had to grow to match the magnitude of the new political territories, and class pride was no longer sufficient to fill the ranks. Regimes now emphasized for the masses the romantic glory of combat, with an emphasis of service based on emotion that could, as Marshal Foch put it, "overcome lesser considerations" imposed by reason, such as personal safety. The ideal of military service was to uphold justice by preserving the institutions of society (Vagts, 1959: 17, 41–46, 157, 221). Cohen (1985: 23–25, 57) notes that this aim has been achieved as citizens are recruited to military service by calls to "glory, plunder or, above all, security."

Therefore, while the civil conflict literature largely explains recruitment by insurgent groups as opportunism, either for bounty or for political concessions, there is also present in effective mobilizations for armed service the communication of the need to defend the nation. Recruiters also act in the name of other types of communities: Islamic fundamentalists claim that their calls for jihad are in defense of the transnational Islamic community, irrespective of state citizenship (Roy, 2004). Transnational recruiters in other instances rely on similar frames of duty and defense, whether of an ethnic group or an ideological faction. However, this raises the question of why recruiters should expect their targets to fight on behalf of an affiliation other than their citizenship, particularly when the demands of the two are in conflict. Why do recruiters employ affiliations such as Muslim or Philhellene in recruitment messaging and expect it to overcome identities and obligations as Algerians or Britons?

How Does Group Identity Facilitate Recruitment?

Sociologist George Herbert Mead proposed that individuals develop a sense of who they are through the reflected appraisals and expectations of others. Identity is therefore a construct of social structure. In social network analysis (SNA), a methodological approach for measuring relational data such as community structures, decision-making processes cannot be reduced to individual choice when all choices are constrained by interactions with others. Relations create identities and their attendant norms of behavior, or "roles" (Degenne and Forsé, 1999: 2, 6). In SNA terminology, *role* is defined as putting into effect the rights and duties that constitute status, or identity as a member of a network (Wasserman and Faust, 1994: 348).

Preferences are therefore determined by social structures that establish roles for members with attendant obligations to the group. This approach is compatible with constructivist claims that structural factors determine decisions rather than wholly individual choice. Sociologist Talcott Parsons argued that individual interest is insufficient to explain most social behavior and that choices are prompted by the interests of institutions that exist to promote their own core objectives. This is why different actors make different choices in a given situation—different courses appear more rational based on prefabricated perspectives imparted by institutions with which the individual is affiliated (Swidler, 1986: 274–277). For example, surveys demonstrate that individuals engage in apparently altruistic or self-sacrificing communal activities, such as donating blood or to charity, because of what they perceive to be their role expectations by other members of an identity group (Call, 1999: 277–278).

Foreign fighters are therefore not actively choosing the political identity most salient to them. Transnational recruiters instead find recruits in roles that make them amenable to messages of duty to the Islamic *ummah*, common Philhellene community, Albanian diaspora, or other such group that encompasses local combatants. The data available from the case studies do indeed indicate that membership in standing transnational organizations provided recruiters access to pools of prospective combatants and that membership roles in existing groups were sometimes used to justify or coerce enlistment.

Structure and Preferences

Stronger ties to others through an identity lead to that identity becoming activated, or more salient. In social identity theory, individuals define themselves by their fit with a group or their perception that they have more in common with members of a given social unit than those outside of it (Stets and Burke, 2000: 226–232). Tilly contends that even nationality and ethnicity are only meaningful as labeled connections between people, not as individual attributes. Therefore, it is *transactions* rather than individuals that define social structures. Identity is based on social ties, and it "becomes stronger according to the multiple of their 1) frequency, 2) intensity and 3) range of behavior." Transactions produce ties, and ties to various actors produce social networks, including political affiliation. "Some lead to mobilization and collective action, others do not. The same persons participate in collective action under different identities on different occasions, and the risks people are ready to take on behalf of one identity or another vary enormously" (Tilly, 2002:19, 48, 49).

Studies of large organizations such as religious groups and fraternities demonstrate that appeals from fellow members of social network channels are far more effective in recruiting than are appeals by strangers. Recruitment is therefore not based on individual psychological profiles so much as it is on the microstructural social factor of how tightly an individual is tied into a given social network. Those with connections to other groups will develop commitments to them as well and not be as responsive to a given group as individuals with fewer crosscutting ties (Snow, Zurcher, and Ekland-Olson, 1980: 787–794).

Ties other than those to the institutions of the state are frequently activated by factions in ethnic and sectarian conflicts and made more salient than national identity. Connor (1994: 41, 49, 81, 82) argues that nationalism is too often misrepresented as loyalty to the *state*, particularly by American scholars who do not recognize that nationalism elsewhere is founded on myths of consanguinity. Citizenship is a political and juridical construct, but other identities hold stronger sway because they are more immediately present and salient to members.[3]

Oberschall found that mass-society theory, which holds that marginal individuals with the fewest social ties join mass movements, is not empirically valid. Those who mobilize for contentious politics tend to be segmented from the rest of society but have strong ties within their subgroups. Typically, they have been previously active within specific social or political milieus, a finding that reinforces the theory that groups minimize costs by building on existing social structures (Tilly, 1978: 81–83). These close ties to specific communities relative to overall society produce strong identification with the substate group over the state polity.

Jesse and Williams (2005: 8) argue that because identities are constructed, they can be reframed, thus leading to a lower degree of salience assigned to identity-based conflicts. They recommend implementing policies within divided societies that promote consociation because broad, overlapping identities are less likely to trigger conflicts than those that highlight stark divides.

Movement activists are typically linked by both public and private social ties well before they engage in contentious politics (Diani, "Introduction: Social Movements, Contentious Actions, and Social Movements: 'From Metaphor to Substance'?" in Diani and MacAdam, eds., 2003: 1–10). People become involved in political activities because they were asked to by someone they already know. Spontaneous political participation is not as common as recruited activism, perhaps because established acquaintants possess characteristics in their relationships that aid persuasion. The two primary attributes in relationship-based recruitment are leverage (in which the relationship provides the incentive to agree, such as with a supervisor) and closeness (by which knowledge of the recruit's individual characteristics permits use of the most effective appeal). Recruiters to political activity therefore tend to concentrate their efforts on elites who can bring in others. Similarly, recruitment efforts are directed toward those with some history of prior activism because past participation is the best indicator of future political activity (Brady, Schlozman, and Verba, 1999: 153–155).

Transnational Identities and Contentious Politics

But while these local ties explain subnational affiliations, they also apply to groups with memberships across national boundaries. Transnationalism has been described as the "process by which immigrants forge and sustain multi-stranded relations that link together their societies of origin and settlement" (Basch, Schiller, and Szanton-Blanc, 1994: 3). The existence of diasporas ensure that what Shain (2007) calls "the politics of belonging" routinely transcends states and formal relations between them (Brinkerhoff, 2009; Hersman, 2000; Hockenos, 2003).

Traditionally, transnational identities have been linked with ethnic diasporas, but recent decades have seen the rise of purely sectarian transnational identities, such as the Muslim diaspora, transstate movements such as

Pan-Arab, and normative communities including those in global civil society movements who identify more as cosmopolitans than as nationals (Sheffer, 2003: 65–68). These phenomena provide evidence that political identities are broader than shared ethnic or cultural history and that imagined communities that provide identity can be constructed on various bases.

Tarrow (2005: xiii, 53, 54) observes that many transnational activists who become involved in civil conflicts are actually "rooted cosmopolitans" concerned primarily with local and national issues. Among them are "birds of passage" who utilize the safety afforded by operating in an outside host country to organize campaigns of violence within their home states. Many are ethnic émigrés who settle within diaspora communities abroad and, because these organizers do not have to ultimately reach a modus vivendi with the opposition, they are able to maintain extremely hard-line positions that often do not keep pace with the views of the community in their homeland.[4]

The solidarity of local insurgents with outsiders is often dependent on the most uncompromising members of diaspora communities who provide material support and may encourage the use of force more stridently than those still in the homeland. For example, Balkan émigrés in the United States and Canada who returned to participate in the civil wars of the 1990s had been extremely active within their respective local immigrant communities but not within the broader host society (Hockenos, 2003: 10–11).

Nondiaspora Transnationalism

Florini and Simmons (in Florini, 2000: 7) ask of transnational civil society activists, "Why should people in disparate parts of the world devote significant amounts of time and energy, for little or no pay, to collaborations with groups with whom they share neither history nor culture?" Their explanation, that "they are bound together more by shared values than shared interest," applies only because the individuals in question conceive of themselves as part of some grouping beyond the state. These epistemological communities organize into what Keck and Sikkink (1999) term *transnational advocacy networks* (or TANs) that share resources to influence political outcomes in contentious politics in a variety of contexts and across state boundaries, including antiglobalization riots such as the Battle of Seattle.

But would adherence to an ideology constitute as compelling an identity without the institutional ties of religion or ethnicity? Geertz defines *culture* as constitutive "sense-making tools," and Williams (1996: 371) distinguishes

ideology as pertaining particularly to organizing principles regulating political arrangements: "Ideologies emerge as comprehensive systems of meaning at
times when current cultural systems seem unable to handle social changes." On
an organizational level, shared ideology leads to membership in groups, ranging from the Communist Party to College Republicans, and produces new levels of collective identity. Ideology can therefore be a form of identity because
cohorts share constitutive sense-making tools, which other members possess
and outsiders do not. In the tumultuous 1930s, recruiters of combatants for the
Spanish Civil War promoted the broadly shared ideological identity of antifascist as significant enough to overcome divisions between disparate groups of
recruits with divergent political goals from dozens of countries.

Is Islam the Answer?

In a recent example directly relevant to transnationalism, the 7/7 London
bombers, who claimed to act on behalf of a pan-Islamic identity (being three
ethnic Pakistanis and a Jamaican convert protesting the British presence in
Iraq), were involved in local Muslim community institutions even if not integrated into the broader British society. As group leader Mohammed Khan
stated in the will he left behind: "I am directly responsible for protecting and
avenging my Muslim brothers and sisters. Until we feel security, you will be
our targets" (House of Commons, 2006: 13–19).

Across Muslim states, at least pre–Arab Spring, the domestic Islamist
groups that served as channels for popular discontent were either severely
suppressed or integrated into mainstream politics and therefore viewed as
compromised. The natural outlet for "idealists" has therefore been through
a "Muslim foreign legion" (Fuller, 2002: 48) that carries the fight for change
to less centralized and more malleable societies where they can make a difference (Roy, 2004: 313). In effect, the result is the reverse of the boomerang
effect predicted for TANs in which outside assistance is brought in (Keck and
Sikkink, 1999); instead, the politically repressed or frustrated move to new
arenas to fight their battles and gather strength to return home. The motivation of these fighters stems from a sense of besiegement by the West and
a feeling that they are victims of a Western-led system that is tilted against
their societal framework and interests: In the interest of maintaining its own
power, the United States is seen as propping up regimes that are not responsive or responsible to the populations they govern.

Similarly, religious and ethnic leaders view the spread of foreign ideas as
threats to their position of social control and seek to foreclose the emergence

of alternate networks of influence. To actors who consider themselves in a domain of loss, foreign expansion, though not in the form of state military force, could readily be perceived as hostile action (Watson, 2002). Thus a group of Australian Muslims charged with plotting to plant bombs around Sydney were not seeking an offensive advantage through terrorism, often described as the weapon of the weak, but instead, in the words of the prosecutor in the case: "They believed Islam was under attack...jihad was an obligation for every Muslim" (Australian Associated Press, 2007).

Ranstorp (in Howard and Sawyer, 2004: 125–140) claims that religious extremists view themselves as fighting a defensive battle to preserve communal values. While this is a widely held formulation for explaining transnational jihadist groups, I argue that the weight of historical evidence shows that there is nothing particular to Islam that produces foreign fighters. Where jihadist recruiters are successful (as Philhellenes, liberals, ethnic diasporas, and both Communists and anti-Communists have been previously) is in the utilization of salient social identity roles to persuade volunteers to sacrifice their individual interests for the needs of the community.

Defensive Mobilization as a Cause of Violence

Organizers can overcome the barriers of individual interest to producing collective action by persuading their audience that their interests will suffer even greater costs with inactivity. What is presented as defensive collective military activity is therefore easier to organize (Niou and Tan, 2005). Political interest groups also emphasize the need to mobilize to protect shared interests that outweigh the costs of membership obligations (Gamson, 1992; Hansen, 1985).

These findings are in line with the expectations of prospect theory, in which individual decision makers and "probably states"—and therefore presumably other units of social organization—have a cognitive bias in favor of maintaining the status quo and will work harder to protect it than they otherwise would to improve it in the absence of a threat. When individuals perceive themselves to be in a domain of loss rather than the status quo or a domain of gain, they will be motivated to assume greater risks to avoid further deterioration of resources or relative position (Levy, 1996: 179–195).

The greater aggressiveness in the face of loss implied by prospect theory is triggered by fear, and recruiters across the various cases of foreign fighters employ this and other emotional devices, such as outrage, as motivators. Kaufman notes that compelling people to act requires evocative, emotionally potent symbols—representing the national group in cases of ethnic conflict—and cites Edelman's claim that support is best mobilized by portraying valued resources as under outside threat. If individuals made all decisions on the basis of pure self-interest, they would switch sides and join more powerful enemies, but group norms of duty prevail (Kaufman, 2001: 21, 27–28).

The recourse to threat can also be explained by other perspectives in international relations theory, notably how the balance of threat can lead to weaker actors balancing against a stronger foe (Walt, 1985). It is also illustrative of the intersubjective process of securitization, in which actors use discourse to present an issue "as an existential threat, requiring emergency measures and justifying actions outside the normal bounds of political procedure" (Buzan, Waever, and de Wilde 1998, 23–30). Norms of legitimacy in the international system also favor casting military intervention as defensive of the international order or of the rights of disenfranchised actors (Bull, 2002: 51–53, 182), even in cases of territorial expansionism such as Iraq's invasion of Kuwait in 1990 or Russia's incursion into Georgia in 2008. A wide array of literature therefore suggests that the perceived necessity of defensive mobilization leads actors with a sense of shared common identity or interest to fight against superior odds.

However, Francois-Rene de Chateaubriand argued: "Men don't allow themselves to be killed for their interests; they allow themselves to be killed for their passions" (Anderson, 1998: 212). Pape, in *Dying to Win* (2006), argues that suicide bombers are motivated by a sense of social obligation to a threatened population that they perceive will be conquered unless desperate measures are taken. The strategic goal, then, is to effect the withdrawal of the occupying power, even if the costs exceed the material benefits for the individual carrying out the attack.

This same logic can be extended to the recruiters of foreign fighters, who emphasize obligations to the transnational communities by which their audiences define their identities. Particular identities are salient because of the structure of the recruits' social relations (typically strong ties to in-group members and relatively few to their broader polities), and these identities carry with them norms that dictate appropriate conduct in relation to the community. Rather than appeals to greed or grievances suffered directly by the target audience, recruiters emphasize *threat*. The duty to defend the recruit's fellows is incumbent because the state will not act, and the threat will eventually come directly to the recruit after having destroyed the rest of the group. The effectiveness of such an appeal depends on the recruiter being able to frame the civil conflict as one that affects not some distant population, but a broader transnational community to which the local combatants belong.

Framing Conflicts to Recruit Outsiders

Kumar (in Florini, 2000: 115–129) describes the enlistment by the armed Zapatista rebels in Chiapas, Mexico, during their insurrection, of a coalition of various transnational advocacy organizations as advocates and witnesses (but not combatants). By serving as an information conduit, these groups ensured that foreign media attention would be focused on any violent government reprisals, and they also permitted the rebels to gain support from a wide variety of foreign sources, requiring the Zapatistas to alternatively portray themselves as indigenous rights activists, environmentalists, or anticorporatists, depending on their target audience.

The Technique of Framing

The implementation of mass transnational activism depends on the successful process of framing a political conflict as one of global concern, leading to internationalization by forming coalitions with outside groups (Goffman, 1974; Snow et al., 1986; Tarrow, 2005). To transnationalize an issue of contention, activists must create an abstraction of their core idea that shifts its meaning from one that is specific to their situation to one that is generalizable to other situations as well. For example, a local civil conflict involving sectarian divisions is represented as a contest between adherents of the different religions (e.g., Serbs vs. Bosnians becomes Christians vs. Muslims). With this shift in claims come shifts both in the identity of the participants and in the scale of the conflict, as well as changes in the nature of the claims and action required to meet them (Tarrow, 2005: 61, 123–128, 204).

Activists also employ the technique of frame bridging: linking two or more ideologically congruent but structurally unconnected frames regarding a single issue or problem. Accomplishing frame bridging allows groups to enlarge the scope of contention by bringing in new participants who previously would have had no direct interest in the outcome. The success of this practice then permits target shift and claim shift (focusing on another conflict and redirecting the attention of the mobilized to it as relevant), as seen in the case of militants successful in Afghanistan who developed the concept of jihad and exported it to other circumstances. A downward scale shift, by contrast, is when an international movement adapts itself to local causes, such as the same jihadi movement's decision to set up shop in Iraq.

The strategy of frame bridging is consistent with the literature on the interest group behavior strategy of conflict enlargement, in which engaging otherwise nonparticipating parties is often the best strategy for the weaker side in the hopes it will tip the balance by creating a new majority. Enlarging the scope of public involvement in political conflicts by "displacement" into the activity of other interest groups brings new resources, and eventually governing majorities, onto the side of the minority party (Schattschneider, 1975: 5, 10, 60, 72).

The emerging strategy of forming "constellations" of groups representing different but related issues, as seen in the Chiapas example, joins the capabilities of different organizations. Fowler (2005: 2–6, 19, 39, 116, 119) argues that the power of contemporary transnational insurgencies comes from the inclusion of people, not the acquisition of territory. The goal of insurgents is therefore to demonstrate that they can project power in distant locations to signal the strength of their network, and recruits can be committed locals with little insurgency training, with skilled advisors brought in from abroad.

Are Foreign Fighters Becoming More Prevalent?

As praxis for transnational contentious politics is adopted by groups in different conflicts, do more transnational insurgencies follow as a result? Descriptions of building activist networks and conducting frame bridging appear in literature on international civil society and in accounts of online activism from the netroots in American politics and on jihadist Web sites. At the same time, there has seemingly been a buildup of anecdotal evidence that foreign fighters are appearing in more conflicts from Colombia to Congo to the Philippines. (In chapter 2, an examination of the data determines whether there actually has been an increase in recent years.)

Assuming that the increased media reports of foreign fighters (see Appendix A) are not simply heightened post-9/11 attention to conflicts in the Muslim world, the question then becomes whether an increased effectiveness of transnational activist groups has produced more recruits. In this section, I outline the argument for this explanation and two alternatives: that an increase in the number of civil conflicts has raised the overall number of insurgencies that successfully recruit transnationally and that processes of globalization make it easier for recruiters to convince target audiences that they share common interests with distant populations.

Role Modeling

Tarrow (2005: 186–187) notes: "New forms of activism do not simply appear in different places automatically. That transfer involves diffusion of forms of activity that can be adapted to a variety of national and social situations." Recruitment of Islamist foreign fighters in Iraq and other contemporary conflicts is predicated on the downward scale shift discussed earlier in this chapter, by which the framing of international contentious political activities is transposed on local conflicts. Sometimes veteran foreign fighters travel between conflicts to set up the organizational infrastructure in the new locale, which notably occurred when al Qaeda first spread forth from Afghanistan to Bosnia, as described in chapter 6.

McAdam (in Laraña, Johnston, and Gusfield, 1994: 41–42) notes that movements are not discrete phenomena, but cultural artifacts that cluster in time and space around the emergence of a master conceptual frame. When an identity emerges, it is appropriated by successive groups. A sit-in protester is therefore not presenting a unique violation of the laws and norms of society, but following the successful and accepted tactics of prior activists. Thus the success of the international jihadi in Afghanistan provided inspiration and legitimacy to emulators elsewhere, even if they had no direct ties between them.[5] Victories enjoyed by foreign fighters should also inspire other insurgencies to isomorphic adaptation to the form of successful groups (Powell and DiMaggio, 1991).

Supply and Demand

Another explanation for a potentially growing number of transnational insurgencies is simply that the number of civil conflicts being fought grew dramatically in the half century after World War II. Rosenau argued in 1964 (5–6) that the number of civil conflicts was growing because great powers sought to engage in proxy wars rather than face devastation by challenging each other with advanced conventional and nuclear arms. Fearon and Laitin (2003) claim that the growth has occurred in weak, largely postcolonial states. Others have pointed to the proliferation in small arms that has permitted more nonstate actors to assume the security functions of states on behalf of their own groups.

MacKinley (2002: 11, 17, 29, 36) noted that the loss of Cold War superpower patronage prompted many insurgent groups to shift their emphasis from popular wars to securing market access to sustain their organizations.

This has led to an increased reliance on transnational clan or ethnic networks, potentially introducing more foreigners in cross-border illicit activities.

An increase in the total number of civil conflicts being fought at any given time would seem likely to increase the probability that more of the total number will feature foreign fighters taking part. However, it would not necessarily increase the proportion of conflicts with transnational insurgencies. In chapter 2, I examine whether the number of wars with foreign fighters is increasing both in absolute numbers and relative to the total.

Think Globally ... Act Locally?

An additional possible explanation for foreign fighter recruitment is that transnational recruiters are able to get individuals to fight because their target audiences have had direct prior communications with the local populations and are not strangers who require education about the conflict before becoming involved. Recruitment is therefore accomplished by appealing to existing active transnational communities, such as diasporas, and the use of mass media that more easily permit individuals to communicate and empathize with those in distant groups. The increase in transnational insurgencies during the twentieth century coincides with advances in global communications and transportation that make it far easier for target audiences to receive messages (and images of menace) from distant conflicts and with the availability of affordable rapid international travel that permits recruiters to release large numbers of foreign fighters without reliance on a military to field them.

Urry (2003: 4–10, 40–41) defines *globalization* as "increased density of international and global interactions, compared with such interactions at the local or national level." He argues that such processes are not causes but the effects of particular nodes in social networks arising that stretch across state boundaries. Transnational interpersonal networks among communities have become increasingly "detached from point-specific locality" (Scott, 1991: 80). Dark (in Ferguson and Jones, 2002: 74) notes that revolutions in communications and transportation have permitted individuals and organizations to interact across state boundaries in an unprecedented fashion.

Tarrow (2005: 44–45) examined the *Yearbook of International Associations* and discovered that the number of transnational social movement organizations has increased dramatically in the past half century, with fewer than 100 in the 1950s to more than 1,000 in 2003, with a quarter of them being human rights groups. This development indicates that more people do perceive themselves as part of a transnational civil society not bound by state citizenship, one that presumably carries normative obligations along with identification. Vertovec and Cohen (2002: 2) claim that more individuals are conceptualizing themselves with more complex affiliations beyond the nation-state, which they largely attribute to migrants in ethnic diasporas.

Olesen (2005: 18–21, 41, 104), in examining the Chiapas case, argues that rather than simple framing, participants evidenced the emergence of a "global consciousness" that views the lot of humanity as common and interconnected and forms the basis for transnational civil society. These activists employ a social constructionist approach, using framing to create a common understanding of issues so that they are seen as a question of justice that resonates with those who would otherwise not be directly impacted. However, the distinction is worth noting that not all transnational activists conceive of a global civil society in which all of humanity are members or of equal concern; many instead focus exclusively on the interests of particular groups and take sides in political conflicts.

Conclusions

Although international resettlement, communication, and transport may be faster and cheaper today than in the past, recruiters for transnational insurgencies have always made use of the communication and transportation technologies available at the time, dating back to the dissemination of Lord Byron's writings on Greece. Still, what appears to be a growing propensity for combatants to hop borders and ally with nonstate armed groups challenges operating assumptions about sovereignty and represents a challenge for counterinsurgency planning and peace building.[6] Additionally, transnational insurgents have in many instances caused more casualties than locals have. Understanding the differences in their behavior, and potentially limiting the flow of foreign fighters, requires recognizing the differences in the ways in which they are recruited.

Effective calls to arms are predicated on defense of the community (whether nation-state or transnational religious sect) and upholding the institutions of society. Recruiters find emotive appeals particularly effective and employ symbolic imagery of threats to strategic values and duty to the community to motivate collective action.

Rebellions arise over local political grievances or when recruiters mobilize insurgents through the opportunity for material gain. But insurgencies begin conflicts as the weaker side, and some attempt to exploit foreign connections to gain additional support to change the balance of forces. By framing the conflict as one that affects the interests of a wider community of outsiders, recruiters attempt to convince foreigners that they should bear the risks and costs of joining a distant war. The easiest way to persuade their target audience to do this is to demonstrate that they are likely to eventually face greater losses if their cohort loses the war. While recruiters have practiced this technique throughout modern history, globalization and weapons proliferation have made it easier for more groups to arrange the logistics necessary to introduce foreign fighters into their ranks.

In the next chapter, I examine the historical record of foreign fighters to determine how widespread the phenomenon is, in what ways it has changed over time, and what differences there might be between foreign fighters in different types of conflicts. Are there really more in the twenty-first century than there were in the nineteenth? Chapter 2 presents empirical data to test the theoretical arguments I have introduced.

A History of Foreign Fighters

GENERAL RASHID DOSTUM, despite his victory in capturing Kunduz, the last Taliban stronghold in northern Afghanistan, had a problem on his hands. His Northern Alliance forces, with the approval of the United States, had granted a general amnesty to the local members of the Taliban who surrendered and disarmed but not to the foreign prisoners. A riot and jailbreak began shortly after a CIA operative attempted to question a foreign Taliban fighter, fellow American John Walker Lindh, and after three days of a brutal standoff, Dostum finally decided to drown the resistance by diverting a water supply into the basement where the foreign fighters held out. Among the survivors was a Pakistani who spoke perfect English and, after asking for tea, claimed, "We wanted to surrender on Thursday. But there was a group of seven Arabs who wouldn't let us" (Worthington, 2007: 5–11).

The 2001 decision by the United States and its allies in Afghanistan to apply different standards to Taliban and al Qaeda prisoners who were not Afghan citizens reified for a global audience the foreign fighter as a distinct and particularly threatening actor in modern warfare. The unwillingness of the prisoners described here to surrender may have been borne out of a realization of the penalties that awaited them in their home countries, most of which have special sanctions against joining a foreign insurgency (at least without state approval). Although state laws and international norms tend to treat transnational military recruitment by nonstate organizations as aberrant, such groups have a very long history in civil conflicts. To determine whether the foreign fighters captured by the Coalition in Afghanistan were recruited in a way that was unique or comparable to other instances of transnational recruitment, it is necessary to develop a clear perspective of the scope of transnational insurgency over time and across the world.

In this chapter, I describe the changing roles of foreign fighters through history, including the rise of norms, and later laws, against transnational insurgency, followed by an examination of other state responses to foreign fighters. With the historical context established, I proceed to present data on the appearances of foreign fighters in modern civil conflicts. This empirical record permits testing the theoretical arguments from the literature presented in chapter 1 and developing a typology of foreign fighters that provides further insights and from which I select cases for comparison of recruitment methods.

Transnationalism versus Sovereignty

As Huntington (1964: 65) noted, "there is no necessary reason why nation-states should be the only socio-political groups maintaining professional forces." The state itself as a legal sovereign entity is a fairly recent concept, originating in Western Europe after the Peace of Westphalia in 1648. The state system was exported, first by colonialism and then by international norms, and has been in place for less than a human lifetime in areas of the Middle East and Africa that have experienced large concentrations of foreign fighters.

Europe before Nationalism

Prior to the establishment of the Westphalian international system of sovereign states, it was more difficult to distinguish combatants as foreign. However, there were notable examples of multinational forces in medieval Europe. Vikings recruited relatives living in different kingdoms to wage war against their monarch, leading to some parties hiring themselves out as mercenaries. These included the Varangian Guard, "an elite corps of Scandinavians and other foreigners in close attendance on the Byzantine emperor" (Cook, 2001: 323). The Crusades period saw the rise of two rival transnational groups, The Poor Fellow-Soldiers of Christ and of the Temple of Solomon (Knights Templar) and the Order of Saint John of Jerusalem (Knights Hospitaller, later Knights of Malta) both of which still exist in some civilian form today.[1]

The Treaty of Bretigny in 1360, which produced a decade-long lull in the Hundred Years War, also left the soldiers of various nations unemployed. Thousands of English, French, and Spanish soldiers formed a loosely organized army that called itself the Great Company, divided along national lines into smaller units called *routes*, which pillaged its way across France and the Holy Roman Empire of its own accord or occasionally at the command of a noble who had hired it to sack a rival (Fowler, 2001: ix, 1–6). Likewise, nearly 500 years later, the end of the Napoleonic Wars led to Simón Bolívar's recruitment of more than 5,000 otherwise unoccupied British soldiers to join his wars of national liberation in South America, of whom only a few hundred survived his many campaigns (Smith, 1999).

The Impact of the Nation-State

By this time, however, the practice of employing foreign mercenary forces was already in decline. The Thirty Years War had not only birthed the Westphalian state system and its attendant economies of scale that could support large militaries but also demonstrated the "success of disciplined armies" on the field against ad hoc collections of mercenaries (Huntington, 1964: 20–21). The Grande Armée of France fought more effectively, attributed to higher rates of morale, than did mercenary forces it opposed, precipitating the development of modern nation-states and the national militaries they employ (Cohen, 1985: 42). The Napoleonic Wars were therefore highly significant in reducing transnational military forces, inaugurating not just a new age of powerful national militaries but also an era of strong nationalism.

The United States, like the other new Western Hemisphere nations formed during this period, relied on foreign troops to secure its independence. Aside from the regular French and Spanish troops assigned to the aid of the rebels, the nascent Continental Congress also sent Benjamin Franklin and other representatives to Europe to secure professional officers who would volunteer to train the Continental Army[2] (Xenophon Group, 2005). Further, 750 volunteer freemen from Haiti, soon to stage its own anticolonial revolution, fought against the British at Savannah in 1779 (Wong, 2002).

State Responses to Transnational Recruitment

Legal and Normative Restrictions

Despite this record, the United States became the first country to pass a law, the Neutrality Act of 1794, making it illegal for citizens or inhabitants to accept commissions in foreign military forces or work to enlist or recruit others, with the loss of citizenship as penalty. (One year prior, an American citizen had been indicted by a federal jury for serving on a French privateer vessel that raided British ships.) In 1817, the law was updated to include not only foreign states but also "colonies, districts, people," thereby applying the standard to insurgencies as well. The law did permit travel abroad to enlist in a foreign military not in conflict with the United States or a friendly nation, but recruiting others to do so was strictly prohibited and remains so today[3] (Thomson, 1994: 78).

The early United States attempted to maintain a policy of avoiding foreign entanglements and, during the 1790s, lacked the resources to confront any major European power aggrieved by the actions of American citizens. However, throughout the nineteenth century, a growing number of states elsewhere adopted neutrality laws as well, many with loss of citizenship as penalty for violation. In some cases, the legislation was in response to past events (Great Britain wished to keep its subjects out of the Franco-Prussian War after failing to keep them out of the American Civil War), but many had not had any experience with foreign insurgents. Instead, norms of the obligations of citizenship in a nation-state crystallized over this period, with the result that, by the outbreak of World War II, two-thirds of the countries in the world had laws against foreign military service (Thomson, 1994: 80–82).

Beyond statutes against transnational military activity, the prevailing attitudes of military and counterinsurgency policy makers also changed over time. As recently as the Spanish Civil War, captured foreign insurgents were given preferential treatment over locals, but this practice had disappeared well before 2001. The Soviets, for example, perhaps mindful of their own history of transnational recruitment and eager to delegitimize interlopers, often termed foreign insurgents as "bandits" or as puppets of former or foreign regimes who were not representative of the local population. They were generally treated as traitors, with courts of "people's representatives" lacking legal training set up to try them, rather than sending them to courts reserved for regular criminals (Radu, 1990: 40–41). This perspective and the application of extrajudicial methods survived the dissolution of Soviet Union.

The Russian Federation maintains the policy, instituted during the civil war in Chechnya, that any foreigner found in Russia "fighting on the side of terrorists will be killed immediately," a threat issued specifically to Canadians after one was killed in Grozny. Some Russian officials claim foreign fighters in Russia are highly skilled specialists there for pay; others insist that they are conduits for illicit funding of insurgent activities. Most appear to concur that mercenary motivations, not religion or nationalism, drive their participation (although one general opined, "Maybe they were simply normal Muslims who had been fed horror stories about the Russian military and were tricked into coming here to protect the human rights of the Chechen people") (Canadian Broadcasting Company, 2004).

The Russian Federation, in contrast to the generous support for insurgents abroad offered by the Soviet Union, moved quickly after Communism to curtail the ability of its own citizens to become foreign fighters. Embarrassed by the (often inebriated) support given by Russian recruits to Serb forces during the Yugoslav secessionist wars, the Duma in 1993 approved a law banning within Russia the recruitment, arming, financing, and training of mercenaries[4] (Bugajski, 1993).

State Efforts to Harness Foreign Fighters

Despite such stark policies, a number of other states have been eager to use foreigners in conflicts. Such practices include recruiting foreign military units to fight on their behalf and enabling their own citizens to serve as insurgents in civil conflicts abroad for strategic purposes. Neither meets the criteria outlined for defining foreign fighters as insurgents, but both indicate a willingness to contravene laws of neutrality and norms of sovereignty.

It is a commonly accepted practice for states to offer citizenship to recruits as an incentive to join the ranks of their armed forces. The United States offers expedited tracks to citizenship not only for military personnel but also for family members, even if they reside in the country illegally (Lavendera, 2007). More recently, it has offered citizenship to temporary workers in exchange for six months of service (Preston, 2009).

The French Foreign Legion also offers citizenship in exchange for service. The legion was created in 1831, when King Louis Philippe, in the wake of the Napoleonic Wars, faced a manpower shortage at home and could not spare civilian labor to rebuild the strength and prestige of the military enough to meet French foreign policy objectives (Turnbull, 1964: ix, 1). "Although French law forbids the Legion to actively recruit beyond French borders, the internet has rendered the law almost meaningless," a development that would certainly bear upon American and other state laws against recruitment as well (Moore, 2007).

Other states have accepted the service of foreign volunteers not under their own chain of command. When the Russian Civil War spilled over into a Russian-Polish territorial contest, nine American former World War I flying aces (only two of whom were of Polish descent) volunteered their services to Poland by forming the Kosciusko Flying Squadron (*New York Times*, 1919). Among them was Captain Merian C. Cooper, who would later direct a number of films, including *King Kong* with its climactic aerial battle (McDonough, 2005). In 1940, American Lieutenant General Claire Chennault commanded pilots whose requests for discharge had been granted so that they might join the 1st American Volunteer Group, or Flying Tigers, in the service of the Chinese Nationalists.[5]

Some states whose regimes were founded by foreign fighters have attempted to export their revolutions abroad, notably Communist Cuba through the efforts of Argentine-born Ché Guevara in Africa and South America. Conversely, Iraqi officials contended that Saudi Arabia encouraged its citizens sympathetic to al Qaeda to become foreign fighters in the neighboring civil conflict so that they would not remain at home to create dissent (Parker, 2007). Some states and insurgencies also continue to import foreign individuals and privately held organizations to provide security and conduct combat operations.

The Question of Mercenaries

The definition of mercenary activity has changed over the past two centuries from the practice of sovereigns hiring out their own militaries to other rulers to individual soldiers hiring out their own services to the highest bidder. In recent years, private security companies (PSCs) have hired personnel from diverse countries to conduct operations contracted by one state to occur in another state. Thus the United States has employed foreigners who, while under contract, are not directly under American jurisdiction to operate in conflicts in Iraq and elsewhere (Avant, 2005: 23, 130).

Although differing from mercenaries of old, PSCs are not a new phenomenon either. In 1860, Frederick Townsend Ward formed the Foreign Arms Corps in Shanghai, using Filipino and Western soldiers for hire against Taiping rebels. This group later became the Shanghai Foreign Legion, comprised of Americans and Europeans commanded by British General Charles Gordon. Gordon would be martyred in 1885, defending the British fort at Khartoum against the Mahdi, a Sudanese self-proclaimed messiah whose ideology of liberation from apostate secular Muslim regimes and their Western backers and harsh fundamentalist applications of Koranic law drew transnational support and volunteers, foreshadowing the rise of the Taliban a century later (Thomson, 1994: 93).

Why Not Count Mercenaries as Foreign Fighters?

For the most part, PSCs would not be considered foreign fighters because in nearly all cases they are employees contracted by state governments and not rebels. Insurgencies would seemingly be unlikely to be able to arrange adequate payment and operational security for outside firms or even be able to conduct them into the conflict state. There are, however, a few notable exceptions—mostly in resource conflicts in Africa—in which PSCs "have also provided assistance and support to rebel groups." For example, South African veterans were recruited in the 1990s by UNITA in Angola and by anti-Kabila forces in Congo, conflicts in which ethnic kin and ideological compatriots from abroad also fought as rebels (Kinsey, 2006: 111). In 1960s Nigeria, Biafran separatists hired South Africa–based Mercenaire International to send dozens of American, European, and South African mercenaries against the central government, despite the presence of other volunteers who claimed humanitarian motives (Thomson, 1994: 93–94). In each of these cases, and in other cases such as the Spanish Civil War, rebels employed soldiers for hire as part of a broader, nonprofessional force of recruits

Mercenaries have also played roles in a number of cases of armed conflict that did not rise to the level of insurgency.[6] Rebels staging a coup in the Comoros in 1975 hired a French mercenary to conduct the operation; three years later, the former regime hired him in its successful bid to regain power (Thomson, 1994: 93–94). The founders of the now-disbanded South African PSC Executive Outcomes, who were among several dozen foreigners arrested for an attempted coup d'état in Equatorial Guinea in 2005, fall in the same category (BBC News, 2005). As these conflicts were not civil wars, the soldiers for hire were not technically transnational insurgents.

A more difficult status question to answer might be whether PSC employees of private companies operating in a foreign state might qualify as foreign fighters. To return to the Nigerian delta, Shell Oil has facilities in Nigeria that are protected by non-Nigerian corporate security forces (Avant, 2005: 184). Shell is a transnational corporation—its holdings cannot effectively be limited to the jurisdiction of one state, and it is not headquartered in Nigeria. If a foreign-held transnational corporation brings armed foreigners into a state, would they not meet the definition of foreign fighters? The answer in this case is that they would not. Although a nonstate entity recruiting transnationally and operating in a third-party state, a PSC in this context is still presumably operating with the sanction of the state. It is not part of a rebellion designed to wrest political or territorial control from the state and therefore would not qualify as a transnational insurgency.

International Law and Exceptions for Transnational Insurgents

Despite the growing use of PSCs by states, international agreements ensure that foreigners offering their services abroad do not become insurgents. The PSCs are licensed by states. Activity outside the scope of that license remains illegal and is regarded as aberrant. Under current international agreement, Additional

Protocol I (1977) to Article 47 of the Geneva Convention defines *mercenaries* as combatants who are neither nationals nor residents of the territory controlled by one party of the conflict, not members of the armed forces of a party to the conflict, and not sent by a third-party state on official duty as a member of its armed forces. However, the criteria further specify mercenaries as "motivated to take part in hostility essentially by the desire for private gain" and exclude those motivated by ideology or religion or who provide training and logistics to belligerents rather than participating directly (Kinsey, 2006: 19).

The 1987 United Nations International Convention against the Recruitment, Use, Financing, and Training of Mercenaries, which came into force in 2002, also defines illegal mercenary activity as concerted violence performed by individuals who are neither residents of the conflict state nor in the armed forces of a state but are motivated by material gain (Avant, 2005: 230–231). As with the Geneva Convention, it is difficult to assess motivation, and these conditions may exclude large groups of foreign fighters if they cannot be shown to be motivated by profit.

Historical Data: Developing a Profile of Foreign Fighters

Determining how insurgent recruiters persuade foreign fighters to join civil conflicts requires first establishing what is known about the historical population of transnational insurgencies. Are most foreign fighters clearly mercenaries, or do more appear to be of the suicide bomber type operating in Iraq who do not appear chiefly concerned with their own survival? Are insurgencies in certain types of conflicts more likely to go transnational than others? To determine which, if any, particular characteristics are representative of foreign fighters, it is first necessary to establish the total population of transnational insurgencies. With this accomplished, I will test two hypotheses pertaining to the various theoretical arguments introduced in chapter 1 about factors influencing foreign fighter recruitment:

H1: Foreign fighters are more likely to be recruited in nonethnic civil conflicts than in ethnic civil conflicts.

H2: Foreign fighters have been recruited in more civil conflicts over time.

The first hypothesis examines the nature of the relationship between recruiters and their target audience. While researchers in the Cold War 1960s (Rosenau, 1964) contended that international intervention in intrastate wars would not be more likely in ethnic conflicts, by the ethnic conflicts of the

1990s, a new generation had arrived at the opposite conclusion (Saideman, 1997, 2001). If most of the conflicts in which foreign fighters appear are ethnic conflicts, I would expect transnational recruitment to be largely based on ethnic appeals made through diaspora connections to readily identifiable audiences.

The second hypothesis relates to the potential impact of globalization. Transnational insurgency is not new, but it is worth knowing if it is becoming more prevalent. If there are more instances of foreign fighters, is this simply because there have been a large number of civil wars since World War II? Given that various transnational insurgencies cite other foreign fighters as precedent, perhaps they learn from each other's successes or even communicate directly with other rebel groups. I look for period effects indicating that increases in transnational insurgency correspond with advances in globalized communications that would permit easier transnational coordination and empathy with distant communities.

Observation Set

The data collected in stage 1 of the project provide the delineation of the universe of possible cases that is a necessary prerequisite to conducting comparative case studies. I researched each civil war in the set and coded recorded appearances of insurgents who are not citizens of the state in which the conflict occurred. I coded simply whether transnational insurgents were documented or not, rather than their numbers or extent of participation, because, even in the best documented cases, reports of the number of foreign fighters present vary by an order of magnitude, and it is often similarly unclear whether they took part in frontline combat. I also coded a number of additional variables, including whether the conflict was an ethnic conflict and—if it was—whether the foreigners were actually of the same ethnic group as the locals.

While there is no formal consensus on the criteria for an ethnic civil war, I am coding using Sambanis's (2001) definition of a conflict for self-determination rights for a nation or ethnic group.[7] I separate religious from ethnic conflicts because these two types of identities do not always overlap. (See appendix B for coding rules.) This distinction is relevant because of cases in which foreigners who were not coethnics intervened in ethno-nationalist rebellions (Islamists in Chechnya, for instance) or in cases where foreign fighters on opposing sides were recruited with ostensibly different motivations. The volunteers who came to 1930s Spain expressly to defend the Catholic Church were Irish, Romanian, and other nationalities who were coreligionists with the Spanish Nationalists but not coethnics.

The distinction is directly relevant to testing my hypothesis and the competing claims in the literature that external intervention is more likely when conflicts are framed as fronts in larger global conflicts over the structure of society (such as transnational Communism or Islam) as opposed to contests between particular local ethnic groups. Accordingly, foreign fighters are also coded by whether they were coethnic with local insurgents: Interventions may be more likely in ethnic conflicts, but how can this be explained if the foreign fighters are not of the same ethnic group as the local insurgents? (Examples include Britons in 1820s Greece and Pakistanis in 2000s Macedonia.) Although the overarching basis of contention in a civil conflict may have been the rights of a particular ethnic group, if the foreign fighters who arrived were not of the same ethnic group as the local insurgents, then it is possible that they had a different rationale for fighting (such as a broad anticolonial agenda).

Beyond questions of ethnicity and time period effects covered in the hypotheses, I took the opportunity to code other variables, including geographic region, whether foreign fighters were observable from states that were not directly adjacent to the conflict zones, and conflict outcomes. Determining where the most foreign fighters are to be found or whether they fare well in the field does not necessarily address recruitment techniques, but it does further establish the scope of the foreign fighter phenomenon. I have included these additional descriptive statistics because they illustrate findings about the potential significance of foreign fighters that may be of interest to readers.

Typology

The two variables (ethnic conflict, coethnic foreign fighters) produce a 2 x 2 matrix of possible relations between the type of conflict and the relation of transnational insurgents to the contention (table 2.1). The typology indicates dimensions of variation between different groups of foreign fighters and permits case studies of representatives of each type to test the influence of the causal variables of social identity and framing of threat. With variation on both the issue of contention in the conflicts and the relation between the transnational and local insurgents, I would expect a different recruitment message to correspond to each type of foreign fighter. However, the logic of defensive mobilization presented in chapter 1 suggests minimal variation in messaging.

Table 2.1 Typology of Foreign Fighters

	Ethnic Conflict	Nonethnic Conflict
Coethnics	Type 1 *Diasporans* (Join with nationalist rebels to advance common nationalist goals)	Type 3 *Encroachers* (Join with secessionist rebels in adjacent state to expand political control to neighboring territory)
Non-Coethnics	Type 2 *Liberationists* (Defend anticolonial rebels to advance shared ideological goals)	Type 4 *True Believers* (Join with ideological rebels to preserve institutions of shared transnational identity)

The descriptive labels of each type are derived inductively from matching the different observations to the appropriate quadrant of the typology (see "Findings"). These labels appear to apply so appropriately across cases that, in future observations of foreign fighters, the basic identity and goals of the transnationals can be ascertained by determining the type of conflict and relation between local and foreign insurgents.

If H1 is correct, I would expect to see more foreign fighters in nonethnic conflicts than in ethnic conflicts because, per Rosenau, interest from abroad would be drawn by conflicts over the structure of society rather than which group controls a particular state. If H2 is correct and more foreign fighters have been appearing over time, then I would expect that type 4 noncoethnics would comprise a growing proportion of foreign fighters as globalization has fostered transnational affiliations not dependent on hereditary or geographic ties.

Findings

Of the 331 civil conflicts contained in the combined data set, I was able to document the presence of foreign fighters in 70, or just over 20 percent. It is likely that recruitment attempts are even more common, but the data cannot provide evidence of this. Indeed, it would be particularly difficult to discern failed attempts to recruit abroad because of a lack of public records or media coverage. For this reason, it is possible to make only inferences about successful recruitment and not to distinguish between characteristics of successful and unsuccessful recruitment.[8] Some of the 70 civil conflicts featured multiple groups of foreign fighters, some antagonistic to each other or even on opposing sides of the conflict. As the data set counts conflicts, these each receive only one listing.

I address the first hypothesis by the variable in the data set determining whether the civil conflict is primarily an ethnic conflict. I find that only 36 percent of all conflicts 1816 to 2005 could be classified as ethnic conflicts. Among conflicts featuring foreign fighters, only 43 percent were ethnic conflicts, indicating that the first hypothesis is correct: Foreign fighters are more prevalent in nonethnic conflicts. (See figure 2.1.) Additionally, of the 43 percent of conflicts featuring foreign fighters that are ethnic conflicts, more than half (24 percent of the total) were Liberationists (type 2), meaning that they were not coethnic with the local group with whom they fought.

As a number of Liberationists appear to participate in some ethnic conflicts to advance ideological goals (Islamism, anticolonialism, etc.) rather than out of an affinity with the particular rebel group, the number of foreign fighters participating in civil conflicts based on ethnicity stands to be even lower. The data therefore support H1. The finding that only 28 percent of foreign fighters are coethnic with local insurgents raises questions about the value of ethnic homogeneity.[9] Only a quarter of foreign fighters are members of transnational ethnic groups coming to aid their kin (figure 2.2). And although instances of foreign jihadis in civil wars are increasing, they represent only about a third of the historical total.

The data also provide evidence that foreign fighters are not simply cross-border kin dragged into wars by spillover effects. While a greater proportion of foreign fighter conflicts are ethnic wars than the overall number of civil wars, the majority of instances of foreign fighters have not occurred in ethnic conflicts (figure 2.3).

Further, in half of the cases, the foreign fighters arrived from noncontiguous states, indicating extensive recruitment and mobilization efforts (figure 2.4).

Controlling for geographic region indicates that for much of the world, notably the Middle East, there is little correlation with the location of the conflict and the presence of foreign fighters (figure 2.5). Africa, however, appears to have more than its share of transnational insurgencies, whereas the Western Hemisphere has few foreign fighters in proportion to its overall share of civil conflicts. The data on the Americas could likely be attributed to geographic separation from other regions (no cases of foreign fighters were found in Oceania) and possibly to a high concentration of strong states. The disproportionately high percentage of foreign fighters found in Africa might best be explained by the concentration of weak states that do not hold as

	Ethnic Conflict	Nonethnic Conflict
Coethnics	**Type 1** *Diasporans* (Join with nationalist rebels to preserve shared nationalist goals) 1) 1936–1948 Palestine, Diaspora Jews vs. British Mandate 2) 1948 Israeli War of Independence, MACHAL on Jewish side, Arab Liberation Army on Arab side 3) 1960–65 Congo, Angolan Katanga tribesmen 4) 1961–1974 Angola, Zaire refugees in FNLC 5) 1961–1996 Iraq, KDP, PUK 6) 1963–1973 Guinea Bissau and Cape Verde residents in PAIGC vs. Portugal 7) 1972–79, ANC in Rhodesia 8) 1974 Cyprus, rogue Greek National Guardsmen arrive, fight 9) 1990, RPF in Rwandan Tutsi uprising 10) Diaspora Rwandans in 1990–94 Civil War 11) 1991–92 Croatia, diaspora Croats 12) 1991–94 Nagorno-Karabakh, diaspora Armenians 13) 1997, Rwanda vs. PALIR, Congo Hutus 14) 1998 Kosovo, Homeland Calling recruits Albanian diaspora into KLA 15) 2004 Sudan, Chadian Furs	**Type 3** *Encroachers* (Join with secessionist rebels in adjacent state to expand political control to neighboring territory) 1) 1835 Texas Revolution, Texas Army 2) 1948 Malaya, Chinese Communist Organization, Indonesian volunteers 3) 1963 Brunei rebels vs. British-backed sultan, Indonesian volunteers 4) 1962–70 Yemen, Yemeni-Saudis, Egyptians 5) 1980–1988 Uganda, Rwandan Tutsi refugees join Tutsis in National Resistance Army

(Continued)

	Ethnic Conflict	Nonethnic Conflict
Non-Coethnics	**Type 2** *Liberationists* (Defend anti-colonial rebels to preserve perceived shared ideological goals) 1) 1821 Greece, Philiki Etaireia 2) 1903 Macedonia, Bulgarians in Macedonian VMRO 3) 1946–53 Cambodia, Vietminh 4) 1946–53 Laos, Vietminh 5) 1954 Algeria, Tunisians in FLN 6) 1964–74 Mozambique, ZAPU, Tanzanians, Malawis join Frelimo 7) 1967–70 Nigeria, Biafra Babies 8) 1978–91 Ethiopia, pro-Tigrean Muslims 9) 1978–92 Afghanistan, Islamic Society 10) 1991–94 Georgia vs. Abkhazia, Russians and Chechens 11) 1992–95 Bosnia, Islamists 12) 1992–95 Liberia, Burkinabe and Libyans 13) 1994–ongoing Chechnya, Islamists 14) 2000–ongoing Israel, 2 Britons 15) 2002 Macedonia, Pakistanis 16) 2002 Cote D'Ivoire, Liberians	**Type 4** *True Believers* (Join ideological rebels to preserve institutions of shared identity) 1) 1835–45 Brazil, Garibaldis 2) 1861–65 US, "Wild Geese" 3) 1863–77 China, Muslim Uzbeks 4) 1910–14 Mexico, Villa's Yankees 5) 1917–21 Russia, International Brigades 6) 1918 Finland, Anti-Communists 7) 1934 China, Comintern 8) 1936 Spain, International Brigades & Catholic anti-communists 9) 1946–48 Greece, Communists 10) Cuba 1958–60, Communists 11) 1960–62 Laos, Vietcong 12) Cuba 1961, Brigade 2506 13) 1963 Laos, Vietcong 14) 1966–ongoing, Colombia, Israeli, IRA trainers with FARC 15) 1975–1990 Lebanon, Islamists 16) 1975–1991 Angola, Anti-Communists 17) 1978 Nicaragua, Argentinean Revolutionary Coordinating Junta

Ethnic Conflict	Nonethnic Conflict
	18) 1980 Chad, Libyan Pan-African Legion
	19) 1981–82 Iran, Arab Mujahidin
	20) 1982 Iraq, Iranians in SCIRI
	21) 1989 Chad, Libyan-backed Arabs
	22) 1990 Liberia, rebels from Guinea, Cote d'Ivoire
	23) 1991–ongoing Somalia, Islamists
	24) 1991 Sierra Leone, Liberian NPFL, Libyan-trained Burkinabe
	25) 1992 Tajikistan, Islamists
	26) 1992–2001 Afghanistan, mujahidin
	27) 1996 Zaire, Ugandan, Rwandan rebels
	28) 1996 Ethiopia, Somali-led insurgents, Afghan, Yemeni Islamists
	29) 1998 Tajikistan, Islamists
	30) 1999–ongoing Dagestan, Islamists
	31) 2000 Guinea, Sierra Leonean RUF
	32) 2000–ongoing Uzbekistan, Islamists
	33) 2001–ongoing Afghanistan, Taliban
	34) 2003–congoing Iraq, Islamists

FIGURE 2.1 *Historical Typology of Foreign Fighters*

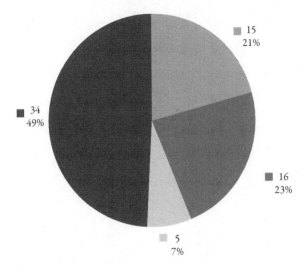

15
21%

34
49%

16
23%

5
7%

▦ Type 1 Coethnics in Ethnic Conflict   ▦ Type 2 Noncoethnics in Ethnic Conflict

▦ Type 3 Coethnics in Nonethnic Conflict   ▦ Type 4 Noncoethnics in Nonethnic Conflict

FIGURE 2.2 Foreign Fighter Prevalence by Type

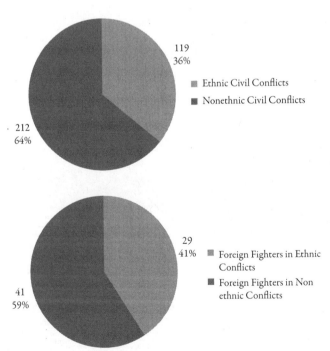

119
36%

▦ Ethnic Civil Conflicts
▦ Nonethnic Civil Conflicts

212
64%

29
41%

▦ Foreign Fighters in Ethnic Conflicts

▦ Foreign Fighters in Non ethnic Conflicts

41
59%

FIGURE 2.3 Are Foreign Fighters More Likely in Ethnic Conflicts?

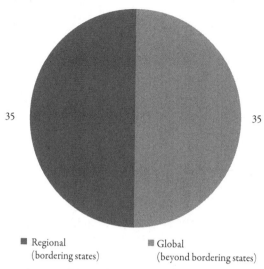

35   35

■ Regional   ■ Global
(bordering states)   (beyond bordering states)

FIGURE 2.4 Geographic Origins of Foreign Fighters

much loyalty as tribal or other transnational affiliations and by the inability of a number of these states to secure their borders against trespass.

For the second hypothesis, the data clearly indicate that foreign fighters do tend to be appearing in more civil conflicts over time, both in absolute numbers and as a proportion of the rising number of civil conflicts (figure 2.6).

Not only does the hypothesis appear to conform to expected conditions of globalization but also it suggests that Dark (in Ferguson and Jones, 2002: 74) is correct in asserting that new patterns of interaction produce realignment of identity. Transnational civil society organizations have proliferated with advances in communications technology that permit members to interact and establish ties seamlessly across national borders, as have diasporas and religious sects.

As the data indicate (figure 2.7), the proportion of type 4 foreign fighters (True Believers) has been increasing, and this type now accounts for most foreign fighters, far outstripping either type of participants in any form of ethnic conflict. Perhaps not surprisingly, the increase is primarily due to Islamist mujahidin appearing in a growing number of civil wars. This finding supports the prediction that globalization coincides with the growth of transnational identity groups.

In addition to the possibility that more individuals are willing to fight for a transnational rather than an ethno-national affiliation, another possibility might account for the growing number of foreign fighters appearing in civil conflicts: the old adage that nothing succeeds like success. If insurgents are

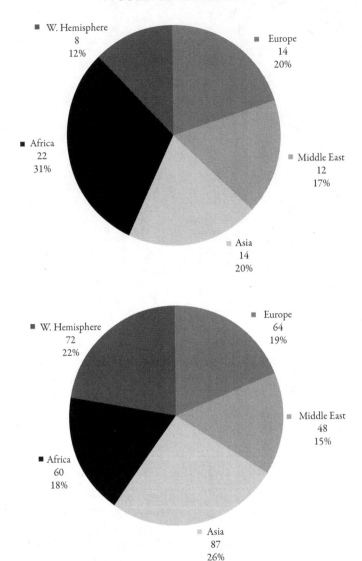

■ W. Hemisphere
8
12%

■ Europe
14
20%

■ Africa
22
31%

■ Middle East
12
17%

■ Asia
14
20%

■ W. Hemisphere
72
22%

■ Europe
64
19%

■ Middle East
48
15%

■ Africa
60
18%

■ Asia
87
26%

FIGURE 2.5 Foreign Fighters versus All Insurgencies by Region

the weaker side in a civil conflict, they are likelier to lose than to win most civil conflicts, and the data confirm that this is indeed the case. Recruitment would therefore seem to be a tough sell, as the prospect of either material or political gains, let alone survival, would be improbable, given the likeliest outcome. But as foreign fighters proliferate, there are more success stories to inspire other movements elsewhere.

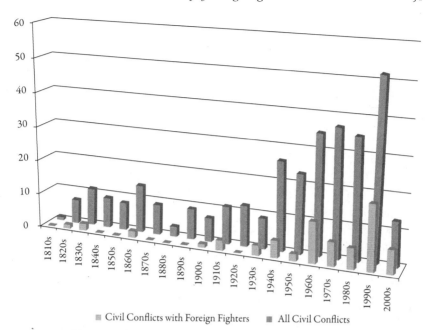

Civil Conflicts with Foreign Fighters   All Civil Conflicts

FIGURE 2.6 Foreign Fighters versus All Insurgencies over Time

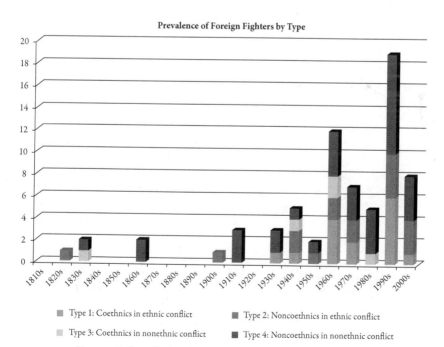

Type 1: Coethnics in ethnic conflict   Type 2: Noncoethnics in ethnic conflict

Type 3: Coethnics in nonethnic conflict   Type 4: Noncoethnics in nonethnic conflict

FIGURE 2.7 Foreign Fighters by Type over Time

Finally, another possibility must be considered: The apparent rise in the number of foreign fighters may be merely an artifact of the data available. The global communication age has produced a growing amount of information as mass media, literacy, and electronic reporting have proliferated, and it is entirely possible that older cases of foreign fighters or cases that occurred outside areas with independent media coverage remain unrecorded. If this is true, then the apparent increase in foreign fighter occurrence may not be as pronounced as it might appear.[10] It also would mean that foreign fighters are yet even more common than might be expected.

The data also indicate that insurgencies employing foreign fighters tend to be disproportionately successful. (See figure 2.8.) Data from my observation set indicate that incumbent governments won 60 percent of all modern civil wars, a finding consistent with other studies that have found that insurgents win only 41 percent of the time (Stoker, 2007; Michaels, 2007). Foreign fighter–driven insurgencies still lose most of the time, but the figures are significantly better for these particular rebel groups (table 2.2).

This correlation certainly does not prove causation; it is difficult to argue conclusively that the arrival of foreign fighters tipped the balance to the side of the insurgents in enough cases to produce these dramatic results. Indeed, it may simply be the case that the best-organized and most effective insurgencies

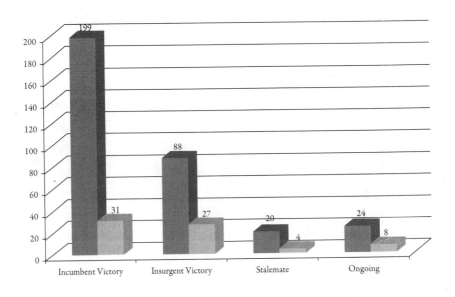

FIGURE 2.8 Do Foreign Fighters Win More Civil Conflicts?

Table 2.2: Conflict Outcomes

Civil Conflicts 1816–2005	All Conflicts (331)	Foreign Fighters (70)
Incumbent Victory	199 (60%)	31 (44%)
Insurgent Victory	88 (27%)	27 (39%)
Stalemate	20 (6%)	4 (6%)
Ongoing	24 (7%)	8 (11%)

were those that also had the capacity to recruit abroad. However, the qualitative data presented in the case studies indicate that recruited veterans of other wars with technical proficiencies, as well as raw recruits who are willing to sacrifice their lives in response to a perceived existential threat to their people, have made a difference on the battlefield. Foreign fighters in Iraq and Mexico engaged in more aggressive attacks against their opponents than did the local insurgents (resulting, for example, in the capture of San Antonio after the locals had folded their tents for the winter). In other cases, they brought specialized military skills that are generally accepted to have prolonged conflicts (Spain) or directly changed their outcome (Israel).

In either event, the finding is important. If it is simply a case that insurgencies that are organized well enough to draw foreign recruits are more likely to win anyway, this arguably indicates that more formidable insurgencies recruit transnationally. The significance for both theory and policy includes questions of state sovereignty and, as demonstrated in the introduction and in the cases in subsequent chapters, the participation of actors who tend to be responsible for higher levels of violence.

Evaluation: A Growing Source of Instability

Transnational insurgencies have been becoming more prevalent since the birth of the modern international system despite the development of national laws and international norms making recruitment by nonstate groups an unacceptable activity. Modern states that have relied on foreign fighters outside their direct control to serve as security forces—such as the Spanish Republic and Taliban Afghanistan—now do so simply because they lack the resources to either defend themselves or challenge these transnational forces when they do not act in accordance with the goals of the host. Otherwise, states have acted to affirm their monopolies on violence and thwart or disclaim citizens who act against their strategic and diplomatic interests.

Over this period, the number of conflicts in which foreign fighters appeared increased dramatically. Although there was a spike in recruitment as foreign Communists entered a number of civil wars in the years following the Russian Revolution, most of the shift occurred in the second half of the twentieth century, first as the collapses of colonialism and Communism triggered struggles for national liberation, and later as transnational Islamic fundamentalist groups attempted to duplicate their efforts in 1980s Afghanistan in other theaters of conflict. It seems likely that increased globalization—advances in communications and transportation that aided both the logistics of recruitment and the likelihood that recruits would view themselves as connected to distant insurgents—facilitated these developments.

The observation set data support both hypotheses: First, ethnic conflicts constitute a minority of both the total number of civil conflicts and those that feature foreign fighters, and the percentage of foreign fighters that share the same ethnicity as local insurgents is even smaller. This finding supports Rosenau's argument that civil conflicts over the basic structures of society, such as ideology and religion, rather than which individual or ethnic group controls the mechanisms of power of the state are more likely to draw foreign involvement. This is also significant because the data show that about half of transnational insurgencies involve foreign fighters arriving from farther away than just the neighboring state, indicating that spillover effects and local ethnic ties do not sufficiently explain the phenomenon.

Second, the number of instances of foreign fighters has clearly increased not only in absolute numbers but also as a proportion of civil conflicts fought. Consistent with my expectation, type 4 foreign fighters (those who have no ethnic affiliation with local combatants and are fighting for causes other than nationalistic) have increased in proportion to other transnational insurgents. Processes of globalization—particularly advances in communication and transportation—have permitted participants in contentious politics to recruit participants beyond state boundaries in a growing number of cases. In part, this is because the ability to communicate globally with like-minded individuals has permitted identification and mobilization not previously available along ideological rather than national lines.

Case Studies

In the following chapters, I present case studies of diverse transnational insurgencies to explore the influence of the variables of ethnic conflict and coethnicity on recruitment messaging. I also examine the arguments presented in chapter 1 that participants in contentious politics are recruited from existing social structures (whereas this would seem less apparent if recruits were simply responding to offers of bounty) and that recruiters frame conflicts as threats that require defensive mobilizations. I therefore test two hypotheses using cases from each quadrant of the typology:

H3: Insurgencies recruit foreign fighters from transnational communities linked to local insurgents rather than randomly or by targeting experienced mercenaries.

H4: Recruitment appeals are predicated on the necessity of defending transnational communities rather than on opportunities for material gain.

I examine primary and secondary source material concerning recruitment in each case examined, looking for evidence that distant intrastate wars are framed as threats to vital interests of some identity community shared by recruiters and their target audiences. Although individuals may have incentives to lie (or at least misremember noble motives for fighting), original recruitment material has been preserved in each case in the form of propaganda pamphlets, posters, speech transcripts, audio and video recordings, and other media. From these sources, it is possible to observe what rationales for participation were offered to recruits. Additionally, surviving foreign fighters have penned memoirs or granted interviews about their mobilization, and these are useful to determine whether the messaging used by the recruiters was absorbed and reflected in these accounts.

From each primary and secondary source, I recorded evidence of framing: attempts to explain the significance of the conflict and what benefit the recruit can expect to achieve by fighting. While I expected that messaging would focus on defense against threat, I also looked for disconfirming evidence in the form of proffered material rewards and alternative frames portraying the conflict (the opportunity to acquire land, etc.). The preponderance of examples determines the main type of messaging employed.

To assess whether particular messages were used because they were designed to motivate targeted members of transnational identity communities, it is also necessary to examine how messaging related to the overall process of recruitment. For example, does an examination of the demographics of the target audience tell us anything about the messages the recruiters selected? As for the messengers themselves, did they record why they selected particular frames for the civil war and how they decided to reach their target audiences? Did different recruiters—or different institutions affiliated with the effort—utilize different frames for the same conflict? It is also important to examine the experiences of foreign fighters as they mobilized and fought in the field. Did their experiences lead to alterations in the messaging? Were early recruits held up as exemplars to inspire later volunteers?

For all case studies, I conducted a structured, focused comparison of the recruitment messages put forward by the different types of insurgencies to analyze whether and how such messages change based on interactions of the variables of ethnic conflict and coethnicity of transnational insurgents. In each case, foreign fighters were successfully recruited. As in stage 1, the lack of reliable data militates against comparing measures of success in terms of numbers of foreign fighters. Among successful cases, variation in numbers of recruits may have resulted from smaller potential pools of recruits or fewer available organizational resources rather than more or less effective framing. The study was therefore limited to comparisons of the messages and dissemination structures between cases of each type, regardless of the known numbers of recruits in each observation. For each case, I compared results of the following inquiries:

1. How did the insurgency frame the issue of contention to potential recruits?
2. Were the primary stakes framed in terms of gains or losses, and for whom?
3. What specific rationale(s) were offered for why the recruits themselves should participate as opposed to merely locals?
4. What, if any, selective incentives were offered for participation?
5. By what means or media did recruiters disseminate their appeals?
6. Who did the target audiences appear to be?
7. To what extent were most recruits affiliated with the target group(s) and the local side in the civil conflict?
8. Did recruits report their understanding of the conflict in the terms and the rationale for participation in similar terms to those in the recruitment messages?

In conducting case studies, those that permit the most useful inferences are not necessarily the most generalizable to the widest populations, but instead those that present well-defined types with high degrees of explanatory richness (George and Bennett, 2004: 30–32). Cases that have a narrow range of variation, or all experience similar particular outcomes, can "provide a better opportunity to gain detailed knowledge of the phenomenon under investigation" (Collier, Mahoney, and Seawright in Brady and Collier, 2004: 87). The goal in selecting cases to meet the research objective is therefore not to provide a representation of median cases among the universe of observations, but to determine which best illustrate the causal mechanisms of the previously unexplained phenomenon.

In selecting case studies, I quickly discovered that successful large-scale mobilizations were also the only cases likely to have left useful records. Even in the case of Diaspora Jews in the Israeli War of Independence, who made significant contributions resulting in statehood and official archives containing their efforts, all involved in the recruiting effort abroad were ordered at the end of the war to destroy their recruitment records and materials. Fortunately, many recruiters and veterans wrote (largely consistent) accounts of their efforts. By contrast, the apparently unsuccessful effort to organize an African American contingent to liberate Ethiopia from fascist control left no trace but footnotes in historical accounts written about Black antifascists. I therefore operated under the constraint of selecting cases that not only were representative of each type but also could generate enough primary and secondary source data to answer the eight questions I use to structure my comparisons of each of the four types. I selected cases from each permutation of the type of conflict featuring large-scale mobilizations of foreign fighters that not only provided the greatest potential for available records but also permitted the greatest opportunity to observe variations in messaging among the greater number of message recipients.

In seeking evidence to test the hypotheses and through valid comparisons using the questions listed for analysis, I present the cases representing recruitment in each type of transnational insurgency in a narrative format. Each case history appears in sections corresponding to each stage of messaging and mobilization: Background to the Conflict, Institutions of Recruitment, Target Audience, Framing and Messaging, Mobilization, Experience in the Field, Outcome and Legacy.

I proceed chronologically, beginning in chapter 3 with an analysis of transnational recruitment in the Texas Revolution during the 1830s.

3

The Texas Revolution (1835–1836)

HERMAN EHRENBERG HAD already traveled far from his native Prussia when he arrived in New Orleans in October 1835 and attended a meeting to promote the cause of Anglo-Saxon settlers in the Mexican state of Coahuila y Tejas. After hearing speeches by Texan settlers and New Orleans business leaders, Ehrenberg and 120 other volunteers signed up to enter Mexico as separatist insurgents. Each was issued a rifle, pistol, and matching gray "work clothes which we found in warehouses of the city." Ehrenberg departed by ship the following afternoon and arrived in Texas as part of a 65-strong paramilitary contingent that included other Germans, Britons, Canadians, "six Irishmen, and natives of seventeen of the twenty-four commonwealths of the United States" (Ehrenberg, 1968: vii–3).

A great deal of irony accompanied the transnational insurgents of the Texas Revolution. The New Orleans Greys and other groups of foreign fighters, in being essentially wiped out by heavy casualties taken during reckless missions shunned by local Texan fighters, were instrumental in building international support for independence from Mexico. Rebel leaders like Stephen Austin and Sam Houston heavily recruited them, praised their contributions, and then desperately hoped to rid themselves of them. And while many veterans or their survivors accepted promised awards of land for their service, a number—including Ehrenberg, who was entitled to additional bounty as the survivor of a major massacre—left the country they had fought to free without claiming their reward.

In this chapter, I examine the Texas Revolution as a case of how insurgent recruiters continuously redeveloped their framing of the conflict to make it sufficiently salient to generate transnational intervention. In this civil conflict, "a relatively few Anglo settlers aided by outside adventurers revolted and wrestled away a very large section of land from Mexico" (Brown, 1999: v). The opportunity to own large tracts of land certainly attracted both settlers and combatants, and the fledgling Texan government offered land grants as incentives to both. However, it had been widely known that access to land was available in Texas for some time before the conflict, and even advertisements promoting land for military service generally included other messaging as well. Why did recruiters employ these frames, and why was any framing necessary at all if land bounties supposedly motivated recruits?

Representing a type 3 transnational insurgency, coethnics in a nonethnic conflict, the civil war between Texas and the Mexican federal government was a nonethnic conflict. Although it featured foreign fighters who were largely coethnic with the local insurgents, it was rooted in a broader ideological civil war in 1830s Mexico of state rights against central political and military authority. Consistent with other type 3 cases, the foreign fighters in this instance were Encroachers, seeking control of territory while defending members of their group across the border. However, I expect to find messaging used by recruiters that framed the threat to the Texan settlers as one that would ultimately menace their fellow Americans, if left unchecked.

The Texas Revolution generates a great deal of passion, and not only among Texans. A wider audience in the 1950s and 1960s grew up with the legend of the Alamo presented in movies and television, and many regarded it as a parable for the necessity to stand firm against advancing Communism. (See Roberts and Olson, 2001, for a description of the threats and accusations made against researchers who attempted to develop an accurate account of the demise of Davy Crockett.) With this in mind, I present this conflict, and those in the following chapters, to offer a functionalist perspective of the commonalities and differences between transnational recruitment efforts, not to suggest equivalence between Travis at the Alamo and bin Laden at Tora Bora.

Even the terminology for the land and inhabitants in 1835 can be contentious, with different scholars applying different terms. Most accounts term the territory of the current state as Texas rather than Mexico, and I maintain that distinction. However, it is important for contemporary audiences to recall that, in 1835, the border of the United States extended only to Louisiana and the Sabine River, and everything on the other side was Mexico. Additionally, in referring to the different groups attempting to claim the territory, I adopt the terms Texian to refer to the Anglo-American settlers residing there prior to the conflict, American or foreign to refer to those who came to Texas from outside Mexico during the war to fight, Tejano to describe Texas residents of Hispanic lineage, and Mexican to describe all other Mexican citizens.

In addition to the widely published historical works on the subject, I relied on the Daughters of the Republic of Texas Library (DRTL) on the grounds of the Alamo for access to its archive of original letters, broadsheets, and periodicals. I also received the assistance of the Texas General Land Office, which maintains the state records of land awards, including those made to volunteers in the revolution. Unlike other conflicts that saw numerous foreign survivors publish memoirs, the accounts of only a handful of Texas volunteers are available for analysis, and, due to the lack of records kept, there are no precise data concerning what would appear to be the more than 2,000 who participated. Obtaining an accurate depiction of the workings of the complex transnational insurgency that descended on Mexican Texas from the United States therefore requires an examination of the principals responsible for their recruitment.

Background to the Conflict

Texas historian William Brinkley (1952: 2) declared that the revolution had been widely misunderstood and described variously as "part of a deliberate design of the South to extend the slave territory of the United States, as a plot of speculators to enhance the value of their investments, and as a spontaneous uprising of outraged freemen against the threat of tyrannical oppression" but that "serious study [shows that] none of these are accurate." However, each of these influences *was* present in the stated aims of rebellion leaders, the efforts of Texian settlers and Louisiana mercantile barons to recruit combatants to weaken the Mexican central government, and the propaganda and recruitment effort that spread from New Orleans to New York and beyond.

The American Revolution of 1776 had drawn French forces, in the form of both regular troops and volunteer foreign fighters, who carried back with them the ideals of republicanism. The growth of this movement contributed to toppling the French monarchy and the eventual reign of Napoleon Bonaparte. The installation of his brother Joseph on the Spanish throne disrupted ties between Spain and New Spain and led to Mexico's declaration of independence in 1810 (Brown, 1999: 15–17). Years of instability led in 1822 to the seizure of power by General Antonio López de Santa Anna, whose stated goal was building a liberal republic modeled on the United States. The result was the Constitution of 1824 that established a decentralized federal government (Reid, 2007: 6).

"Inconvenient Neighbors"

The region of Texas offered fine agricultural land but had remained under-populated wilderness off the main Mexican trade routes and subject to perpetual Indian raids. Santa Anna therefore continued a Spanish plan to colonize the area and prevent the territory from being overrun by the rapidly expanding United States. The Mexican federal government gave Moses Austin, a Missouri resident who retained Spanish citizenship from the period when Spain controlled the Louisiana Territory, the position of *empresario*, which entitled him to settle 300 families on the Brazos River. Each family received 4,500 acres, exemptions on taxes for 10 years and customs duties for 7, Mexican citizenship, and the requirement to practice Catholicism (Davis, 2002: 32).

Poor economic conditions in the United States soon prompted many others to follow. "The panic of 1819 and the termination of the credit system" (Brinkley, 1952: 2) led to emigration.

> During the 1820s some ten thousand Americans migrated to Texas, many of them burdened by debt and looking to escape their financial obligations and the penalties of the law. G.T.T. (Gone to Texas) became infamous letters when left on the doors of abandoned homes by delinquents wishing to avoid the debt collector and the sheriff in southern states.... Largely isolated in eastern and central Texas, Anglo-American settlers not only outnumbered Mexicans but also remained in relative independence from the predominantly Mexican settlements of Béxar and Goliad. (Davis, 2002: 26)

The Santa Anna regime then grew concerned that a clash of civilizations would erupt from unchecked Anglo-American immigration into Mexico. As Alexis de Tocqueville observed, "Daily, little by little, the inhabitants of the United States are infiltrating into Texas and, though submitting to the country's laws, establishing there the empire of their language and mores. The province of Texas is still under Mexican rule, but soon there will, so to say, be no more Mexicans there"[1] (Davis, 2002: 76). A British agent, observing in 1825 that only one Englishman had applied to live in Texas, predicted that the Texians would prove "inconvenient neighbors. In the event of a rupture between this country and the United States, their feelings and earlier connections will naturally lead them to side with the latter..." (Reid, 2007: 16). Sharing this concern, in 1830 the government barred further immigration from the United States and established garrisons to ensure compliance with Mexican law (Brinkley, 1952: 6).

Filibusters and Encroachers

There was ample evidence for an increasingly authoritarian Santa Anna government to view the Texians as a Trojan horse. American presidents since the Louisiana Purchase had attempted to obtain Texas by sale, treaty, or direct pressure (Reid, 2007: 10). In 1810, a Tejano named José Bernardo Gutiérrez, along with his conspirator, U.S. Army Lieutenant Augustus Magee, "with the tacit support of the United States traveled through Kentucky, Louisiana and Tennessee" to recruit the "Republican Army of the North"—"a motley army of hunters, trappers, Indians, and Tejano rebels…some hoped to liberate Mexico from Spanish oppression; others yearned for nothing more than land and loot."[2] Setting out from Louisiana, between 1812 and 1813 Gutiérrez and his followers eventually took Béxar (present-day San Antonio), where he claimed sovereignty. His mixed force of 1,000 to 1,400 was eventually destroyed at the Medina River by the Spanish army, launching the career of nineteen year-old Lieutenant Santa Anna. (Roberts and Olson, 2001: 62–63)

The destruction caused by the Gutiérrez-Magee expedition may have reduced the population of Texas by half; after a subsequent filibustering expedition launched from the United States by Dr. James Long in 1819, perhaps only 2,000 Tejanos remained in the territory, with their dwindled ranks subject to Comanche raids (Reid, 2007: 10–11). However, the Cherokee proved a greater threat in 1821 by forming an alliance with Anglo squatters and declaring the sovereign Republic of the Red and White Peoples, also known as the Republic of Fredonia. Mexico eventually ended the Fredonian Revolt with the support of most of the Texian *empresarios* (Resendez, 2005: 40, 45). Moses Austin's son Stephen, who became the voice of the Texians to Mexico City upon his father's death, went so far as to declare, "I am a Mexican citizen and officer, and I will sacrifice my life before I violate my duty and oath of office" (Brands, 2004: 109).

The Revolution Begins

Although Austin and the established landholders identified themselves as Mexicans, this view was not shared by all Texians, and increased repression by the Santa Anna regime soon produced unrest. The main issues of contention were efforts by the federal government to make slavery illegal in Texas as it was in the rest of Mexico, the refusal to permit the Texians to form their own local governments, and the requirement that all Texians be Catholics, even though this had not been closely enforced. The immigration ban was also widely ignored, and many radical Texian leaders had immigrated to Mexico illegally from the United States. Newer immigrants without large estates of land tended to be more readily aggrieved by the political conditions and formed underground prowar parties that advocated violent confrontation and secession.[3]

Still, no major incidents of rebellion materialized until June 1832, when federal troops attempted to collect tariff dues from which the Texians had previously been exempt. A meeting of the prowar faction passed a resolution of the necessity to defend their rights under the Constitution of 1824, and a radical faction organized a successful attack on the garrison post at the port of Anahuac, leading to the withdrawal of the troops posted there since 1830.[4] Many *empresarios* protested that they were being forced into a war that was being arranged by land speculators hoping to profit from the end of Mexican control, but the Mexican crackdown after the attack began to radicalize even the propeace faction (Brinkley, 1952: 5, 7, 49, 56–61).

In October 1832, representatives from each Texian settlement held a convention that called for the repeal of the immigration ban, reductions of tariffs and customs, the right to organize militias, and the separation of Texas from Tejano Coahuila. In April 1833, Austin took the resolution to Santa Anna but was arrested on his return trip for having endorsed sovereignty in a letter to the Texian leadership. He would not be released until July 1835, and both he and the Texian community became more radicalized during his imprisonment (Brinkley, 1952: 8–11).

Civil War in Mexico

Santa Anna should hardly have been expected to grant greater autonomy to Texas, given events unfolding elsewhere in the country. The national government had never fully consolidated power, and the regime struggled to maintain power by increasingly siding with reactionary factions of the military who argued for the recentralization of the federal government. The ideology of centralism became the defining issue of Mexican politics in the 1830s, with disappointed liberals and many state governments accusing the man who had described himself as "the Napoleon of the West" of creeping toward military dictatorship (Brinkley, 1952: 41).

The Texas Revolution was therefore simply one theater of a broader Mexican civil war that pitted militarists and centralists against liberals and federalists (Reid, 2007: 2). Elsewhere in Mexico, the Republic of Yucatán declared independence and did not submit to Mexico City until 1848.[5] In May 1835, the restive state of Zacatecas staged an armed rebellion against central authority, prompting Santa Anna to crush it ruthlessly and order summary executions for all Americans captured, an edict that included not only filibusters aiding the rebels but also accountants in the local banks (Roberts and Olson, 2001: 26). The Texians could therefore convincingly argue that an expansionist and militarist Mexican dictatorship was mobilizing to attack Anglo-Saxon civilization.

Another consequence of the centralist approach was the failure of the Mexican government to develop adequate commercial ties to Texas (Brinkley, 1952: 22). As a result, the Texian settlements "developed essentially as economic outposts of Louisiana," integrating with Gulf commerce, not with that of the Mexican interior (Resendez, 2005: 38–39). As a result, many business interests in the southern United States had close financial ties not only to land developers in Texas but also to liberal Mexican politicians who had hoped to encourage trade with the United States but now fled there instead as political refugees. Together, they conspired across the border to hobble the centralist regime.

Meanwhile, on October 2, 1835, the Texian community of Gonzales repulsed an effort by Mexican centralist troops to remove the town's cannon, and the message "Come and take it" flown on a flag during the skirmish became the battle cry for a spreading revolution. By the end of the month, the Texian insurgents had won several key battles, seizing the presidio of Goliad and laying siege to Mexican troops inside the Alamo at Béxar. At the consultation to form a Texas government in November, delegates proclaimed the legitimacy of their actions as a defense of the Constitution of 1824, soon to be a rallying cry against Santa Anna (Crisp, 2005: xiii).

On November 2, the provisional government under President Austin passed an act to raise an army of "permanent volunteers" who, in exchange for enlisting for six months, would receive 640 acres of land, the only currency the rebels had to offer[6] (Reid, 2007: 98). Already, however, the "permanent council" that had served as the temporary government had on October 11 authorized "Thomas F. McKinney to go to the United States and borrow $100,000, and appeal to the citizens of the United States for men, money, and supplies" (Barker, 1904). Given the particular connections of the Texians and dissident Mexicans to the United States, there could be little doubt where this effort would be organized.

Institutions of Recruitment

New Orleans in 1835 was "a haven for exiled revolutionaries and scheming filibusters." Its economy was based on shipping cotton and sugar, so its powerful business community eagerly sought the addition of Texas to the Union as a slave state. The New Orleans Association, a conglomeration of local business enterprises, had by 1835 already provided financial backing to the Gutiérrez-Magee expedition and several other transnational mercenary efforts at annexation. Mexico had also accused it, and other businessmen in the Red River trading port of Natchitoches, Louisiana, of aggravating its troubles with the Indian nations by supplying them with arms in exchange for stolen cattle (Miller, 2004: 4, 26, 32, 43).

Operating out of this network was Adolphus Sterne, organizer of the Committee for Texas and the landlord of General Sam Houston of the new Texas Army (Roberts and Olson, 2001: 291). Sterne had previously moved to Mexico and converted to Catholicism to obtain citizenship but was arrested for arms smuggling and sentenced to death before being permitted to leave the country. His committee, in consultation with Texian leaders, organized the recruitment of Americans and other foreigners to wrest Texas away from Mexican sovereignty. This group was the "speculators" who worried the old Texian *empresarios*, and "membership on the committee was a step toward protecting their Texas investments."[7] The committee formed a public front group called Friends of Texas to raise funds, disseminate messaging, and recruit combatants. Despite its nativist members, its leadership had counterparts across the border who "were exclusively Mexican in terms of agenda and planning" (Miller, 2004: 41, 62–67).

The Black Legend

The link between checkered New Orleans businessmen trying to profit from the expansion of slavery and Mexican federalists, who viewed themselves as more liberal than the United States because they had outlawed slavery, was their highly salient shared identification in a transnational community: Freemasonry. The Freemasons had originated in Britain in the late 1500s, and Masonic groups were operating in New Orleans by the 1700s. Membership was driven by otherwise marginalized immigrants (including Jews like Sterne and Latin American exiles like his coconspirators) who wanted to establish business connections. Subsequently, French Masons established the Scottish Rite branch in Mexico in 1806 (Miller, 2004: 24–26).

Freemason lodges were "simply social venues where political opinion was shaped in the absence of formal parties." In a system promoted by officials who had experienced it in Europe, members met to exchange information and to jockey for government positions and contracts. The Scottish Rite also promoted the establishment of a republic, and, just as they had in the American Revolution, lodges played a key role in organizing the revolt that led to the republican 1824 Constitution. However, in 1825, the American ambassador to Mexico incorporated the rival York Rite, which promoted direct elections, looser federalism, and closer relations with the United States (Resendez, 2005: 61, 62).

Mexican centralists and aristocrats now joined the Scottish Rite to oppose American influence, while liberal federalists joined "Yorkiño" lodges. Thus, "in the late 1820s Mexican Freemasonry became the battleground on which federalists and Centralists vied for power in the Mexican government… [and it] took on a political dimension of immense proportions not seen in the United States," as the establishment of York Rite lodges came to be seen by the conservative elements of society as manifestations of foreign intervention. Adolphus Sterne was reportedly freed by a judge who was a fellow York member. "The Black Legend" of the role of a Masonic conspiracy in the eventual loss of much of its territory would persist in Mexico well into the twentieth century (Miller, 2004: 26, 33, 41, 44).

Amid this conflict, Yorkiños collaborated with York Rite members among the Texians. Mexican liberals saw the American experiment as one to be emulated, and, as Santa Anna increasingly aligned with the centralists, dissident liberal Mexican politicians turned to Texas as a haven. Fellow Masons won the best development contracts, and ultimately the Texian political leadership, including Austin, was largely Freemason.[8]

> The entire colonization experiment in Texas was guided by liberal ideals. The [Yorkiño] state officials' notorious preference for Masonic empresarios and Anglo-American settlers stemmed precisely from this faith in the power of liberalism.… The colonization experiment in Texas became a crucial test, an ideological battleground of the virtues of liberalism. The hopes of liberals in Mexico rode on its success.[9] (Resendez, 2005: 64–73)

Many Mexican political exiles therefore used their Texian Masonic business connections to establish themselves in New Orleans. One of these was General José Antonio Méxia, who "had become an agent of the Galveston Bay and Texas Land Company, a conglomerate of businessmen and lawyers in New York and New Jersey who had bought out the empresario contracts of [prominent Texians]." Méxia, and other Mexican federalists, hoped that the Texas Revolution would not result in secession but would provoke uprisings in other northern states and restore looser federalism to Mexico; however, he promised his network of Yankee capitalists that if they helped him defeat Santa Anna, he would annex Texas to Louisiana. In New Orleans, the Committee for Texas collaborated with him to raise his own paramilitary force; using their transnational Freemason connections, American businessmen traveled to Mexico City on his behalf and organized meetings of liberals to prepare support for an invasion from the north (Miller 2004: 27–29, 87).

Framing and Messaging

With the Texian government sending an agent to the United States to offer bounties of land to military volunteers, and with the evident willingness of the Committee for Texas to invest in procuring a mercenary expedition, it would be perfectly reasonable to assume that foreign fighters in this front of the Mexican civil war were simply responding to appeals to greed. However, while recruiters did emphasize the reward of large tracts of land for service, they also framed participation in the conflict as a defensive imperative, a frame echoed by many recruits in their descriptions of the issue of contention. Recruiters modulated the message of which precise interest required defense as the situation in the field soon changed, but, in the beginning, the rationale offered to potential recruits was very welcome to Yorkiños.

Transnational Identity: "The Principles of 1776"

As previously noted, the early nineteenth century featured a number of conflicts that fit within a broad frame of liberalism versus authoritarianism. For the target audience in the United States, the various specific issues at stake in the conflict and the broader Mexican civil war

> all blurred into an epic battle of democracy versus dictatorship, freedom versus oppression, the United States versus Mexico. And they knew they were not alone in the world; men were bleeding and dying in similar wars over similar issues on distant battlefields. Many of the men arriving in Texas considered themselves liberals fighting to rid the world of absolutism, aristocracy, and privilege. (Roberts and Olson, 2001: 93–94)

Following the Greek War of Independence were other "uprisings against conservative, centralist regimes," and "in Europe and the United States, liberals followed the rebellions closely, hoping to see democracy and freedom unfold." Sam Houston, in his first speech in the U.S. House of Representatives (as a congressman from Tennessee), called for assistance to the Greek insurgents. Organizers of the incursion to take Texas therefore expected American audiences to consider the repression of fellow liberals and the advance of centralism in neighboring Mexico as a direct threat to their way of life (Roberts and Olson, 2001: 93–94).

As a result, the revolution was "portrayed by its leaders as the 'last rallying point of liberty' for the 'republicans of Mexico.'" The Texian General Council declared that it sided with "any Mexican liberal, whose cause is our cause, as opposed to military despotism" (Crisp, 2005: 42). In adjuring Americans to put down the threat of Santa Anna, Frank Johnson, a commander of the Texian army, framed it as part of a larger, necessary struggle against despotism:

> Louis Philippe of France, faithless to his oath, now sits side by side with the monarchs of Russia, Austria, and Prussia, and Spain, and the minister of Santa Anna is among them.... (Roberts and Olson, 2001: 94)
> To arms! then, Americans, to aid in sustaining the principles of 1776 in this western hemisphere.... It is more than probable that the freedom of Mexicans has been sold to tyrants, and that a European force is to sustain the diadem on the head of the traitor Santa Anna. Not only Texas and Mexico, but the genius of liberty, demands that every man do his duty to his country, and leave the consequences to God. (Reid, 2007: 87)

Austin, committed to independence after his imprisonment, attempted at a Louisville, Kentucky, stop on a fund-raising tour to legitimize intervention by Americans by comparing it directly to these past conflicts. Liberty was the goal of the Texians, he proclaimed, and "on this principle the Greeks and the Poles and all others who have struggled for liberty, have received the sympathies or aid of the people of the United States... on this same principle Texas expects to receive the sympathies and aid of their brethren, the people of the United States, and the freemen of all nations" (Austin, 1836: 27, DRTL).

Among many broadside posters carrying similar messages was one in Oxford, North Carolina, that preceded contact details for emigration arrangements with the message:

> To the Brave and Generous! When Poland struggled for her liberty, her arm was nerved by the exhaustless bounty of the free. The armies of

Greece were augmented by our noblest youth, and her coffers replenished by the benevolence of the rich....A very few years ago, when General La Fayette landed upon our shore, and millions and millions laid their gratitude at his feet, who would have thought that an opportunity to be like him would have passed unnoticed and unimproved....Arise young men and middle aged, and go with us to Texas; there is a theatre for your valor, and a reward for your labors. Let not her brave sons and virtuous daughters go down unaided and unmourned, the hapless victims of tyranny and oppression. Like the three hundred Spartans they can, they will, live free or die....(DRTL—microfilm Reel 24, 1209)

While the Greeks of the 1820s may have been victorious, the invocation of their defeat at Thermopylae is evidence that recruiters did not simply promise loot to mercenaries. The Friends of Texas, rather than merely advertising bounty to all recruits, legitimated their activity by adopting the master frame (as described by McAdam in chapter 1) of noble foreign volunteers in struggles for democracy. This approach permitted appeals to adventure seekers who otherwise would not have been interested in becoming farmers in the southwestern wilderness, and it motivated idealists to fund and form their own militias to set forth and join the cause of their own accord.

After the Battle of Gonzalez that sparked the revolution, newspaper advertisements began to appear in the United States hailing this "Lexington of Texas" in the cause of justice against oppression: "Of what avail would the mere expression of our sympathies be? Do our prayers or wishes give them a shield against knife or bayonet? Of what use are paper resolutions if not backed by money and men? Rise then, good men and true, and march to the aid of your brothers in Texas" (Elliott, 1947).

Joseph H. Barnard, a Chicago physician and author of one of the few memoirs of a foreign insurgent in Texas, was recruited to New Orleans by such a message appearing in his local newspaper. Clearly reflecting the framing of the conflict, he wrote: "They were in arms for a cause that I had always been taught to consider sacred, viz.: republican principles and popular institutions." He included along with his account a quotation of Byron's poetry, signaling his professed solidarity with the Philhellene freedom fighters (Barnard, 1885: 1, 31).

Changing Rationales: My Fellow Americans

Thus it was that proannexation New Orleans businessman James Ramage, secretary of the Friends of Texas recruitment organization, declared at a rally that on the preservation of Mexico's Constitution of 1824 "hangs all the Law and the Prophets" (Miller, 2004: 85). Rather than initiating conflict to obtain plunder, the broad opposition in Mexico was a conservative defense of liberty; "not Partisan war but Constitutional war, as did our forefathers" (Lack, 1992: 36). This strategy of continually claiming that the civil conflicts in Mexico were an extension of the American Revolution rested on the assumption that Texas would be just one front in the effort to weaken Santa Anna and that promotion of the cause of Mexican federalism was necessary to build support for the wider war. However, this rhetoric soon shifted as the Mexican federalist efforts failed and the Texians and their supporters found that their success depended more on American volunteers (Crisp, 2005: 42).

The Texian leadership began to distance itself from its previous self-identification as Mexican and took every opportunity to emphasize kinship with Anglo-Americans living across the border. After the Gonzalez incident, the Permanent Council of Texas circulated a message that informed an American audience: "You are united to us by all the sacred ties that can bind one people to another. You are, many of you, our fathers and our brothers—among you dwell our sisters and mothers—we are aliens to you only in country, our principles, both moral and political, are the same—our interest is one" (Stout, 2008: 47).

The Texians and their allies soon focused on issues of infringement of their rights by the central government that they believed would have particular salience to a wider American audience. Austin claimed: "Our fathers in 1776 flew to arms for much less. They resisted a principle, 'the theory of oppression,' but in our case it was the *reality*—it was a denial of justice and our guaranteed rights—it was oppression itself" (Austin, 1836: 10). In particular, the lack of freedom of religious expression figured in his messaging, with the Protestant Texians portrayed as under the heel of Hispanic Roman Catholics. In another speech, Austin described the cause of Texan independence as setting "free from the trammels of religious intolerance and other anti-republican restrictions" (Roberts and Olson, 2001: 324). A broadside inviting volunteers to join a group "under the protection of Colonel Owings, Commander in Chief of the Kentucky Legion," declared the revolution to be a case of "Liberty Triumphing over Tyranny and Priestcraft!" (DRTL—microfilm Reel 24, 1212).

Among the recruits in another group of foreign fighters, the New Orleans Greys, was one introduced in a letter to Austin's brother as "Mr. Stiff...who visits your Country as a volunteer in defense of your rights...in your contest against the usurpers of power, the perfidious advocates of central government."

(The letter also mentioned that "Mr. Stiff's pecuniary circumstances render it perfectly unnecessary that he should visit your country in quest of fortune") (Brown, 1999: 2). After the war, Colonel Edward Stiff would write a book critical of the use of fear tactics concerning religion in recruitment:

> [The recruits] left their dear relations and peaceful firesides to stay, as they thought, the desolating progress of a sanguinary invader; and whether they had been misinformed or not, the prompting motive was a noble one, and should endear them to the friends of freedom throughout the world.... [But the mobilization had been the work of] a combination of land speculators and smugglers of merchandise and negroes, who did not scruple to allure ignorant and well-meaning men into the country.... Agents from Texas had long been domiciled in most of the large cities of the Union, but until a recent date had worked by stealth; by gradually paving the way for public operations, interesting men of influence in Texas lands, and rousing the honest indignity of our religious communities, by pathetic appeals on behalf of their priest-ridden Protestant brethren west of the Sabine.... [Texians had actually enjoyed] perfect religious freedom...[and] all pains were taken by the wire workers in Texas to prevent the dissemination of correct information. (Stiff, 1840: 229, 239, 273–274)

Racial Frames

The shift in framing the conflict as a defense of fellow Western Hemisphere liberals to a defense of fellow Anglo-Americans under foreign rule resulted in a new emphasis in the rationale for war. "Earlier, the expression of ethnic prejudice had been restrained by political prudence—many had expected anti-Centralist uprisings in the interior which might keep the war out of Texas. When this hope failed, Anglos began to express both open hostility toward Tejanos and a belief that fundamental cultural-political differences dictated the need for independence" (Lack, 1992: 78).

A prowar faction on the Texian General Council declared: "The Mexican people and the Anglo-Americans in Texas never can be one and the same people" because of differences in religion, language, and "ideas of civil liberty" (Crisp, 2005: 42). David Burnet, later interim president of the Republic of Texas, wrote a letter to U.S. Senator Henry Clay that the causes of the war boiled down to a fundamental dissimilarity between Texians and Mexicans: "The first are principally Anglo-Americans; the others a mongrel race of degenerate Spaniards and Indians more depraved than they" (Roberts and Olson, 2001: 143).

James Fannin, who had immigrated to Texas only in 1834 (and would later lead scores of foreign volunteers to their deaths), sent an appeal that insisted that "the design of Santa Anna [is] to overrun the country and exterminate every white man within its borders" (Roberts and Olson, 2001: 144). "Frantic" that external support for the Army of Texas was insufficient to match the massive Mexican military, he found that "the threat of racial violence was an effective mobilizer when all else failed":

> Can it be possible that they—that any American—can so far forget the honor of their mothers, wives, and daughters, as not to fly to their rifles, and march to meet the Tyrant and avenge the insults and wrongs inflicted on his own country-women on the Rio Grande? What can be expected for the Fair daughters of chaste white women, when their own country-women are prostituted by a licensed soldiery, as an inducement to push forward into the Colonies, where they may find fairer game? (Brown, 2000: 102–103)

Texians used "the specter of interracial rape" as an effective rallying point (Jackson, 2003: 377), and this same appeal to chivalry and the threat to the purity of the women of the community would be echoed by jihadists some 175 years later against American occupation forces in Iraq.

Austin also warned of planned ethnic cleansing, claiming in speeches that Mexicans wanted to wipe out all Anglos in Texas and turn the territory over to Blacks and Indians (Davis, 2003: 175), a message that no doubt resonated in a South recently shaken by the Turner slave rebellion. Austin went so far as to directly argue that prying Texas from Mexico would serve the strategic interests of slaveholding America:

> Texas will become a great outwork on the west to protect the outlet of this western world...to keep far away...from the weakest frontier in the nation...all enemies who might make Texas a door for invasion, or use it as a theatre from which mistaken philanthropists and wild fanatics might attempt a system of intervention in the domestic affairs of the South, which might lead to a servile war.... (Austin, 1836: 29)

"To suppose that such a cause will fail when defended by Anglo-Saxon blood, by Americans...would be calumny against republicanism and freedom, against a noble race," he declared, particularly when the Greeks and Poles he celebrated in his speeches had succeeded, even though "they had not been Anglo-Americans, but we are" (Austin, 1836: 27).

Thus, even though the issue of contention in Texas had not been the concerns of an ethnic group with less standing than other Mexican citizens, the failure of Mexican federalists and of an anticipated pan-American liberal movement to materialize prompted the shift in recruitment messaging to the defense of the Texian population. As the conflict progressed and atrocity stories received publicity, "the war assumed something of the aspect of a crusade, and men felt it was their Christian duty to drive the Mexican from the land desecrated by his presence" (Tapp, 1973: 9). Volunteer Creed Taylor recounted, "I thought I could shoot Mexicans as well as I could shoot Indians, or deer, or turkey; and so I rode away to a war" (Roberts and Olson, 2001: 47).

The Alternative Rationale: Follow the Money

Despite the deliberately constructed and evolving messaging, it would be disingenuous to ignore the fact that most of these defensive appeals accompanied some notice of the cheap and bountiful land available in Texas and the reward of land the Texian government offered to volunteer foreign fighters. This mixed messaging was evident in an October 5, 1835, announcement written for newspapers in the United States, in which Houston declared:

> War in defense of our rights, our oaths, and our constitutions is inevitable in Texas! If volunteers from the United States will join their brethren in this section, they will receive liberal bounties of land. We have millions of acres of our best lands unchosen and unappropriated. Let each man come with a good rifle, and one hundred rounds of ammunition, and come soon. Our war-cry is "Liberty or death." Our principles are to support the constitution, and down with the Usurper!!! (Roberts and Olson, 2001: 269)

Austin (1836: 25, 28) also offered multiple rationales for volunteering, often in the same speech. In Louisville, he reflected on the death of Kentucky-born Ben Milam in taking Béxar, exhorting "his countrymen to embark in the holy cause of liberty for which he died," and also described "our cause of religious toleration and pure religion." But he abruptly shifted to the availability of good agricultural land. Later, he paired the idea that "the march of the present age" would bring liberty to "benighted Mexico" with the argument that freeing Texas would "open vast areas for free enterprise" and for those who wished to escape "cold weather."

Branch T. Archer, president of the consultation developing a constitution for the Republic of Texas, noted as early as November 3, 1835, that men and money were already coming in from abroad but "that those who would come should know that deeds of heroism and chivalry would be rewarded," and he addressed a letter to the Committee for Texas in New Orleans emphasizing that "any who embark in our cause in the Army or Navy shall be liberally rewarded in land and money" (Miller, 1971: 28). The constitutional convention held in the town of Washington offered even more generous terms, as reported in the *New Orleans Commercial Bulletin*: The offer of 640 acres for a six-month period of service would be doubled for those who stayed for the duration, and in case of death, the land would go to the volunteer's heirs (Elliott, 1944).

Broadsides noting this quickly appeared in New Orleans (DRTL—microfilm Reel 24, 1191). Another broadside said "emigrants desirous of assisting Texas at this important crisis of her affairs may have a free passage and equipments" by applying at a New Orleans hotel and that "now is the time to ensure a fortune in Land," with acreage based on length of service (DRTL—microfilm Reel 25, 1246).

This blend of greed and grievance in recruitment messaging was clearly reflected in the statements of some of the recruits defining the issue of contention. Kentuckian Daniel Cloud, an Alamo defender, was able to simultaneously hold forth against "monarchical, tyrannical despotism" and to note that Texas was "immense in extent and fertile in its soil" (Davis, 2002: 109). Michajah Autry wrote: "Be of good cheer Martha, I will provide you a sweet home. I shall be entitled to 640 acres of land for my services and 4444 acres upon condition of settling my family here" (Roberts and Olson, 2001: 103). And Abishai Dickson, a member of the Alabama Red Rovers fighting group who was soon to die with most of his compatriots, insisted "at this time there is not an armed Spaniard in all of Texas.... I have some hopes yet of making a little fortune" (Correspondence, December 29, 1835, Dickson Papers, DRTL).

It is unquestionable that some recruits were motivated by the desire for personal profit, but this rationale is insufficient to explain the scale of the foreign participation in the affairs of Texas.[10] The shifting casus belli offered by recruiters in Texas and New Orleans was intended to widen the scope of conflict to involve the largest possible audience. Evidence for the eventual success of the framing effort comes from the large donations for the Texan cause made across the United States. As described in the following chapters, similar fund-raising drives accompanied subsequent foreign fighter recruitment efforts, and it stretches credulity to assume that donors expected direct returns. Had every donor been a relative of a foreign fighter hoping to increase the odds that they would win land, it seems far more likely they would have invested in supplies and arms for the volunteer, rather than contributing to the collective capacity of Texian independence forces.

Additionally, the Neutrality Act of 1800 was in effect, although not enforced in this case with very much vigor by the pro-Texian Jackson administration. Offenders were liable for fines of $1,000 and three years of imprisonment for fighting for a foreign entity, with penalties of three times those amounts for anyone organizing a military expedition. However, a significant loophole in the law was that violators could be prosecuted only after the event, once supplies or troops were dispatched. Recruiters were therefore careful to advertise for "emigrants" rather than troops and did not solicit the public for weapons, but instead for other necessary supplies (Reid, 2007: 73). Rather than recruiters pushing the defensive frame of the conflict only as moral justification for mercenaries, it is evident that insurgent leaders also used the availability of farmland as an opportunity to stay within the law while advancing their political causes.

Another strike against a purely greed-based model for attracting recruits comes from the fact that so many volunteers returned home without collecting their bounty. Some reported being frustrated by a *lack* of opportunities for combat, and others who stayed for the duration appeared uninterested in securing their due reward. Although it is impossible to gauge individual motivation even with recorded statements of intent, an examination of general information about the recruits who went to Texas will illumine those whom recruiters developed their messages to target, and why the grievance portion of the message may have been more effective than greed.

Target Audience

Texian Noah Smithwick identified a taxonomy of the Texas forces as local Texian soldiers in defense of their country, "another class" from the United States come to aid their "countrymen," some adventurers, and some "actuated by no higher principle than prospective plunder" (Lack, 1992: 141). Smithwick, who had relocated from North Carolina in 1829, recalled of the foreign volunteers: "Some were for independence, some were for the Constitution of 1824; and some were for anything, just so long as it was a row"[11] (Hardin, 1994: 13).

With the exception of the large, polyglot New Orleans Greys and Tampico Blues companies organized under the auspices of the Friends of Texas and

General Méxia, most other companies or small groups of recruits were homogeneous, family and friends hailing from the same communities. The New Orleans Greys, however, were recruited largely from among dislocated individuals looking for employment in the port. Lack (1992) reports that although one observer claimed that they were "generally collected from the dregs of cities and towns," most would have been characterized as men of good character for that era, and many had already established their own businesses. Among them, "youth seems to be one recurring factor" (Brown, 1999: 16).

Stout (2008: 52) adds that while records suggest that the "chief inspiration" among recruits appears to have been the desire to right what they perceived as wrongs against their fellow American colonists, "many of the volunteers were very young. Very likely, among those youngsters, the moral impetus was primarily window dressing for what was arguably their greater motivation: to seek adventure." Most were reluctant, despite the promise of material incentives, to commit to a set length of service and probably were not interested in the rough frontier living and hard work necessary to develop land in Texas. Brown (1999: vi) adds that "'the promise of a good scrape with the Mexicans' was the primary attraction for many of the volunteers, especially the younger ones."

Therefore, while Fannin had called for professional soldiers rather than volunteers (Brown, 2000: 31), few of the Greys had any prior military experience. An exception was John Cook, an English artilleryman. Both companies of the Greys had doctors, including one who had been born in the Netherlands and graduated from the University of Pennsylvania's medical school. Another recruit was the son of one of the founders of Reform Judaism, a wealthy Charleston, South Carolina, developer (Brown 1999: 17). An officer from Philadelphia was described as being in the theater business (or "the histrionic profession"); another was only 16. Among the Tampico Blues, of 31 captured by Mexico, 16 were Europeans, and most of the rest were from the New York region (Reid, 2007: 192). Herman Ehrenberg, one of six Germans among the Greys, was the son of a liberal Prussian court officer who had been forced to flee after participating in student demonstrations[12] (Roberts and Olson, 2001: 290–292).

Evidence for impetuous adventurism contributing more to the pool of recruits than the prospect of homesteading is found among the few surviving accounts of volunteers. Dillard Cooper (1895: 1), a 21-year-old Alabaman from a prosperous family, "had long felt the desire to take part in some great adventure of this kind and this was my first opportunity." He waited two weeks for a local company to organize and, without informing his wife where he was going, set off to join up with a group of 90 others in the Alabama Red Rovers.

John Duval (1892: 13–15) recounted: "A volunteer company was organized in my native village, and although I was scarcely old enough to bear arms, I resolved to join it. But it was no aspiration for 'military fame' that induced me to do so...." Rather, the descriptions of Texas by a family friend prompted "an ardent longing" to see the territory.

> By joining this company I thought an opportunity would be afforded me of gratifying it which perhaps might never again offer itself, and so, in spite of the opposition of relatives and friends, my name was added to the muster roll. I purchased a good Kentucky rifle (with the use of which I was already acquainted)...[and, departing,] I fell into ranks and amid the waving of handkerchiefs and cheering of bystanders.

Gone to Texas: Mobilization

New Orleans was abuzz before the first public meeting of the Committee for Texas. Ehrenberg (1968: 1) arrived to find every street corner in the city posted with two-foot-high placards calling citizens to a rally. Wagons went through the streets to collect arms, and "many veterans of the Battle of New Orleans sorrowfully gave up rifles for the Texian cause" (Miller, 2004: 77).

The meeting, held on October 13, 1835, attracted an overflow crowd and had to be moved to a large shopping center. Even then, so many had not been able to get inside that they repeated the entire presentation again downstairs for new arrivals. Attendees heard resolutions put forward by a Mexican political exile that included "aid and support" to save the Texians from "the tyrant's military rule" and to establish other committees throughout the United States "in favor of the same sacred cause which our fathers in '76 defended." Sign-up sheets for volunteers were left in the coffee houses for several days afterward (Miller, 2004: 59–62).

However, the first night of activity succeeded in raising $10,000 in donations, and the audience witnessed 115 volunteers enroll to travel into Mexican Texas for combat.

Ehrenberg, one of those recruited, heard numerous speakers from Texas and local Masonic business leaders appeal to their patriotism and remind the audience that the people who asked for assistance were fellow Americans (Ehrenberg, 1968: 2–3). The Committee for Texas obtained artillery pieces for the company and hired a U.S. Army veteran to conduct training drills with them. It also paid travel expenses for the first group, and Committee for Texas President Adolphus Sterne personally provided muskets to the first 50 volunteers. Subsequent groups of recruits would travel to Texas by either land or ship, depending on their sponsor on the committee. Recruits purchased their own uniforms, but the committee or individual sponsors provided the weapons (Miller, 2004: 71–79).

Recruiters also conducted separate efforts at the port of New Orleans, as well as on the docks of other major American cities. In November, the provisional governor of Texas signed an order issuing letters of marque and reprisal to attract privateers to harass Mexican commerce. Sailors of diverse nationalities joined the effort, including former Navy personnel recruited by their old commanding officers. Unlike the foreign fighter regiments, these crews of privateers drew strong condemnation in the United States because of the concern that piracy would become endemic if raiders could claim to be serving Texas (Jordan, 2006: 26, 38). For this reason, the Texian General Council required all raiding ships to sail under a Mexican flag with "1824" emblazoned on it to signify that they were not pirates (Davis, 2002: 202). A large recruiting office opened on Front Street in New York's Lower East Side, sending multinational groups of sailors, most armed only with swords, to the Gulf of Mexico. In at least one instance, they were arrested by the British and held for months at Nassau, where "the Europeans, who are Poles, French and Germans, applied to be separated from the Americans"[13] (Reid, 2007: 112).

Texian leaders were otherwise sensitive to concerns about the U.S. Neutrality Act and "instructed volunteers to formally organize and declare their intentions only after reaching Texas." There were, however, no laws against exporting weapons or supplies (Stout, 2008: 46), and the simple gray jackets worn by the recruits and the rifles they carried, considered legitimate defense for frontier families, made impeding them difficult (Reid, 2007: 73). Although the New Orleans district attorney had warned the committee that he would prosecute any organizing of troops, he concluded that "it does not appear that any regular enlisting or entering as soldiers has taken place within the meaning of the statute" (Miller, 2004: 77).

Recruitment Efforts Elsewhere

While New Orleans was home to the recruitment effort, Texian supporters extended their efforts throughout the United States and, in the process, inspired individuals to recruit their own groups from their local communities. Recruiters staged public rallies in Boston, New York, Philadelphia, Mobile, Nashville, Lexington, Cleveland, and Baltimore, and in the six months between October 1835 and April 1836, more than 1,500 Americans joined the war in Texas. A few went individually or in small private groups, but most joined companies formed at recruitment rallies, such as the Tennessee Mounted Volunteers and the Georgia Rattlers (Roberts and Olson, 2001: 95–96).

On October 17, 1835, Texian agents organized a rally at the Shakespeare Theatre in Mobile, Alabama, that raised $1,500 and enlisted several recruits. On October 20, at the Mobile Courthouse, another meeting passed a resolution that "the struggle then in progress was similar to that in 1776 and that it deserved all the assistance Alabamans could give." At a mass meeting held on November 30 in Montgomery, "as an inspiration to the Alabamans there were present at this session approximately one hundred volunteers from Macon, Georgia, on their way to Texas" (Elliott, 1947). This Macon group originated with a public rally promoted by the headline of the *Macon Messenger* (which also appeared in other Georgia newspapers): "The cries of our fellow countrymen of Texas have reached us calling for help against the Tyrant and Oppressor! Let all who are disposed to respond to the cry, in any form, assemble at the courthouse, on Tuesday evening next, at early candle light" (Elliott, 1944).

Shades of Greys and Other Groups

In December, Austin noted with satisfaction to a New Orleans audience that there was now a "Louisiana Battalion, a Georgia Battalion, a Mississippi Battalion, an Alabama Battalion, and a Tennessee Battalion" (Brands, 2004: 324–325). Some of the groups were the product of the Texian recruitment apparatus, but others were evidently homegrown emulators. "In most instances local communities provided the essential clothing and equipment.... Colonel James Saunders, then a child helping to make the [infamous Red Rover] uniforms, recalled 'We were wonderfully proud of our part in the work and felt in our hearts that we were helping to free Texas'" (Jenkins, 1965: 107–108).

While the initial force that departed from New Orleans came to be called the New Orleans Greys after their uniforms, many groups would also later use the name Greys (or Grays) and their ranks sometimes overlapped. (Various members of the original group were also known as the San Antonio Greys and as Cooke's Greys, and they also eventually merged with the Mobile Greys and the Montgomery Greys, etc.) No records of the original muster of the New Orleans Greys survive, but before leaving the city, it had already divided into two companies—two different men had assumed the role of commander—with records in Texas indicating approximately 60 in each group. The only apparent distinction in membership between the companies was that the Europeans had joined one of them en masse. However, most non-Americans were still from Anglophone countries, and language had probably not been an operational concern. All members enlisted as privates, with commanding officers elected once they reached Texas. "The Greys, with their distinctive uniforms and new weapons, added an element of professionalism to the Texan army and bolstered morale immensely. Later, several Texan leaders including Stephen F. Austin would credit the Greys' arrival with preventing the collapse of the army and, therefore, the revolution itself"[14] (Brown, 1999: 11–19, 24, 46).

Meanwhile, other groups coming over the border openly named themselves with flamboyant titles like the United States Independent Cavalry Company or simply named themselves after their home localities, like the Lynchburg Volunteers and the Paducah Volunteers. In defiance of the Neutrality Act, many state arsenals supplied military firearms to recruits, and two Alabama groups, the Red Rovers and the Huntsville Volunteers, bought or borrowed hundreds of muskets from the state (Reid, 2007: 74, 94–95).

The Red Rovers are remembered for their heavy casualties in the Goliad massacre and for the outlandish uniforms that inspired their name. The company was raised by Dr. Jack Shackleford, a wealthy 45-year-old community leader in the small town of Courtland, Alabama, who responded to a "Down with the Usurper!" advertisement in the *Huntsville Democrat* and organized a drive for recruitment and donations. He succeeded in raising $1,000 and approximately 60 volunteers, while the townswomen made "uniforms of fringed shirts in red, green and brown checks with bright red trousers."[15] They were joined by three other groups from Alabama, with a contingent of roughly 160 Alabamans ultimately reaching Texas (Stout, 2008: 48–49).

Elsewhere, the city of Macon hosted the largest gathering in its history in November 1835 in support of Texas. By the end of the month, nearly 80 recruits had departed for Mexico, and this contingent gained strength as it stopped in various cities along the way, including the volunteers from the rally in Mobile. The party described themselves as "emigrants" to avoid violating the Neutrality Act, but their intent was obvious (Stout, 2008: 46). Supplemented by many recruits in their "early teens," many of whom would return to Georgia after the war rather than settle abroad, the Macon enlistment ultimately grew to a force of 200 by the time it reached New Orleans (Brown, 2000: 78).

Accurate records pertaining to these groups are rare and questionable. Their overall numbers are not known, and different sources provide starkly different information about even the better reported groups. For example, one source (Young, 1986: 7) states that the Kentucky Mustangs were originally an eight-man squad that grew to 20 by the time it reached New Orleans, while another (Tapp, 1973: 11) claims that 54 Mustangs left Kentucky in November 1835. Also, data concerning recruiting failures are nearly impossible to locate, although not every recruitment effort was successful. Georgian Thomas Jefferson Chambers reportedly spent more than $23,000 to recruit a 1,000-man volunteer reserve army, but neither he nor they ever made it to the field (Stout, 2008: 52).

Still, small groups inspired by the efforts of the Committee for Texas, but probably not directly affiliated with it, were the main element of the force of foreign fighters that entered Mexico during the civil war. In January 1836, Dr. Barnard of Chicago reached New Orleans by his own efforts, where he watched a fund-raising play dramatizing the Texian victory at San Antonio and obtained his military supplies. Traveling onward by boat, his party encountered the Alabaman group, which "greeted with three cheers, which were heartily returned," and he soon joined their ranks (Barnard, 1885: 3–7). If this account is accurate, it would seem unlikely that separate mercenary groups, who would presumably be competing for the best plots of land, would be so excited to encounter each other on their way to the field.

The passage from their home communities into Mexico was generally the easiest element of the journey for the foreign fighters. Commanders at border posts had orders to stop them, but they were easily evaded by staying in the homes of sympathizers and sneaking through woods (Ehrenberg, 1968: 6). In some instances, a number of soldiers in the U.S. Army serving on the Louisiana border "deserted with the tacit approval of their commanders in order to fight with the revolutionaries" (Davis, 2002: 210).

Sporadic newspaper coverage followed them, "heralding them as heroes even before they arrived at the scene of war," and they were honored at stops along the way on both sides of the border. On arrival in Texas, the Greys were presented a flag by local prominent ladies of the community, knelt and kissed the soil, and took the Texas oath of citizenship (Miller, 2004: 80–83). In Nagodoches, Adolphus Sterne arrived to fête them at a "feast of liberty" (Brown, 2000: 164). And yet, per Brinkley (1952: 97):

> As these American volunteers left their homes, full of enthusiasm for the Texan cause, they could not foresee that by the time they reached their destination the apathy, mismanagement and confusion in Texas would place them in a position where they seemed to be continuing a resistance which the Texans themselves had apparently abandoned.

The Experience of the Foreign Recruits in the Field

Almost immediately, differences over strategy erupted between the Texian settlers and the foreign fighters. When the Army of Texas decided to end the siege of San Antonio de Béxar for the winter, 250 to 300 of the foreigners deserted out of frustration, with the generals "begging" them not to leave. Texian Ben Milam disobeyed orders and, with the aid of the Greys, took the town in urban combat (although dying in the process). This rift led many foreign volunteers to refuse to accept the orders of Texian officers. Major Robert Morris of the New Orleans Greys wrote to Houston that "there are now 225 men, nearly all from the United States, who on no consideration will enter into any service connected with the Regular Army, the name of which is a perfect Bugbear to them" (Hardin, 1994: 67–68).

Many members of the regular Texian army, comprised of local volunteers, believed that they had succeeded in eliminating the presence of Mexican occupation and prepared to return home, but the recently arrived volunteer companies were dissatisfied with this result[16] (Reid, 2007: 52, 62).

> The Greys reached the rebel camp at a critical time for the Texas revolution. With many of the colonists among the insurgents returning to their homes, the new arrivals kept the rebel column from disintegrating entirely. And having traveled so far to engage the Mexicans in battle, they had no desire to return home with their carbines unfired and their Bowie knives unbloodied. (Roberts and Olson, 2001: 295)

Other volunteers, having just arrived on the scene, viewed the capture of San Antonio as anticlimactic and immediately sought to join an expedition against the garrison at Matamoros over the objections of Houston and other officers of the Texian army. Delays in mounting that expedition led more of "the most impatient members" to abandon Texas and return home in frustration, and the well-prepared Mexican forces at Matamoros easily eliminated a force that had dwindled from more than 600 to just 450 (Brands, 2004: 318–320). This outcome occurred in part because the Texian and American commanders in San Antonio would not acknowledge each other's authority and command broke down. In the process, two-thirds of the garrison in San Antonio departed, leaving only a few remaining local Texians, less than half of the Greys, and a "small rump of Peacock's United States Invincibles" to protect the Alamo (Reid, 2007: 67–68).

"The Conduct of Wild Savages"

Part of the difficulty in coordinating between the settlers and the foreigners lay in the total lack of military discipline among the volunteer groups. In addition to electing their own officers, recruits shifted between different companies at will. Before the march to Matamoros and the other calamities that followed it, there had been so many volunteers in different small groups that Houston compelled them to reorganize into two battalions, Georgia and Lafayette. Houston sent some of the more popular leaders of the militias to serve as recruiters back in the United States, and in many cases, their followers simply left with them (Brown, 2000: 119, 120).

Many of the volunteers had never had military training; "they fought best when breaking ranks and fighting hand to hand." Rather than a lack of courage, the volunteers seemed unwilling to stop fighting. Pinned under fire during the siege of Béxar, the Greys voted to fight to the death rather than surrender and afterward protested that the terms of surrender were too lenient on the Mexicans. Houston had to intervene to stop Fannin's policy of paying volunteers with "spoils taken from the enemy," and heavy drinking and brawls were common among the bored volunteers. Some members apparently committed deeds that were unacceptable even under these conditions: Without elaborating, Texan records of the Greys note two members who were "expelled" (Brown, 1999: 62, 70, 117, 125, 158, 294, 305). Under such circumstances, it is not surprising that the foreign volunteers soon exhausted their welcome among the Texians, with one writing to Austin to complain that they had "treated the wimon of this place worse than all of the Comanshee nation could have done and dragged me out of the house and nearly beat me to death.... The conduct of wild savages would be preferable to the insults of such Canebols" (Roberts and Olson, 2001: 49).

Ehrenberg's account of service in the Greys hardly contradicts this portrait. He reminisced that when reveille was called, "We Greys, particularly the Europeans, looked at each other greatly amused by this specimen of Texian military discipline." The foreign fighters would arrive at muster half-dressed, and only if muster did not interfere with their impromptu barbecues. During the siege of Béxar, "we all thought this cannonading huge fun" and the "merry laughter of the men around the guns" rolled through the campsites. Upon learning of the decision to attack Béxar, the Greys "romped and yelled with joy," and then played "Yankee Doodle" when going into battle. At Goliad, Fannin ordered them to stay with the wounded, whereas most Greys thought it "better to sacrifice a part than the whole." Ultimately, the volunteers used the threat of violence to secure their own delegates to the Texian constitutional consultation, and they installed hard-liners who pushed for independence (Ehrenberg, 1968: 39, 43–45, 48, 68, 105, 137).

Given the dissension they introduced within Texian ranks and their propensity to support his political rivals, even Austin privately wished to rid himself of the foreigners. "In the name of Almighty God," he wrote, "send no more ardent spirits to this camp—if any is on the road turn it back" (Roberts and Olson, 2001: 49). But the foreign recruits continued to arrive and to be involved in embarrassing incursions that set back the Texian cause.

"Cannon Fodder": The Case of the Tampico Blues

Chief among these was the fate of the group recruited by the previously described Mexican federalist exile José Antonio Méxia. The group did not have an official name at the time of its mission but was later known as the Tampico Blues. Their blue uniforms were surplus from the 1815 Battle of New Orleans (Davis, 2002: 210); the other half of their name referred to Méxia's intended target, which, unknown to the recruits at the time, was not even in Texas.

Méxia was reportedly "advertizing as a broker offering land to settlers, and he signed on several dozen Americans, who had no clue about his real intentions....When they learned of the expedition's military nature, most of the recruits balked, but it was too late" (Roberts and Olson, 2001: 71). The 150 recruits believed that they were going to Brazoria, Texas, but the expedition leaders told them that a storm had blown them off course and so they were putting into Tampico, well south of the boundaries of Texas.

This scheme was part of Méxia's broader goal of leading an anticentralist revolt throughout Mexico, but the invasion on November 15 did not generate wide enough federalist support to avoid being decimated by the Mexican army, and other boats had to come to perform an emergency rescue. (The 31 recruits left behind were all killed.) Those who returned home were not honored like the Greys and other foreign fighters who went to Texas but broadly denounced as "pirates and traitors." Miller speculates that the Blues may have been deliberately sent as cannon fodder by the Committee for Texas as a way of eliminating undesirable elements in New Orleans. After Tampico, Méxia realized that federalism was on the wane in Mexico and stopped working with the committee[17] (Miller, 2004: 94, 104, 106).

Counterinsurgency

Santa Anna had hoped to put down the Texian revolt quickly as well, before support for intervention could be raised in the United States, as he feared the inevitable loss of California and New Mexico if Texas were to fall. With this threat looming, he declared that "the foreigners" had "audaciously declared a war of extermination to the Mexicans and should be treated in the same manner" (Davis, 2002: 199, 203). It was therefore a matter of Mexican policy to execute any American prisoners, whom Santa Anna differentiated from the Texian insurrectionists (Santa Anna in Castañeda, 1928: 25).

However, Brinkley (1952: 97) noted, "The effect [of this order] was to confirm the conviction that the Texans were at war to save themselves from a military despot and to strengthen the determination of Americans to come to their assistance." Santa Anna's argument was that norms for the treatment of prisoners of war did not apply to foreign fighters:

> The invaders were all men who [were] moved by their desire of conquest.... What can we call them? How shall they be treated? All the existing laws, whose strict observance the government had just recommended, marked them as pirates and outlaws. The nations of the world would never have forgiven Mexico had it accorded them rights, privileges, and considerations which the common law of peoples accords only to constituted nations. (Santa Anna in Castañeda, 1928: 17)

From Mercenaries to Martyrs

Given the Mexican policy toward foreign fighters, it was inevitable that the Anglo-American recruits would pay the heaviest price. Part of the reason that so many were captured, however, was their insistence on engaging in highly aggressive missions. The Matamoros expedition had been an attempt to shift to an offensive strategy and engage the Mexican army before it could regroup after the loss of San Antonio. Brinkley (1952: 90–93) suggests that the strategy was "undoubtedly due partly to a desire to keep the newly arrived volunteers occupied." Houston declared such an effort to be unwise, but he had no authority to order the volunteers, who were outside his chain of command. Other operations designed to support the failed attack on Matamoros subsequently drew away even more of the foreign recruits from the Alamo garrison.

Still, with most local military personnel having returned to their homes, the majority of Alamo defenders were foreign fighters rather than Texians.

The New Orleans Greys and Mobile Greys constituted the bulk of the garrison, with many others being recent arrivals from Kentucky and Tennessee, such as the party that included Davy Crockett (Brinkley, 1952: 96). Alamo records currently list 189 defenders, with only 10 born in Texas—nine of whom were Tejanos—and 29 Europeans (http://www.thealamo.org/battle/defenders.php).

The Mexican siege to retake the Alamo lasted from February 23 to March 6, 1836. Given the surrender policies of both sides, it is not surprising that there were virtually no survivors once the vastly larger Mexican force overwhelmed the fortifications. The New Orleans Greys, with their new long rifles provided by the Committee for Texas, were reportedly the best armed defenders (Brown, 1999: 179). Their blue company standard had flown at the Alamo during the siege, and Santa Anna ordered it removed and publicized as proof that the Texians were traitors and that most of the trouble was caused by "Anglo-Americans who had entered illegally"[18] (Hardin, 1994: 156).

Although the Alamo remains firmly entrenched in American popular imagination, a subsequent mass execution of foreign fighters shortly afterward attracted just as much outrage in the United States at the time, and it remains memorialized in Texas. The largest concentration of foreign volunteers in any battle of the Texas Revolution occurred at Coletto Creek, when a force comprised largely of recent arrivals under the command of Colonel James Fannin, himself a recent immigrant, surrendered to the Mexican Army on March 20, 1836. They were subsequently marched to the barracks at Goliad, where at least 342 prisoners were executed with no warning on Palm Sunday, March 27, as others escaped by fleeing during the confusion.

Among the fatalities were most of the company of Red Rovers, who came from a community of only 300 (Young, 1986: 1, 5), but of whom 52 of 60 were killed in the Goliad Massacre (Simpson, 1978: 3). Their commander, Jack Shackleford, was spared because he was a surgeon and of use to the Mexican troops—and this also saved Dr. Barnard of Chicago who had joined him—but his son, nephews, and close friends died within his hearing (Brands, 2004: 405).

Of the 10 companies that surrendered with Fannin, three originated in Alabama, three in Georgia, and two in Kentucky, and the other two were largely foreign recruits as well (Brinkley, 1952: 96). The New Orleans Greys present "were among the first to be marched out unarmed and massacred" (Brown 1999: vi). Roughly 140 Alabamans (Elliott, 1947) and 85 Georgians were killed, and meetings of Texas sympathizers continued in Georgia as late as September 1836, well after the conclusion of the revolution (Elliott,

1944). Until the American Civil War, a quarter of a century later, Goliad marked largest single-day loss of American combatants in U.S. history (Stout, 2008: xii).

Among the survivors who fled was Ehrenberg, who would recount that a German officer in the Mexican army had invited his fellow Germans who were prisoners at Goliad aside and offered to have them spared if they would switch sides. Ehrenberg rejected the offer, later writing: "It was mere nonsense to talk of belonging to different nations when feeling and misfortune made us one.... We were no longer English, German, or American; we were Texans" (Roberts and Olson, 2001: 403). With news of the Alamo and Goliad spreading, a similar transformation occurred in American and European public opinion and foreign policy, which swung decisively in favor of Texan independence from the apparently barbarous Santa Anna.

Brinkley (1952: 97–98) noted the irony of the Mexican policy on foreign fighters and posed an interesting counterfactual: "It would be interesting to speculate...that if these prisoners had been paroled and landed on the wharves at New Orleans, each with his painful story of Texan mismanagement and neglect, Texas' standing with the American people would have fallen to a new low...." Less noticed among the calls for revenge emanating north of the border was the fact that, of the 700 killed in action or taken as prisoners during the spring of 1836, less than 20 percent had been Texas residents for longer than six months.

Outcome and Legacy

With the foreign insurgents mostly dead and Houston's small force in retreat, Santa Anna assumed that the military conflict was over and had with him only a relatively small force that was easily captured in a surprise counterattack at San Jacinto on April 21 (Reid, 2007: 153–154). Santa Anna was taken prisoner, and he agreed to cede Texas north of the Rio Grande and recognize its independence in exchange for his release, although his government refused to recognize this claim and he was—temporarily—toppled from power. More immediately, the surrender agreement was nearly scuttled by a newly arrived volunteer force from New Orleans that opposed releasing the Mexican leader and instead seized and held him for a time under its own guard (Brinkley, 1952: 108, 112).

Subsequently, a third company of New Orleans Greys entered Texas after the surrender and tried again to take Matamoros (Brown, 1999: 253). This was not an isolated phenomenon. Texan military records indicate that approximately 900 Texans fought at San Jacinto, but fewer than 200 of them remained in Texas in July, meaning that an astonishing number went home immediately after the victory without staying to collect land claims. However, by the end of the summer, the Texan army had more than 2,500 on its muster rolls. Nearly all of the soldiers in the now sovereign Republic of Texas were new arrivals. Many had come for vengeance and were disappointed that the fighting was over and the Mexican president left alive.

> [The newcomers] had neither homes nor rights in Texas to defend. The attention of most of these newcomers had been attracted to Texas by dramatic stories of Mexican atrocities at the Alamo and Goliad, and by promises of liberal land bounties made by desperate Texian agents in the United States during the dark days immediately preceding San Jacinto.... They proved to be a turbulent and troublesome group.... President David Burnet realized that they constituted a serious threat to the civil authorities, but he was in no position to disband them. [Officials] told agents in New Orleans not to send any more volunteers, and sought to employ those there by sending them to fight Indian tribes. (Brinkley, 1952: 113–115)

Still, neither the Texians nor newcomers could be sure that the war was actually over, so many of the late arrivals may have actually believed that they could still help to secure sovereignty. Undoubtedly, however, one attraction for new arrivals was the continuation by the Texas Congress, over the veto of President Houston, of bounties for foreign military volunteers, extended to October 1837. Administration of the bounties was lax and corrupt, and "probably no one will ever know the exact number of headright certificates issued nor the amount of land conveyed by them." However, 7,469 bounty warrants for volunteer service were issued (many of these for individuals who came after the revolution), totaling more than 5 million acres, and 1,816 battle donation grants were subsequently awarded to heirs or survivors of key battles like Goliad, totaling more than 1 million acres. Only 115 were issued to the heirs of Alamo defenders, however, an indication that many who were entitled to Texas land did not collect it (Miller, 1971: 31–34, 49). For example, Tapp (1973: 15) reported that there was no evidence that any heirs of the Kentucky Mustangs ever applied for the land due to them.

One reason for the apparent short number of claims by foreign veterans of the revolution was the very economic underdevelopment of Texas that had initially prompted offers of land as payment. Although the republic was initially grateful for the opportunity to build a standing army to defend against potential Mexican efforts to reclaim territory, it soon became evident that the fledgling sovereign state could not afford to maintain this force, and it made cuts that left hundreds unemployed and crime rates high. Many veterans were unable to pay the surveyors' fees required to stake a claim and instead sold their bounty certificates at cut-rate prices. At the outset of the republic, President David Burnet questioned the need to fill "our country with an unprofitable tribe of needy adventurers" (Hardin, 2007: 21, 69, 125, 137–139, 146).

Still, despite the poor economy of Texas, which would soon contribute to the end of its sovereignty and lead to its annexation by the United States, the fact that foreign fighters were no longer welcome took some time to register among Americans. In late 1836, the outraged "Messrs. Wilson and Postlethwaite of Kentucky" published a warning to other would-be volunteers that their battalion of 300 from Lexington had not been welcome or offered any bounty of land (DRTL—microfilm Reel 24, 1184).

In 1842, a group of 20 from Tennessee, responding to reports that thousands of Mexicans had retaken Texas and editorials that "new hands must pick up the banners" of the 28 Volunteer State natives who died at Alamo, raised $900 and made their way south to find nothing but "ingratitude." That July, President Houston told the Senate that volunteers from the United States "are expensive as they have heretofore proved useless to our country" (Altom, 1997: 3, 11).

Some of the foreign fighters did rise to distinction, with one of the original Greys promoted to Houston's general staff (Miller, 2004: 166) and another elected to the Texas legislature. Other surviving Greys returned in 1836 for more tours of duty but were honorably discharged that fall and left. One, John Rees, returned to his native Wales and helped lead an insurrection against the crown. Herman Ehrenberg returned to Europe and published in German a best-selling account of his time with the Greys. Among many other accomplishments, he grew wealthy as a mineralogist, surveying numerous claims during the gold rush, and served in the Mexican-American War and as a federal representative to Indian nations. But despite his self-reported cry of "Texas Forever!" he never returned to claim land (Brown, 1999: 254–257).

Conclusions

Cartoons used to teach history lessons to Texas schoolchildren claimed that the revolution was the inevitable product of the "age old prejudice of race," and historian Eugene Barker called it a fundamentally racial or cultural conflict (Crisp, 2005: 23). However, an examination of the messaging used to recruit those who fought the revolution demonstrates that recruiters first stressed common ties to Mexicans and a shared enemy in advancing military despotism. Both greed and grievance featured in messaging, as recruiters tried different formulations in attempting to build a self-perpetuating crusade. The ultimate message of the necessity of defending the transnational Anglo-American community was the frame bridging of a conflict over local issues such as tariffs and property rights. Ironically, the initial coalition that launched the recruitment effort had been an Anglo-Mexican transnational community of classical liberal free traders.

The available data largely supported both hypotheses in this case: First, recruitment of most groups of foreign fighters occurred in small, rural Southern communities in which social pressure exerted through local recruitment drives enabled the mobilization of large groups of relatives and existing acquaintances. (See the chapter "Conclusion: Responses to Transnational Insurgency" for how this strategy has been employed in contemporary cases.) Also, advertising directed recruits to mass community rallies where they joined existing groups rather than encouraging them to go across the border and fight individually. The second hypothesis on defensive mobilization is also mostly supported: Potential recruits were promised individual rewards of land, but these were often covers to skirt laws against foreign recruitment, and recruiters still employed the frames of the threat by military dictatorship and, later, race war by Hispanics against Anglo-Saxon Americans. Neither of these frames would seem likely to encourage homesteaders or strategic mercenaries to settle on the front lines. Many recruits turned around and went home indignantly as soon as they realized that their participation in battle was not required by the Texians. However, regardless of the casus belli offered, the framing was defensive rather than expansionist.

The immediate consequences of this recruitment effort were the hundreds of foreign fighters killed in Texas and at Tampico by a regime committed to preventing any transnational incursions threatening its territory. By pursuing this policy, however, Mexico gained international opprobrium, and the United States and European powers recognized Texan independence. As Santa Anna feared, the loss of Texas led to the loss of the rest of upper Mexico, and the United States expanded to be a continental power that was within sailing distance of Asia.

It is unclear whether the Committee for Texas influenced recruiting practices in any subsequent conflicts, but 150 years later, the fruits of its labors would inspire a Texas congressman to arm mujahidin in the Afghanistan War (see chapter 6). One conclusion that might be drawn from its experience is that, in the nineteenth century, shared ideology was not as significant as ethnonationalism in building working transnational coalitions. This dynamic began to change in the twentieth century, as ideology became more salient in political identification, and comrades with no ties of ethnic kinship whatsoever joined to fight for shared interests in the outcome of foreign civil wars.

4

The Spanish Civil War (1936–1939)

IN THE EARLY hours of November 8, 1936, as Nationalist forces closed on Madrid, the defending Republican population was startled by the arrival from behind their lines of "well-uniformed soldiers wearing large blue berets and pulling machine guns on rubber wheels behind them...singing the *Internationale* in a foreign language." According to Eduardo de Guzman, a journalist on the scene, "they fought magnificently, with a military organization and discipline the militias by and large had lacked. In some ways, they taught the militias how to fight. They dug foxholes which no one had thought of doing before" (Fraser, 1979: 263).

Who were these foreigners who aided in the successful defense of Madrid, and how did they suddenly appear in war-torn Spain? Where did they obtain the military training that the locals lacked? The impact of the International Brigades was immediate and overwhelming, as the embattled Republican faction turned the tide and put the Nationalists on the defensive for months, prolonging the Spanish Civil War by two years and leading to an influx of foreign fighters on both sides of the lines.

It is not a completely straightforward matter to label either of the sides as the insurgents in the Spanish Civil War. Both sides had foreign recruits serving in the regular military, as well as in irregular militias. The elected Republican government was not the stronger faction in the face of a Nationalist military insurrection, and, although it paid the salaries of most of its foreign fighters, for much of the war they were not under its control, but that of the Communist International (Comintern). Likewise, the Nationalists had the strong backing of major institutions within society, notably the Catholic Church, and received direct military assistance from other states while the Republicans did not. Foreign fighters for the rebel Nationalist faction were mostly, but not entirely, placed in the Army of Spain or the Spanish Foreign Legion. The historical conditions that produced these complex arrangements were also the reasons that so many outside parties believed the civil war to be their fight as well.

The self-described Republican faction (actually a coalition of socialists, communists, anarchists, and democrats) that nominally controlled the government at the outset of the war was immediately at a material disadvantage because it did not control most of the military resources of the state. The military-backed fascist faction (first named the Nationalists in propaganda by supporters in America), joined by the German, Italian, and Portuguese armies, actually received more international recognition and support than did the Republicans. For these reasons, the Republican faction was completely on the defensive, resorting to militias and irregular warfare conducted by foreign fighters (as depicted in Hemingway's *For Whom the Bell Tolls*). Comintern recruiters made the case to nearly 50,000 foreigners to join what was clearly the losing side for all but about four months of the three-year war. However, if the Republicans can be described as the government side, then the Nationalists were the insurgents, and the more than one thousand private volunteers on the fascist side count as foreign fighters. There were foreign volunteers on both sides of the Spanish Civil War, and valid arguments can be made for counting either or both as foreign fighters.

The Spanish Civil War represents a type 4 transnational insurgency, a nonethnic intrastate war in which the foreign fighters were noncoethnic with the local Spanish insurgents. Without any ethnic dimension around which to polarize a community of transnational volunteers, even the "Nationalist" side that proclaimed itself to be "Sons of Spain" fighting foreign invaders recruited from coreligionists of varying ethnicities who were not even Hispanophones. Consistent with other cases of this type, the foreign fighters in this instance would be expected to be True Believers who view the local civil conflict as just one front in a larger transnational struggle in defense of their group. In this case, most foreign recruits on one side in Spain were Communists, and on the other side they were Catholics, both groups having been told that they faced an existential threat at the hands of the other.

Although the Spanish Civil War is perhaps the best documented civil conflict featuring foreign fighters, there is no repository of information whatsoever on the subject in Spain. Instead, in addition to previously published histories and memoirs, I obtained dozens of original letters and propaganda material by going through the full catalog of the largest collection devoted to the war, the Southworth Collection in the University of California San Diego's Mandeville Special Collections, as well as all the files in the Abraham Lincoln Brigade Archive at New York University's Tamiment Library to produce a representative sample of recruitment messaging and response.

The available data therefore provide a great deal of information on recruitment in the United States and other English-speaking countries, and less on the French, German, and Italian recruits who constituted the bulk of the International Brigades. The large numbers of personal histories offered by Americans appears to be a cultural artifact, with veteran organizations in the other countries publishing a very limited number of memoirs.[1] Thus, while continental Europeans constituted the vast majority of volunteers, my data are not a fully representative sample. The story of foreign fighters in the Spanish Civil War has largely been told by outsiders.

Background to the Conflict

Spain had been a constitutional monarchy since 1876, but chronic instability led to a succession of military dictatorships supported by the crown. The further upheavals caused by the Great Depression led in 1931 to the establishment of a "Republic of workers of all categories" that implemented an ambitious program of landholding reform to modernize Spain's still essentially feudal system. This government's failure to consolidate power led to conservatives sweeping back into power in the 1933 elections, and they quickly set about trying to undo the agrarian reforms. They also took a hard line against striking miners in Asturias, sending a military response and imprisoning hundreds of thousands of their supporters.

Dissent continued, and, in 1936, an unwieldy working-class socialist-led coalition of republicans, communists, and anarchists won the elections with a mandate to reinstitute some of the agrarian and social reforms. The new Republican government was opposed by a Nationalist countercoalition of fascists, royalists, and conservative Carlists. A series of tit-for-tat assassinations of leading figures on each side provided the pretext for a cadre of generals, led by Francisco Franco of the Army of Africa stationed in Spanish-controlled Morocco, to issue a pronunciamiento on July 18, 1936, calling for the government to allow the military to assume political power to restore order. The demand was rejected by the leftists, and the Army of Africa and most of the regular military forces launched their assault, with logistical and material support from the fascist regimes in Italy, Germany, and Portugal (Eisenwein and Shubert, 1995: 8, 11, 16, 21–26, 32).

Militias immediately formed (or existing ones swelled) on both sides, and foreigners inflated the ranks of the separate Communist-, anarchist-, and republican-armed groups in particular. Many were leftist and anarchist refugees from fascist European states who had already sought shelter in the Spanish republic, and others had arrived in July for the People's Olympiad, which was meant to be an alternative to the Olympics being held in Nazi Berlin. Estimates of the number of foreign combatants who joined militias in Spain prior to international recruitment efforts by the Comintern range between 1,000 (Richardson, 1982: 29) and 15,000 (Johnston, 1967: 28).

International Context

Monteath's description (in Romeiser, 1982: 17) of the reaction of the international community to these developments can no doubt be applied to other, more recent conflicts involving foreign fighters: "The great powers of the day saw their foreign policy interests vitally at risk in a nation which, ironically, had exerted no major political influence on the world community in recent times, except perhaps to mark its own decline." Having failed to act to halt Italy's invasion of Ethiopia in 1935 or the remilitarization of the German Rhineland earlier that year, Spain's neighbors moved quickly to contain the crisis so that it would not draw in other European states, as civil unrest in Bosnia had done in 1914. The United Kingdom unilaterally banned arms sales to Spain on July 31, and France closed its border to military traffic on August 8 (Fraser, 1979: 127).

Later that month, 27 states signed the Non-Intervention Agreement, which prevented sales of arms to the Republican government, but this did not stop Germany—which sat on the League of Nations drafting committee—from sending aid to the outnumbered Nationalist faction (Rosenstone, 1969: 26). The agreement also created a Non-Intervention Committee to oversee compliance. Its three aims were (1) to control port and ground shipping, (2) to discourage foreign volunteers, and (3) to encourage the withdrawal of already deployed volunteers. The United States and Canada never entered the agreement, but in 1937 Canada passed the Foreign Enlistment Act, which made it a criminal offense to participate on either side in Spain. The U.S. Neutrality Act, passed more than a century earlier, remained in effect to prohibit American participation, but the United States continued to sell oil to both sides (Howard and Reynolds, 1986: 13–14). And while Germany, Italy, and Portugal supplied troops and matériel to their fascist cohorts in the Nationalist forces, only Mexico and the Soviet Union supplied arms to the Republic (Monteath in Romeiser, 1982: 18).

Comintern Intervention

While the Soviets were anxious to forestall the rise of a militaristic fascist regime allied with Hitler, Moscow remained typically cautious and initially unwilling to do more than covertly sell the Republic arms. Prime Minister Francisco Largo Caballero was not a Communist, and, although some of his coalition partners in the Popular Front government were, there were only 3,000 registered Communist Party members in Spain. General Secretary Josef Stalin did not consider their fates to be worth risking resources or strategic position (Krivitsky, 1939: 78; Southworth Collection, UCSD).

It was pressure within the Comintern that led to the decision in September to recruit sympathizers to counter the fascist troops pouring into Spain in open defiance of the League of Nations. A number of parties claim credit for the impetus to form the International Brigades (IB). Mario Nicoletti, an Italian Socialist leader in exile in Spain, met with Communist Party officials in Madrid at the outset of the war to arrange the formation of an Italian Legion independent of the command of the Spanish General Staff. Caballero, while grateful for foreign contributions, wanted all volunteers to join existing Spanish units and did not extend assistance (Johnston, 1967: 33–36).

Many of the foreigners present in Spain when the conflict began, particularly Communists and Socialists, joined *centuria* militias that came to be organized by nationality.[2] With the realization that a large international force would generate publicity and sympathy, French Communist leader Maurice Thorez flew to Moscow to argue that the Comintern should be used to recruit International Brigades (Howard and Reynolds, 1986: 16–17). Willy Muenzenberg, the Comintern propaganda chief for Western Europe, traveled to Moscow to second Thorez's suggestion. By the end of September, the Comintern had coordinated with its representatives in Italy, France, and Spain to organize the volunteer Italian column. With the initial results promising, the executive committee quickly decided to form columns in as many countries as possible[3] (Thomas, 2001: 438–439).

Why did Stalin permit this course of action despite his misgivings? According to Walter Krivitsky, the Soviet chief of military intelligence in Western Europe in 1936, Stalin maintained a very low opinion of the Comintern, which he liked to call the *lavotchka* ("the gyp joint"). Its members were "nothing but hirelings on our Soviet payroll. In ninety years they will never make a revolution anywhere." No longer concerned with world revolution himself, Stalin viewed the Comintern as a bumbling but occasionally useful arm of Soviet foreign policy, one that was worth placating with minor concessions. If help in organizing a transnational insurgency earned the grati-tude of his supporters in Western democracies, then that was preferable to having them criticize Soviet passivity in their popular presses (Krivitsky, 1939: 74, 76; Southworth Collection, UCSD).

The real impetus for the sponsorship of the IB was for Moscow to gain control of those already in Spain or arriving on their own. Stalin sent a seed force of 500 to 600 foreign Communists who had arrived in the Soviet Union as political refugees, whom he had wanted to unload for some time, and never permitted any Soviet citizens to join the IB. Soviet military advisors were sent to Spain once more than 15,000 other foreigners had already arrived, but they expressly served as consultants to the Spanish army, not in the IB (Krivitsky, 1939: 93–95; Southworth Collection, UCSD).

Institutions of Recruitment

The International Brigades, a term initially used during the Russian Civil War to describe Communist volunteers from abroad (some of whom were no doubt among the first sent to Spain), was headquartered in Paris. There, Josip Broz (later to be known as Josip Tito, president of Yugoslavia) had set up in local trade union offices an underground railroad to smuggle Communists from central and eastern Europe into France. His forged passport distribution center was now rededicated to the intake and indoctrination of recruits, who would then be sent over the Pyrenees into Spain (Thomas, 2001: 439–441).

The Comintern Executive Committee feared that if too many members joined the IB, then class struggles in home countries would suffer, and it therefore denied many activists permission to go to Spain[4] (Collum, 1992: 25). Instead, Moscow gave local Communist Party branches abroad recruitment quotas and instructed them to focus on trade unions and "democratic orga-nizations." Few in the Comintern leadership structure had experience with military recruiting, so the work was assigned to rank-and-file party organizers (Johnston, 1967: 9–10, 36). Georgi Dimitrov, the Bulgarian who headed the Comintern at the time, told an American correspondent in Moscow that the hope was to recruit Jewish nationalists, socialists, and liberals under an anti-fascist umbrella (Rosenstone, 1969: 88).

Workers of the World

Although a highly centralized, top-down operation, the Comintern ordered that volunteers should appear to be spontaneous and self-directed, as Stalin hoped to maintain plausible deniability about Soviet involvement in attacks against German forces (Richardson, 1982: 32). After the outset of the conflict, the quotas provided to party branches were usually higher than could be met. Volunteers who were not party members were subjected to examinations by NKVD secret police investigators and a doctor. During the course of the conflict, the IB produced an estimated 35,000 to 50,000 recruits, although probably no more than 18,000 were in Spain at any time (Thomas, 2001: 439–441).

The French were the largest contingent, with Germans and Italians in exile from their native fascist regimes also a substantial component of the IB. As the ranks grew, recruits were organized into brigades along largely national lines (Carr, 1984: 22–23). Ultimately, these all merged and were reformed as mixed brigades. There were just five brigades of international recruits—the XI through XV—which were variously known as "international," "mixed," or "mobile"[5] (Johnston, 1967: 45–46). While brigades were mixed, battalions were divided by nationality for linguistic purposes. One battalion was comprised of recruits who all spoke a little Russian or German and could therefore function together[6] (Richardson, 1982: 66).

The XI was the German-speaking Ernest Thalmann Brigade ("German, Austrian, Scandinavian, Dutch, and Swedish comrades fighting in brotherly unity"); XII was the Italian Garibaldi Brigade; XIII was the Slavic-speaking Dombrovsky Brigade comprised of Czechs, Poles, Yugoslavs, and Bulgarians; the XIV was the French "Commune de Paris"; and the XV was known as the Mixed International Brigade (Dahlem, 1938: 445; Southworth Collection, UCSD). The XV included the English-speaking units, the British Battalion, the Irish Connolly Column, the Canadian Mackenzie-Papineau Battalion, and the American Abraham Lincoln and George Washington Battalions, as well as the 59th Battalion, Spanish speakers from Cuba, Mexico, and the rest of Latin America (Gerassi, 1986: 14). It also included the mixed Balkan Dimitrov Battalion (Rosenstone, 1969: 36), which was reportedly named after the Comintern chairman because its diverse members could not agree on any one of their respective national heroes (Richardson, 1982: 75).

Sources differ on the total number of IB recruits, with most estimates falling in the 30,000 to 50,000 range. Sympathetic sources tend toward higher numbers, although, perhaps inflating the threat they faced, different fascist sources made the highest claims of 125,000 to 150,000 Communist-allied foreign fighters. Additionally, many foreign recruits in Spain did not actually serve in the IB. For example, George Orwell (Eric Blair) was not accepted because of his membership in a Trotskyite organization, and he therefore served in a militia of the Worker's Party of Marxist Unification (POUM). His strongly negative experiences in Spain made him a committed anti-Stalinist, as forcefully expressed in his novels *Animal Farm* and *1984* (Richardson, 1982: 24).

Despite such schisms, the IB experienced initial success in recruitment, with 6,000 to 8,000 brought to Spain by the end of November 1936 and more than 30,000 by February 1937 (Richardson, 1982: 46). Recruited and transported by the Comintern rather than the Soviet Union and serving in military units outside the command of the Spanish regular army, the International Brigades were truly that, not a foreign legion or a state-sponsored militia. The 2,000 international defenders of Madrid were viewed by the faithful as the fulfillment of the Marxist call "Workers of the world, unite!" (Carroll, 1994: 12).

Recruiting the International Brigades

While refugees from fascism and others who were immediately threatened by it joined the IB by the tens of thousands, the Comintern found that greater efforts were necessary further afield. Earl Browder, executive secretary of the U.S. Communist Party, told the Party National Committee in December 1936 that it could not afford to send large numbers of recruits to the IB but instead should encourage "honest democratic people to go to Spain." In addition to the possibility of not being able to meet the established quota and the expense and logistical difficulties of arranging ocean passages, the Communist Party in the United States faced the danger of being caught in violation of the Neutrality Act. It therefore decided that recruitment must occur clandestinely, through organizations that could maintain plausible deniability.[7]

All American volunteers, regardless of the unit in which they served, came to be known in the popular media as the Abraham Lincoln Brigade or ALB. The Communist Party therefore established two organizations to further recruitment among non-Communists: the Friends of the Abraham Lincoln Brigade (FALB) and the American Society for Technical Aid to Spanish Democracy. The FALB, and several front groups operating out of the same office, represented the public face of the foreign fighter recruitment drive, organizing fund-raisers and publishing information pamphlets and newsletters to gain public support. While FALB did not publicly offer to induct anyone into the ALB, nonetheless it did not escape government suspicion, nor did its successor, the Veterans of the Abraham Lincoln Brigade (VALB), which was founded ostensibly to help combat casualties recover and find employment.[8]

The Society for Technical Aid proclaimed its objective to be the recruitment of Americans for work in Spanish factories so that Spaniards would be
able to join their army and fight for their country themselves. Even aside from
the apparent lack of appeal of working in a factory in a war zone, the society's
goal was evident on its face, and its officers were all senior Communist Party
officials. Most American newspapers refused to print the society's ads, which
consequently appeared mainly in the Communist press (Lovin, 1963: 157–158,
176, 177; Southworth Collection, UCSD).

    In Canada, the Communist Party had an easier time operating the Spanish
Aid Committee, which held rallies in Toronto that collected thousands
of dollars and recruited openly until the law changed in 1937. Recruits did
not have to be party members but needed to show liberal tendencies, and
no one who had been a Mountie or a member of Trotskyite organizations
was acceptable. A thousand to 1,200 Canadians were recruited to serve in
the Mackenzie-Papineau Battalion, which also included a large number of
Americans.

    The depression had produced organizations of unemployed workers who
lived in Canadian government unemployment relief camps. There they performed labor for the state, which feared the workers would otherwise conduct
public strikes. Instead, alienated laborers joined together to stage intracamp
strikes for better working conditions, often ending in armed clashes with
law enforcement. Unlike in many comparable Civilian Conservation Corps
facilities in the United States, the 170,000 men who passed through these
camps had no connection while there to their families, and radical leftist
organizations found fertile recruiting territory. The Comintern concentrated
Canadian recruitment efforts in these camps, and "the radicalized didn't
require much soul-searching."

    More than 60 percent of Canadian recruits were over the age of 30, as
compared with just under 30 percent of the Americans. One possible reason
for this difference is that Canada maintained a more open immigration policy, and many recent arrivals of working age, disaffected by their inability
to assimilate or prosper, looked for some opportunity to return to Europe
by remaking society there. In fact, two-thirds of the Canadian volunteers
for whom records exist were immigrants (Howard and Reynolds, 1986: 9,
27–29, 31, 38).

    In Great Britain, open recruitment was also legal until January 1937, when
the Cabinet decided to make the Foreign Enlistment Act of 1870 applicable
to the war in Spain and threatened persons guilty of an offense under this act
with imprisonment for up to two years or a fine. Scotland Yard shadowed

the London recruitment office, but it was difficult to prevent British foreign fighters from traveling out of their jurisdiction because a passport was not necessary to go to Paris. The British Battalion, which was not the only unit in which Britons served, had at least 2,500 recruits. "No monetary inducements were offered to the volunteers and there was no promise of pensions." Even a promised allowance could not be guaranteed because it depended on volunteer contributions (Rust, 1939: 9, 10–12, 25; Southworth Collection, UCSD).

In those early days, when the outcome of the war appeared to be influenced by the IB, Britons interested in going volunteered directly to the party. The forerunner of the KGB, OGPU, conducted investigations of all volunteers and "eliminated" those suspected of being informers. Sometimes officials from the Communist Party headquarters on King Street talked to young Communists and hinted broadly that perhaps they should go to Spain, but there were many reasons for exemption, such as if student party members were in their final year at the London School of Economics (Brome, 1966: 17, 25).

However, certain national political circumstances militated in favor of moving the entire operation to Spain itself. In Italy, Carlo Rosselli, leader of the antifascist Giustizia e Liberta Party, determined that he could best accomplish his political objectives in Italy by assuring the defeat of Mussolini-backed fascists in Spain. His strategy was to demonstrate through a large Italian presence in Spain that the war there was simply one front in a global struggle against fascism (Mangilli-Climpson, 1985: 28; Southworth Collection, UCSD).

Adopting the slogan "Today in Spain, tomorrow in Italy," Rosselli's objectives in bringing his supporters to Spain were to provoke antifascist reaction in Italy, both through military success and symbolic sacrifice on behalf of the IB, and to gain military experience that could later be used in Italy itself. Recruits were informed that they were part of a broader movement against fascism and that service in Spain would therefore lead to international intervention at home (Slaughter, 1972: i, 2). Rosselli's strategy and messaging, original at the time, appear to have been adopted in the twenty-first century by transnational Islamist groups for recruitment in various civil conflicts.

Framing and Messaging

Janice Thomson (1994: 9) characterizes the IB as an authoritative rather than a market deployment of nonstate violence, meaning that the transnational insurgents were not mercenaries but were following directives from the Comintern. However, this assessment only partly captures the basis of recruitment. Estimates are that 60 percent of Americans who fought in Spain were members of the Communist Party before the war started, and another 20 percent joined while there (Carroll, 1994: 14–17). Records indicate that foreign fighters in the IB were indeed volunteers—party members were not directly ordered to go to Spain and, in Great Britain, some promising young party figures, particularly those who had special propaganda skills, were told to stay and avoid the risk of death[9] (Brome, 1966: 25).

If they were not under marching orders, it is still apparent that, the motives of particular individuals to the contrary, IB recruitment was not on the basis of material incentives. Although propaganda portrayed volunteers often engaging in leisure activities, it did not mention the availability of loot or promises of substantial pay commensurate with the risks and hardships involved. Much of the propaganda plays explicitly on the theme of sacrifice, and even the *Daily Worker*, distributed as the newspaper to volunteers as well as abroad, reported earnestly on casualties with pieces on how happy foreigners were to "die smiling" for the Republic (Fisher, 1998: 166).

Although there was censorship of correspondence, few pains were taken to conceal that the soldiers ate a daily diet of only chickpeas, occasionally supplemented by burro meat (Edwards, 1997: 22). One noted that a swim he took on a free day was "my second wash in seven weeks" (Nelson and Hendricks, 1996: 137). And some volunteers wrote letters home insisting that they were not mercenaries. American John Cookson, who was ultimately killed in action, informed his aunt that he was not in it for the money: The pay, in nonconvertible Spanish pesetas, was equivalent to 18 cents a day, 21 if at the front lines. As an officer, he received 75 cents a day and returned 50 cents of it to the party (Nelson and Hendricks, 1996: 37).

Profiling the Recruits

It is always problematic to accept the explanations of individuals for their political activities, but useful indicators of what constituted an effective recruitment frame can be gleaned from the recollections of IB veterans, as well as from statistical data of the profiles of the approximately 3,000 Americans who joined the XV International Brigade. The average American volunteer was between the ages of 21 and 27, lived in an urban industrial center with active radical political parties, was likely a manual laborer or a student, came from a family that was among the working poor even before the depression, and was a first- or second-generation immigrant whose family paid closer attention to

European politics than did other Americans. Perhaps a third were of Jewish descent.[10] Nonetheless, the ranks also included elites, such as the sons of the governor of Ohio and the mayor of Los Angeles, relatives of congressmen, and scions of prominent banking families (Rosenstone, 1969: 98–99). As a whole, the American contingent was younger than other nationalities, perhaps because it did not include refugees of varying ages fleeing fascism in their home countries and drifting to Communist recruitment centers (Johnston, 1967: 63). A possible related factor may have been that a significant number appeared to be orphans or from broken homes (Carroll, 1994: 17).

Ethnic ties appear to have played some role in recruitment. Approximately 10 percent of American volunteers had Hispanic surnames, but appeals to ethnicity or homeland do not appear to have been employed in this nonethnic conflict. Instead, the New York Cuban and Puerto Rican communities that arrived in the wake of the Spanish-American War had mixed with Spanish refugees, many of whom were involved in antifascist movements, making them receptive to IB messaging (Fernandez, in Carroll and Fernandez, 2007: 87).

Gerassi (1986: 2–3, 44, 53) claims that 31 percent of the ALB were immigrants, with as many as 45 percent of the total being Jewish, as compared with just 16 percent for the IB as a whole. Gerassi speculates this rate of participation may have been because Jews facing discrimination had a harder time finding jobs in the United States and faced lower opportunity costs. Carroll and colleagues (2006: 2) reported that "of the 2,800 ALB volunteers who went to Spain, at least 1,250 were Jews, with approximately 300 Italian-Americans, more than 80 African-Americans, and 54 women among them." Most were second-generation Americans, the children of immigrants who still retained at least affective ties to Europe. "Most men and women on the Left knew that if fascism triumphed, the labor and progressive movements would be destroyed. Communists, and many Jews and African-Americans, were certain that they would be the first victims" of a fascist putsch.

The Necessity of Sacrifice

Both sides in the war, conscious of the unprecedented international media coverage of the conflict, worked assiduously to define the terms of the conflict through propaganda. The results were examples of the frames by which the conflict was defined and made salient to the prospective pool of antifascist recruits. Just as during the Texas Revolution, laws against service in transnational insurgencies prevented recruiters in the United States and elsewhere from directly soliciting combatants. Instead, the distant conflict was defined in personally threatening and affective terms. Alongside requests for donations were thinly veiled exhortations to arms.

With totalitarian states closed to Spanish propaganda, the messages were tailored for audiences in the Western democracies. The Nationalists tried to portray the Republic as a Trojan horse for international Communism; the Republicans presented an image abroad of working people threatened by exploitive plutocrats, their democracy trampled by a military-clerical conspiracy (Stradling, 2003: 17, 101, 103). One propaganda pamphlet sold in the United States to raise money for the Republican cause opens with a discussion of the land reform program initiated by the prior government, immediately framing the conflict as a class issue. The discussion then turns to the threat to European democracies, and how America might be next (Ward and MacLeod, 1936).

Evidence that recruitment was based on fear rather than the opportunity for profit is found in the propaganda released on behalf of the IB, which calls for necessary sacrifices to stave off threat. In England, the Communist Party distributed pamphlets such as *Spain Calling! Their Fight Is Our Fight* and *Save Peace! Aid Spain*. Published in 1937, they reflect changes in British law, in that the most they ask of the reader is assistance with lobbying and donations. However, the latter pamphlet insinuates what must be done:

> From every country in the world they came. These men know that a victory for fascism anywhere means a weakening of the stand for liberty in their mother countries.... Hundreds of Britishers have proudly offered their lives in just this spirit. Many have already died. It is idle merely to applaud their sacrifice unless we of the British working-class movement are also straining every nerve to ensure the speediest possible victory over fascism in Spain. (Southworth Collection, UCSD)

A booklet written in English titled *Greek Volunteers to Spain* claimed that 500 Greeks were serving with the ALB (presumably this meant in the XV Brigade). The author claimed the Greek members of the IB were "paying our national debt to the Philhellenes of 1821.... From the entire continent of Europe, and from America, volunteers, idealists, and freedom loving people rushed to [our] help...." This reference to the foreign fighters who joined the successful Greek War of Independence against the Ottoman Empire was intended to confer legitimacy on the IB as upholding a noble tradition of humanitarian intervention. The author singles out a number of names for praise, particularly Lord Byron, and also references the American Revolution, in which "people from all over the world came to help" (FBI File 25, ALBA, Tamiment Library, New York University).

The pamphlet *Americans in Spain: New England Fights for Spanish Democracy* takes the analogy a step further, comparing the ALB in 1937 to "Boston patriots of 1776" and adding that "France did more than applaud" during America's War of Independence. It justifies serving as a foreign fighter in Europe by noting the litany of Von Steuben, Kościusko, "Irishmen of the Old World," and other Europeans who joined or aided the Continental Army during the American Revolution, and "German exiles fighting slavers" during the American Civil War (FBI File 14, ALBA, Tamiment Library, New York University). This framing was echoed in turn by recruits. In a letter to his mother, Joe Dallet compares himself to Lafayette aiding an emerging American democracy (Dallet File, Box 1 File 11, ALBA).

Ben Leider: American Hero, a five-cent pamphlet published by a FALB front company, adds to this portrayal of selflessness with the story of the pilot and ardent Communist it erroneously identifies as the first American killed in Spain. He is described as "a volunteer without pay, a volunteer for a cause that he saw as his own.... He was not content to sit in a ring-side seat and watch. When he saw that democracy was in danger, that fascism was about to sweep on to new conquests, he left the sidelines once and for all." In what would appear to be subtle instructions to potential recruits, it notes that Leider was "never given to self-glorification, he told only a few of his closest friends" before departing. Somewhat at odds with other accounts of his fatal crash, the fund-raising pamphlet describes how Leider sacrificed his life to bring his plane in safely so that it might be used by other Loyalist forces, dying of blood loss after a perfect landing rather than ejecting in time. The back cover provides contact information and a checklist of options for the reader. Besides donating money or selling pamphlets, there is also the vague pledge "I will volunteer my services to the work of the fund"[11] (Southworth Collection, UCSD).

In addition to celebrating martyrdom, both sides heavily employed atrocity propaganda in courting international support. The regular FALB newsletter *Among Friends* ran in its Spring 1938 issue pieces by celebrity supporters such as Ernest Hemingway and Dorothy Parker. Among them were photos of dead children accompanied by a statement by FALB Chairman David McKelvy White: "This fire is the fire of burning Spanish towns. It shines from the charred bodies of women and children. It must command our attention. It must direct our every action" (Joseph Brandt, File 7, ALBA, Tamiment Library, New York University).

Other FALB-published material included a magazine titled *The Spanish People's Struggle*, in which a clearly doctored photo depicts an armed policeman inserted over a fleeing crowd under the title "Police firing on the people." Also presented were gruesome photographs of the cruelty of fascist guards toward political prisoners, with warnings that such practices would be exported if the Republic fell. Such images were juxtaposed with cartoons of the Spanish Inquisition, no doubt to delegitimize church claims of atrocity against clerics and to imply that the fascists wanted a return to the Middle Ages.

The Crimes of Francisco Franco continues in this vein, arguing that on the generalissimo's hands was the blood of "loyal Catholics," women and children. Among the evidence presented against the defendant is an interview with the Scripps-Howard News Service in which Franco states that "the new Spain will progress on the lines of a totalitarian state." In keeping with the Comintern outreach message, the pamphlet charged that Franco's real enemy is not Communism, but democracy, and he was therefore the enemy of all Americans (Joseph Brandt, File 3, ALBA, Tamiment Library, New York University).

In attempting to vilify Franco and expand the scope of the conflict to those who might not otherwise be sympathetic to Communist internationalism, the Republicans and their allies pointed markedly to Nationalist reliance on the Army of Africa. Approximately 100,000 of Franco's forces were Spanish colonial subjects from Morocco, black Muslim Moors (Gerassi, 1986: 15). Although they were troops in the regular Spanish military, the Moroccans were singled out as an alien threat to European civilization. As *The Crimes of Francisco Franco* put it, "From Morocco came Franco, with his Foreign Legion of hired adventurers and his shock troops of barbarous Moors, to whom rich rewards of rape and pillage had been promised."

A book of cartoons published by the Republican Propaganda Ministry in Spanish, French, and English, *30 Caricaturas de la Guerra*, depicts Prussians in pickelhaube spike helmets associating with stereotypes of large-lipped blacks in turbans. One image, meant to imply the hypocrisy of the church, shows the pope blessing the Nationalists "in the name of Mohammed and Luther" (Joseph Brandt, File 3, ALBA, Tamiment Library, New York University). Another American publication, *The Truth about Spain*, perhaps aimed at what was perceived to be a racist American audience, states succinctly: "Civilization does not mean Moorish pillage" (Joseph Brandt, File 7, ALBA, Tamiment Library, New York University).

Leaving aside the issue of whether an Islamic invasion would be more terrible than a fascist one, the question that emerges is why citizens of neutral states far removed from both the civil conflict in Spain and the menace of Mussolini and Hitler would become engaged to do anything. More recent international fund-raising campaigns for victims of conflicts in Sudan, for example, have not directed donors to organizations that might send them to Darfur as combatants. More than just humanitarian interest was invoked by these pamphlets. Implicit in their messages were appeals to self-interest and to duty.

Transnational Identity: "My Duty as an Antifascist"

The economic upheavals of the 1930s had made class politics salient in the United States and produced a polarized subculture of radicals. The refusal of corporations to permit labor unionization, and the resultant clashes with private security and national guard forces brought in to put down unrest, led many in the labor-worker movement to accept that violence would be necessary to achieve political change. As well, fascist groups were already springing up in the United States. Intellectuals, liberals, and minorities—and there was often considerable overlap between these categories—had every reason to believe that they would be next if fascism continued to gain momentum. The radicalized joined social justice and Communist-affiliated groups in which they shared ideas, reinforced their ideological development, and made contacts that would ultimately serve as the recruitment chain for the ALB (Rosenstone, 1969: 50–55, 61, 68–73).

There were 41,000 members of the American Communist Party at the beginning of the war in 1936 and 82,000 by its end in 1938 (Carroll, 1994: 13). Most Americans who joined the Communist Party in the 1930s did not have the goal of establishing a Marxist state, or even an educated understanding of Marxist theory, but instead saw the party as an agency committed to social justice. As Rosenstone put it, "joining the Communist Party did not produce the motivation to go; rather both actions were reflective of the same impulse." Recruitment efforts therefore did not need to rely heavily upon indoctrination because those who had contact with Comintern-affiliated recruiters were already sympathetic to the aims of the organization (Rosenstone, 1969: 68, 69, 119).

As noted, although some nonmember recruits did eventually become Communists, the party directed its efforts toward recruiting nonmembers by "preaching anti-fascist unity." The ALB veteran Len Norris, who was not a Communist, explained, "I had become an anti-fascist. An anti-fascist meant being opposed to the regimes of Hitler and Mussolini" (Gerassi,

1986: 73, 95). As noted in chapter 1, ideology can be a form of identity because it offers a shared set of constitutive sense-making tools that are particularly salient in times of social upheaval. Framing the conflict as one of importance not just to the Spanish, and not even just to Communists, but to all antifascists allowed the Comintern to perform frame bridging that made the Nationalists a threat to liberals and minorities far removed from the Iberian Peninsula. Records of surviving recruitment material and the recollections of IB survivors indicate that the Comintern was particularly successful in frame bridging the tribulations of Spanish workers and peasants with the global contest between fascism and antifascism and in establishing frame shifts that made individuals concerned with the plight of local workers and minorities view themselves as part of the same transnational community as their imperiled counterparts in Spain.

The very definition of the ideology and identity as antifascist implied the necessity of defense against a counterpart ideological group. Accordingly, during the Spanish Civil War, the Comintern followed Chairman Dimitrov's strategy for recruiting foreign fighters who were predominantly nonparty members and shifted its rhetoric from antibourgeois to antifascist. The ALB veteran William Herrick recalled that when *Life* magazine asked to interview him during the war, he was ordered to tell the correspondent that he was fighting fascism because he was a Jew, rather than because he was a Communist (Richardson, 1982: 6–7, 155). Antifascist became established as a transnational identity that linked disparate individuals who did not otherwise share historical, linguistic, or sectarian ties, and it was furthermore established as an identity under an attack that required the defense of its members.

Based on the explanations contained in the two largest collections of contemporary letters from IB members and later recollections published in a variety of IB histories, recruiters were successful in communicating this frame. Radicalized by the depression, Texas farmer Bob Reed "realized there was an 'us' and a 'them' in America, as well as everywhere else. So when I heard … that the 'them' and 'us' were at it with guns in Spain, in what I thought would be the beginning of the final showdown, I decided to go" (Gerassi, 1986: 42). For some, the conflict was more personalized. Eugene Wolman wrote of his inability to retaliate against oppressive forces at home in the United States, including being struck by policemen. But in Spain, "here finally the oppressed of the earth are united, here finally we have weapons, here finally we can fight back" (Carroll, Nash, and Small, 2006: 17).

It is furthermore apparent that this transnational identity also carried obligations to fellow members of what was as much an imagined community as fellow members of the same nation. Indeed, some veterans reported that the obligations to the transnational identity of antifascist were more salient than their national identity of American, an indication of the recruiters' success in framing the conflict and a result consistent with Oberschall's findings on those who join radical movements, as discussed in chapter 1. Many activists maintained closer ties with members of their antifascist social network than with the broader society and reported that their relationships were primarily built on the characteristic of antifascism rather than another social grouping or polity.

Don McLeod, echoing the sentiments of the pamphlet addressing Spanish land reform efforts, explained that "in the Depression, we poor people began to identify with other poor people in other parts of the world" (Gerassi, 1986: 47). Harry Fisher agreed that "in many ways we viewed the Spanish struggle as an extension of our fight against reaction at home.... We were trade unionists" (Fisher, 1998: 2). Hy Katz neglected nationality altogether in his formulation of interest, explaining in a letter from Spain: "I took up arms against the persecutors of my people—the Jews—and my class—the Oppressed" (Nelson and Hendricks, 1996: 31). And Carl Geiser stated: "I just felt it was my duty as an anti-fascist to go" (Gerassi, 1986: 49).

Alternative Rationales

Psychologist William Pike, head of the IB medical corps, discovered through interviews that many incoming volunteers' primary goal was ego gratification—they expected to be seen as heroes of messianic Communism[12] (Carroll, 1994: 121). And it is evident some went for material gratification as well. As one veteran recounted, he went because he was "out of work and looking for adventure" (Rosenstone, 1969: 98–99).

Director of the FBI J. Edgar Hoover claimed that recruits went on the false promises of liaisons with Spanish women. As Rosenstone put it, this presents a "rather odd picture of young men so sexually desperate that they would journey across the Atlantic to enter a foreign war just for a woman's 'favors'" (Rosenstone, 1969: 94). However, Harold Dahl, a former Army Air Corps pilot who became a flier for the Republican air force, claimed that he went because of his interest in "Spanish women" (Edwards, 1997: 4).

Pilots like Dahl were far better compensated than ground troops, many more had prior combat experience, and the incentives offered varied accordingly. French military writer André Malraux organized 100 recruits for a Republican air force called the Escadre España. His collection of "idealists

who wanted to stop fascism, long in the tooth World War I combat airmen who relished the hunt, and an assortment of neurotics addicted to
adventure" were offered a renewable monthly contract of 50,000 pesetas
and life insurance of 500,000 pesetas—pesetas being a nonconvertible currency. Some swore service oaths to the Spanish Air Force, rather than to the
Republic, to avoid risking their citizenship over loyalty to a foreign state. As
in the Israeli War of Independence a decade later, pilots enjoyed benefits far
beyond those of the average recruit, perhaps because the insurgencies needed
highly trained specialists to fly airplanes and found it necessary to resort to
well-paid mercenaries rather than the usual recruit with a deep connection
to the cause. "With a few shining exceptions, most of these men expressed
no interest in the civil war or repugnance to fascism in general"[13] (Edwards,
1997: 12–13, 23, 31).

An exception was Frank Tinker, a Naval Academy graduate who had been
court-martialed out of the Army Air Corps. He had been disgusted by the
"excessive and cowardly" use of Italian air power against civilians in Abyssinia
and had attempted to volunteer in that conflict, only to learn Ethiopia had
no air force. After his offers to Spanish representatives in America received
no response, he eventually arranged passage with the Spanish ambassador to
Mexico, who offered him a contract of $1,500 per month with a $1,000 bonus
per fascist plane downed (Edwards, 1997: 2–3).

The Ethiopian Connection

Tinker's case illustrates how the successful effort to recruit Americans to fight
in Spain provides an interesting counterpoint to the lack of a comparable
response to the fascist attack on Ethiopia. As with Spain and Americans affiliated with workers' movements, the Italian invasion of Ethiopia led to efforts
by some Black nationalist leaders to set up aid organizations. A few of these
groups did make efforts to recruit Americans to join in combat, but, despite
claims by one that it had 3,000 African Americans training in New York state
as foreign fighters, records confirm only two American volunteers ever having
reached Ethiopia (Collum, 1992: 12).

Ethiopia was viewed as both the cradle of Black civilization and the
source of future redemption in African American nationalist songs of the
time period and in the emerging Rastafarian movement. The Provisional
Committee for the Defense of Ethiopia, run out of Harlem by African
American Communists, "worked tirelessly to redirect anti-white and
anti-Italian sentiment toward anti-Fascism." By early 1937, the Communist

Party had adopted the slogan "Ethiopia's fate is at stake on the battlefields of Spain!" While many Black nationalists rejected this blatant attempt at frame shifting, a number of African American intellectuals publicly supported it (Collum, 1992: 16–18).

Even before the Spanish Civil War and transnational recruitment efforts by the Comintern, some were already attempting the frame bridging and scale shifts that direct international movements to adapt to local causes, as described by Tarrow (2005). The August 1935 edition of *Fight against War and Fascism* featured an article titled "The Rape of Ethiopia" by Pastor William Lloyd Imes of St. James in Harlem, who was organizing an interdenominational day of prayer and protest. The article concluded: "What may come to Ethiopia now may come to many another nation sooner than we think. Americans of African descent should stand as a unit in their defense of this fascist malice and threat" (Southworth Collection, UCSD).

While Black nationalist leaders had been promoting a pan-African identity as the solution to dispossession in America, some did not view nationalism and internationalism as inimical interests. As with a number of Jews involved in the Communist cause, they realized that a push for universal equality meant that they would enjoy relative benefits but that the success of fascism would mean persecution. The nearly 100 African American recruits in Spain were evidence of the success of the Comintern's work to frame the situation in Spain as an extension of Italian aggression.

Black nationalist groups followed suit with propaganda such as the autobiographical pamphlet *A Negro Nurse in Republican Spain*: "The place to defeat Italy just now is Spain…. The outcome of the struggle in Spain implies the death or realization of the hopes of the minorities of the world"[14] (Collum, 1992: 6, 18, 29). However, poet Langston Hughes, who traveled to Spain as a correspondent for *The Afro-American* because he wanted "to write about Moors and Colored People," puzzled that "some of America's most politically aware blacks had left their own troubled country to risk their lives in Spain" (Barbara Dale May, in Romeiser, 1982: 24).

One development in Spain that impressed Hughes was the integration of the ALB in a way that was inconceivable in the U.S. armed forces at the time. Oliver Law, previously a Chicago community organizer in a protest movement of the unemployed, became in Spain the first African American to command white troops when he was appointed to lead the ALB in May 1937. Law and other African Americans featured prominently in Comintern publicity material (Carroll et al., 2006: 2).

Mobilization: Staying out of Jail to Go to Spain

Asking for material and financial support is one thing, but overcoming the collective action barrier to get volunteers to face hardship and death is another. Even with a willing base of volunteers, recruitment efforts needed to be surreptitious. The U.S. Criminal Code imposed a $3,000 fine or one year in prison for citizens found enlisting in a foreign war.

To avoid law enforcement, as well as fascist-affiliated spies, recruits needed someone to vouch for their political credentials and typically had to be a member of the Communist Party, Popular Front, a union, or a student activist group to be advanced through the enlistment process. These logistical requirements not only built on existing social networks but also accentuated reliance on new linkages between affiliated groups rather than pitching enlistment to outsiders. Still, if the law drove formal recruiting underground, it was nonetheless understood what was meant when the Communist Party held mass meetings at union halls and YMCAs featuring returned volunteers as guest speakers and then distributed leaflets with contact information for those who wanted to "do something" (Rosenstone, 1969: 90, 93, 122).

> If the speakers did not openly urge enlistment, their portrayal of the Loyalist cause was designed to produce sympathy and hopefully enlistments. Handbills distributed at meetings were sometimes inscribed with the name and address of an individual who could be contacted regarding enlistment in the Brigades. On occasion, persons recruited at these meetings thought that they were enlisting in the Medical Bureau's ambulance corps or for service in some capacity normally filled by civilians.[15] (Lovin, 1963: 173; Southworth Collection, UCSD)

Lovin (1963: 174) claimed: "Pressure was not effected directly upon a specific individual in the form of orders to go to Spain, [but] the rank-and-file of the party could scarcely avoid exposure to a deluge of propaganda about the importance of the war...." Likewise, the majority of historical accounts, which are sympathetic to the ALB, contend that no pressure was brought to bear on party or trade union members to volunteer. Nonetheless, ALB veterans who cooperated with the FBI during later investigations of Communist activity in the United States painted a different picture.

One interview subject stated that, upon changing his mind about going after being provided with a passport, his contact "kept after him" until he finally left for New York to join the other recruits before departure. Another subject claimed recruiters "continued to talk to him about the advantages of going. He was promised salary to fight and a good job at the conclusion of the war. These men also stated he would not be in the war very long and that they felt the war would soon be over in Spain...no actual fighting on their part" (FBI File, Report 100–1128, File 13, ALBA, Tamiment Library, New York University).

Hyman Jacobs told investigators that his involvement began when he joined a workers' club in the Boston area. He soon discovered that meetings were run by Communists who told Jacobs, who was Jewish, that he should join them to help fight Hitler. From there, the frame bridging proceeded to the topic at hand:

> There was talk at the meetings they got to do something to aid Spain. Then they formed some sort of recruiting. It was done on the quiet, they would approach members and tell them they were going to Spain. Some of them they forced into it by saying you had a choice of being forced out of the Party, or going to Spain. I asked to go before they got around to that. (FBI File, HQ 100–7060, File 11, ALBA, Tamiment Library, New York University)

Jacobs's account, given to the FBI during the McCarthy era, differs from those who presumably remained sympathetic to the party in later years. Still, if accurate, it calls into question whether IB "volunteers" were not simply following orders to go to Spain like the supposed "volunteers" of the German regular army. Although there were implicit and explicit promises made about workplace opportunities to reluctant recruits, it seems unlikely that these would mitigate the risks and hardships of an illegal ocean passage to fight as a rebel in an overwhelmed insurgency. Instead, the recruit's social identity within the Communist Party was at stake. As described in chapter 1, identity is a construct of social institutions, which impose norms and constrain choices. Members of networks derive their sense of self from the judgment of other members and are loath to risk their status in the network. Given that so many IB volunteers came from broken homes or grinding poverty, the sense of self, support of fellow members, and access to social and material benefits of party membership were not something to be discarded lightly. The same factors that lead urban youths to join violent gangs compelled Jacobs and other recalcitrant party members to go to Spain, even if they did not see it in their personal interest.

However, the initial large number of willing volunteers in the autumn of 1936 led the party to shift its efforts from finding recruits to "screening undesirable elements…[it] wanted to exclude mere adventurers who lacked a political understanding of the anti-fascist struggle."[16] Recruiters at first even rejected volunteers without military training but soon relaxed their requirements as the initial wave of interest passed. Those who made it through the security screening were brought in for assessment interviews and subjected to a medical examination. These latter may have been formalities, as a number of recruits were sent to Spain who had asthma or partial blindness, and at least one had a wooden leg.

The party coached recruits on how to obtain passports, and its World Tourist Travel Agency arranged ship passage for all recruits to Spain from New York on fares purchased by the party. Military equipment was not as forthcoming: The party merely provided lists of suggested supplies and surplus stores where individuals might purchase them, along with World War I uniforms. Prior to departure, some drill activities, using broomsticks for rifles, were held in New York union halls (Rosenstone, 1969: 64–67).

The ALB Veteran Harry Fisher recalled his induction:

> [They took us] to a place on 2nd Avenue, where a group of doctors examined us and other people questioned us to see if we were really anti-Fascist. The committee was very somber and serious. They wanted us to know what we were getting ourselves into. One of them said something like "You know, comrades, this is not just another picket line. This is a matter of life and death."…But I could not forget those newsreels of the Nazi storm troopers stomping and spitting on those poor helpless people. I also knew it could happen here. My anger was so strong, I knew I had to go. Fascism simply had to be stopped. (Fisher, 1998: 16)

Fisher then recounted a meeting in New York, the night before sailing in February 1937, in which recruits were told they must not tell their families where they were going and would have to remain inconspicuous to the other passengers on the boat. They were also informed that if they were found drinking or with prostitutes while in France that they would not be allowed into Spain but would instead be sent home as "a disgrace to the working class"[17] (Fisher, 1998: 17).

Ultimately, a mélange of recruits were motivated by different antifascist appeals, and others went for more personal reasons unconnected to the Comintern messaging. Stradling (2003: 106) delineated three categories of volunteers: "the ideologically solid," committed Communists for whom death or suffering was a valid consequence of the necessary fight; "superficial ideal-ists," who experienced an emotional surge to fight for the "good" that most lost in the Spanish trenches; and "selfish opportunists," for whom abstract ideals were essentially meaningless. Stradling argued that the first two catego-ries were the most susceptible to recruitment propaganda.[18]

Recruiting Fascist Volunteers: Onward, Christian Soldiers

Across the lines, Frank Thomas, a Welsh Protestant volunteer for Franco, identified a mirror taxonomy of three types of transnational insurgents on the Nationalist side: "Philosophical-religious crusaders," who were essentially well-educated Catholics; "Fascist types"; and individuals in search of adven-ture. As with other instances of successful transnational recruitment—and despite the fact that the Nationalists were on the offensive throughout most of the war—at least the first two groups joined the rebellion as a defensive cause, responding to the same frame of obligation to protect a transnational identity under threat employed by the Comintern (Keene, 2001: 94).

While most memoirs and histories have concentrated far more upon transnational insurgents on the Republican side, the Nationalists also man-aged to attract approximately 1,000 to 1,500 foreigners into the Spanish Foreign Legion and Carlist conservative militias. Franco downplayed their presence in his eagerness for propaganda purposes to portray the conflict as "the sons of Spain" against world Communism. However, Carlist support-ers of Franco recognized that framing the Nationalists as champions of tradi-tional Western Catholic culture against a new Marxist spearhead into Europe would draw interest elsewhere. Nationalist recruits shared "the conviction that the Republic was Communist-dominated, and that it must be militarily destroyed in order to prevent the establishment of a Soviet-style regime in Western Europe." The effort succeeded as far away as Australia, where Nugent Bull, a devout Catholic with some employment difficulties, volunteered after reading a pamphlet by the Australasian Catholic Truth Society (Keene, 2001: vi, 3, 106).

"Vagabonds" versus "Noble and Generous Volunteers"

In a later report on the war, the Franco regime claimed "the Moscow International" directed all activities of the Republican government and "ordered its members all over the world to lend all assistance possible; and many of them, as well as numerous adventurers and outlaws, enlisted in the

International Brigades, and in this way an international gang of vagabonds began to encamp in Spain" (Ministry of Justice, 1946: 279, 293).

Early in the war, Franco had been caught off guard by transnational intervention on behalf of the Republican government and had nothing to match it. His generals had expected the uprising to last for only a few weeks before they could consolidate power. Eager to accept Axis assistance, he allied with the fascist regimes of Germany, Italy, and Portugal, all of which sent thousands of "volunteers" who were regular military forces under orders by their national commanders (Monteath, in Romeiser, 1982: 18).

By Nationalist figures, at the start of the conflict there were 67 foreigners from 13 countries in the Spanish Foreign Legion, which had remained under Franco's command. By its end, there were a reported 1,248 from 37 countries. The Tercio de Extranjeros swelled from 6 to 20 battalions, including the French "Joan of Arc" and the Irish Brigade (15th Bandera) (Keene, 2001: 8, 29). That the numbers are far smaller than those on the Republican side suggests that potential volunteers went instead as the regular foreign fascist troops and also raises the possibility of the impact of the absence of an effective counterpart to the Comintern to engage in transnational recruitment.

Still, efforts were made to sympathetic audiences to communicate the message that Spanish culture was under assault by a spreading Red Menace. Conservative periodicals in Latin America attempted to frame the conflict in a manner politically relevant to local populations. The September 5, 1937, edition of ¡Arriba! Periodico al Servicio de la Causa Nacionalista, published in Peru, warned that Communism would "end private property and put it in the hands of state officials" (Southworth Collection, UCSD).

In France, Arriba España!... Espagne, éveille-toi! described an advancing Communist threat rather than the strategic challenge of a German ally on the western border. The book describes the opening hours of the war as "a heroic struggle" against numerically superior Communists and concludes that "France is menaced by Sovietization and a civil war. At all costs, another must be prevented" (Riotte, 1936: 24, 127; Southworth Collection, UCSD).

One group with whom this message was probably most effective was Russian refugees from Communism. Like members of Balkan diasporas who returned to participate in civil conflicts in the 1990s, White Russians in the 1930s lived in "enclosed émigré societies," unassimilated into the daily life of their host states. In Paris, Berlin, and Brussels, they plotted the reconquest of the Motherland.

When the conflict in Spain began, the widow of a British general who had fought with the White Army in the Russian Civil War raised the money to send a White Russian contingent, and an accompanying Orthodox priest, to Spain. The editor of the *Sentinel*, the diaspora community's newspaper, conducted the recruitment of approximately 100 volunteers and published their letters home, admonishing their peers that the real place to fight Bolsheviks was Spain, not sitting around in some coffeehouse (Keene, 2001: 192, 197, 200, 202).

The White Russians, however, were the only foreigners not permitted to serve in the Tercio because Franco did not want to provide a pretext for more direct Soviet intervention. Instead, recruits served unpaid in Carlist groups or were slipped into various Nationalist army regiments. Their presence in nonprofessional militias may explain the high casualty rate among the White Russians. Of about 100, at least 34 were killed (Keene, 2001: 195, 208).

Holy War

Aside from the White Russians, while some number of anti-Communists were recruited by the Nationalists, the message that brought the most transnational foreign fighters to the Nationalist lines was not simply anti-Communism but that a Communist-allied victory would constitute a direct and dire threat to their most important identity affiliation: the Catholic Church. The rise of Communism itself may have inspired the neo-Gothic movement in Europe to protect private property, which "profoundly affected the development of fascism." This subculture viewed traditional societal institutions as under threat from secular materialism (Stradling, 2003: 107).

English Catholics in particular were strongly anti-Soviet and worked to foster support for anti-Communist movements abroad. English recruits to Spain who perceived "Victorian virtue falling to social climbing masses, mass consumerism, political leadership failing" at home claimed that in Spain they found again the England of their youths. Reports that churches were attacked or burned, which the Republicans claimed happened only in response to their being used as shooting posts by Moors, and atrocity stories about priests and nuns were the most effective recruitment tools available (Keene, 2001: 53). The *British Catholic Times*, promoting a recruitment drive in Ireland, claimed the first act of Nationalists upon liberating a village from Republican forces was to restore the (apparently removed) crucifix in the village school (Stradling, 2003: 107).

The pro-Franco campaign spread to the United States, where Catholic magazines such as *Ave Maria* attempted to broaden the appeal of Franco's junta of fascists and monarchists by terming them "nationalists" and "rebels" because these labels invoked images of George Washington. The New York chapter of Notre Dame alumni passed a resolution that defined the civil conflict in Spain as "Christianity vs. anti-religion." A counterpart to the FALB groups, the American Committee for Spanish Relief, was established, and through it, the Knights of Columbus sent $110,000 to the Nationalists. Such fund-raisers, held at Carnegie Hall and Madison Square Garden, were still dwarfed by the total donated by a Jesuit campaign alone, indicating strong support among portions of the American Catholic population for the Nationalists (Valaik, 1964: 92, 158, 160, 299–306; Southworth Collection, UCSD).

European efforts to recruit for the Nationalist cause also employed the imagery of the church under attack by godless Marxist or Jewish forces. French volunteers were members of far right or explicitly fascist groups, such as Action Française. Their messaging encouraged volunteers to defend the besieged "Latin spirit and Western civilization." Franco actively encouraged recruitment in France so that there would be French Nationalist foreign fighters he could offer to send home if the Republicans returned their own French contingent, which was the largest national group in the IB.

Although they were a far smaller contribution to the Nationalist forces, student fascist leaders in the ultranationalist Romanian Iron Guards went to Spain for the church as well. Officials of the conservative regime told student leaders that they must join "a worldwide crusade to defend Christ against Satan and his Judeo-Masonic henchmen" (Keene, 2001: 140, 215, 231). A Spanish propaganda pamphlet presented biographies of two Romanian volunteers, with one testifying: "Is it not of great spiritual benefit in the afterlife to fall in the defense of Christ?... We defend the power that is the source of our nation!" (*Los Legionarios Rumanos*; Southworth Collection, UCSD).

Other Nationalist supporters attempted to enlarge the scope of the conflict by making creative efforts at frame bridging between the defense of the Catholic Church and defending religion against Communism. In *The Unpopular Front*, the Catholic Truth Society in London claimed that the Irish Brigade sent expressly to defend the church was 5 percent Protestant and begged, "Is it too late to appeal to those Christians outside the Catholic Church who love Christ more than they hate His vicar, to cooperate with us to form an unpopular front against Atheism?" (Southworth Collection, UCSD).

More interestingly, attacks against Franco's Moorish troops as improbable defenders of the church and Spanish culture were parried by ardent Catholics endorsing jihad. The *Sign*, a Catholic magazine published in New Jersey, argued that the maligned Moroccans were not barbarous mercenaries. Instead, "the Moors were reported to have said 'We also want a New Spain. We do not want the Holy Musulman faith attacked and abolished as it has been in Russia under the Communists'" (Valaik, 1964: 156; Southworth Collection, UCSD). Franco's press secretary, Luis Bolin (1967: 229), claimed that "for the Moors this was a holy war…whoever burns the house of God is an enemy of Allah." He reported that they enlisted "with such zest" that you could tell by the dejected faces which ones had not been permitted the opportunity.

The Irish Connection

The largest contingent of foreign fighters on the Nationalist side, and apparently the one whose members were most eager to record their experiences, was ironically the one whose contribution to this particular civil conflict was the least consequential. Irish exiles and volunteers had an established history of participation in foreign wars and, in the nineteenth century, had fought in civil wars in Spain, as well as the Mexican-American War and U.S. Civil War. These "Wild Geese" had shared with the Greek volunteers in the IB—and Saudi and Egyptian foreign fighters decades later—a deep frustration with their own repressive government and sought the opportunity to influence political outcomes elsewhere. With the establishment of the Irish Free State in 1920, Irish nationalists, "having defeated their English foe, next turned their attention to communism" (Stradling, 2003: 109).

Yet it was internal Irish political struggles that led directly to Irish recruits in Spain. The remnant of the Irish Parliamentary Party (IPP), which had slid into electoral eclipse since the establishment of home rule, attempted to reassert itself by provoking national indignation over atrocity stories and the alleged failure of the de Valera government to prevent them. The IPP conservatives established political-religious groups, such as the Irish Christian Front, to rail against "Red elements in Ireland" and imply the government's association with them, and they also sponsored the fascist Blue Shirt group led by Eoin O'Duffy. "They made the issue very simple. You were either in favor of burning churches and all that or you were against [it]" (O'Donnell, 1937: 239–240; Southworth Collection, UCSD).

Just as Abraham Lincoln Brigade recruits were informed that Franco must be stopped because oceans would not halt fascism, so O'Duffy's organization's Irish Brigade recruits were implored in newspaper advertisements to defend the church before international Communism could obliterate it. Most of these volunteers were from rural communities "where the Church was the main institution and religious affairs provided the glue of social existence" (Keene, 2001: 106, 116–122). They heard priests speak of "vile outrages against nuns and made them see that intervention in Spain was a matter of putting down these outrages...these people had been whipped up to believe that an attack on churches and priests was imminent in Dublin city." O'Duffy drew an initial 670 recruits, though his bombast and the deep political divisions in Ireland led to Irish volunteers on the Republican side in response (O'Donnell, 1937: 245, 255; Southworth Collection, UCSD).

Irish volunteers went first to Lisbon to hear sermons and visit local convents, where they heard themselves described as defenders of the faith. In Spain, they were enrolled in the Tercio de Extranjeros as XV Bandera—Irlandesa (Stradling, 2003: 110). At first, Franco kept them from the front lines, fearing that casualties would damage fund-raising and recruitment efforts in Ireland. After complaints about lack of action, they were sent to the Battle of Jarama in March 1937 without combat training. Assigned to lead a charge against enemy lines, the *bandera* retreated under fire and subsequently refused an order to advance (Keene, 2001: 122–125).

O'Duffy justified his insubordination on the grounds that compliance would have produced "a huge loss of life." Departing the battle, the Irish Brigade was involved in their only firefight when they were attacked by a fascist militia from the Canary Islands that did not recognize their uniforms and mistook them for Reds (Rust, 1939: 8–9; Southworth Collection, UCSD). The deaths of four of the Spanish fascist militiamen in this incident, coupled with the battlefield desertion, led Franco to write to O'Duffy complaining about the "limitation of the military contribution." After this, O'Duffy claimed that the Irish *bandera*'s "six month enlistment" was ending, and the troops voted 654–9 to return home (Keene, 2001: 125–127). Thus even the largest group of foreign fighters on the Nationalist side did not match the contributions made to the Republican side by the IB.

The Experience of the International Brigades in the Field

Like the Irish, other foreign recruits found themselves largely treated as expendable shock troops by their Spanish officers (Johnston, 1967: 79, 172). At the major battle of Jarama, ultimately won by the Republican forces, fresh ALB recruits were used as cannon fodder in World War I–style over-the-trenches suicide attacks against Nationalist forces. Among Harry Fisher's group of 80 that were rushed into the trenches without training, none had ever held a rifle, and only 90 of the 400 Americans in the field survived the battle (Fisher,

1998: 41–44). The prevalence of such reports appears to indicate that local commanders regarded foreign troops as disposable or less valuable. At Jarama, the Americans were told their heroic sacrifices would serve as inspiration to the Spanish troops. The results of that campaign reportedly seriously damaged recruiting efforts in the United States (Rosenstone, 1969: 46, 94, 154). This provides an indication that, even among those instilled with a sense of communitarian obligation, recruits do make some cost-benefit analysis based on the likelihood of survival and success of the effort.

Reinforcing the Message

Some Americans complained that they enlisted with the understanding they would serve in noncombat roles but were instead placed in the infantry, possibly because overzealous recruiters made promises that they did not have the authority to keep (Rosenstone, 1969: 94). A number of French recruits complained that they were told that they would be in Spain for only three months, but none had documents supporting their assertions. Nor did they have their passports any longer, which were supposedly taken for safe keeping upon their arrival in Spain, but in practice made it more difficult for them to desert[19] (Thomas, 2001: 588). Deserters usually sneaked away, rather than face their comrades and possible punishment, and caught merchant ships to foreign ports. The American military attaché to Spain who interviewed deserters trying to return home reported that most did not have strong political convictions and had not expected the level of danger they faced (Carroll, 1994: 148).

By the summer of 1937, the early enthusiasm that had produced such a large pool of volunteers that recruiters could afford to be selective had waned, as more state governments clamped down on recruiting activities and the fascist armies regrouped. France's decision to seal its border with Spain made replacing losses even more difficult, and the Republic was forced to supplement the thinning ranks of the IB with a growing proportion of Spaniards. As a result, on September 23, the Negrin government officially merged the Brigades and the People's Army into a single military force (Carr, 1984: 58).

Both the frustrations of recruits and deteriorating battlefield conditions led Comintern officials to attempt to turn necessity into a virtue. Surviving letters home from Spain appear to have been subjected to minor censorship, and reports of lost comrades were not excised. However, with recruitment levels also dropping considerably, the hardships of war were no longer emphasized as they had been initially. Commissar Joe Dallet wrote home, apparently without a trace of irony, that "I can personally verify that the men eat better than officers here…they say here that if you really want to eat well, what you have to do is go to the trenches" (Joe Dallet Box 1 File 11, ALBA, Tamiment Library, New York University).

By 1938, the IB was undeniably faltering against the superior numbers and firepower of the fascists. Socorro Rojo Internacional (International Red Aid) resorted to an appeal in English, which noted in passing that the XV International Brigade was made up of English speakers, for any who wished to join. It described improving service conditions for recruits who would be treated as well as their Spanish comrades:

> Gone are the old days of the Spanish war when volunteers were drafted to the fronts a few weeks after their arrival in Spain…the breathing space given by the first volunteers to the Spanish people to organize their young regular army has also been utilized by the IB themselves to give the later volunteers a better training than their predecessors for the tasks which lie ahead of them.

The transnational force now apparently included officer training schools, where "everything possible is done to see that those of good character get to advance themselves." Recruits are not "willy-nilly drafted" but are there because they are conscious of the necessity of struggle. The "local population are tremendously interested in these comrades from other lands and they do everything possible to make them comfortable during their stay in the village," and the children even sing songs to them (William Colfax Miller File, ALBA, Tamiment Library, New York University).

"You Are History"

The reality was far grimmer. Of nearly 3,000 American volunteers, a third were dead by the start of 1938, and only half of those who went would ultimately return home (Carroll, 1994: 204). By April 1938, only about 120 Americans were left in the force. More than 70 percent had been casualties at some point, and those who had survived to return home were no longer being replaced by fresh recruits. With no more Americans in combat training, all those engaged in supply duties were called to the front.

Although the IB were retained as distinct units for propaganda purposes, by the battle of Ebro in July, the last major action in which the ALB participated, three-quarters of its ranks were Spaniards. Still, American losses climbed disproportionately, as the Spanish troops and militia drafted into the ALB refused to advance under fire. When the Republican prime minister announced the withdrawal of all international forces on September 21 in a desperate bid to get Germany and Italy to follow suit, there were only about 200 Americans to return home. Their expenses were ultimately paid by the failing government, which also provided each volunteer with $25 in pocket money for personal expenses (Rosenstone, 1969: 296, 314–316, 322, 327, 333–334).

On November 11, a farewell ceremony was held in Barcelona in which 10,000 IB recruits were sent home under League of Nations supervision. Communist spokeswoman Dolores Ibarruri, known as La Passionaria, thanked the recruits for giving their blood and lives for Spain and told them, "You are history." Isolated, the last Republican forces surrendered on April 1, 1939 (Carr, 1984: 73).

Recurring Patterns and Significance

Both Republican and Nationalist propagandists found that framing the civil war as Spain's resistance to a foreign invasion did not produce as much interest abroad as the portrayal of a struggle between global ideological forces (Stradling, 2003: 100, 107). This development appears consistent with expectations that structural wars will generate more international output than authority or personnel conflicts. Framing the civil conflict as central to the struggle against fascism or Communism afforded both sides the opportunity to enlist foreign aid and thereby change the course of the conflict. The fascist attacks on Manchuria and Ethiopia did not provoke the same transnational participation as did Spain, and, while geographic proximity and race may have been factors, IB veterans cite the creation of an antifascist movement as the difference (Howard and Reynolds, 1986: 25).

Claude Pichois (in Romeiser, 1982: 5) notes that another factor allowed recruitment to continue even in the face of what appeared to be inevitable defeat. Unlike the last war experience, World War I, the Spanish Civil War was conducted on a human scale. Stories quickly piled up demonstrating that dogged, ragtag insurgents could be effective against superior professional military forces, and this knowledge attracted not just adventure seekers and mercenaries, but idealists who believed, at least for a time, that they really could defeat the major powers of the day. Such a narrative is employed in current conflicts involving foreign fighters, who can use the Internet and personal videos from the field to publicize their activities in a manner unavailable to the Comintern.

Exporting the Revolution: Legacies of the Spanish Civil War

The available data from both sides of the Spanish Civil War supported both hypotheses in this case: First, recruitment of most groups of foreign fighters on the Republican side occurred through a panoply of identity organizations with ties to the Comintern; on the Nationalist side, the Catholic Church and related organizations were the conduits for most foreign volunteers. The second hypothesis on defensive mobilization was strongly supported: Recruiters on both sides identified target audiences linked to the cause of a local faction and predisposed to fear the opposition; then they set about strategically crafting messages that would be consistent with the frame of specific threats designed to generate the largest possible mobilization.

The impact of the International Brigades on the outcome of the Spanish Civil War remains a matter of contention. Some historians note that the numbers of IB troops present in battles they are credited with winning were small, and their main effect may have been just to provide a pretext for the introduction of more fascist troops, increasing the brutality and lengthening the war. Johnston (1967: 151–152) argues for the benefit of even this conclusion: If not for the IB, the war would have resulted in a rapid Fascist consolidation of power in Spain that would have would have sealed off the Mediterranean as "an Axis lake" during World War II without a costly fight for Gibraltar. Instead, the depleted Franco regime was forced to remain neutral during the war.

The VALB continued its operations after the war, working to release remaining prisoners and shape public attitudes toward the ALB and Spain. At the outset of World War II, during the period of the German-Soviet Non-Aggression Pact, it lobbied to keep America out of the war under the slogan "The Yanks Aren't Coming." This may have been one reason that ALB veterans were not permitted to serve in combat regiments during World War II, despite being among the few members of the U.S. military at the time who had combat experience. Instead, they were relegated to units of German and Italian Americans who had refused to fight their countrymen (Carroll et al., 2006: 45–46).

The VALB still functions as an organization, holding annual reunion meetings, establishing memorials and an archive (ALBA), publishing its quarterly newsletter, and encouraging rapprochement with Spain after the end of the Franco regime in 1975. On the 60th anniversary of the Spanish Civil War, the conservative government then in power in Madrid offered honorary citizenship to ALB veterans and paid the transportation costs of those who could not otherwise afford to attend the ceremony (Fisher, 1998: 169).

This was more honor than they received from the conservative government in power in their own country at the time: During his 1984 reelection campaign, President Ronald Reagan encouraged Americans to join the Nicaraguan Contras at their bases in Honduras. He cited the ALB as a precedent, although adding that they "were, in the opinion of most Americans, fighting on the wrong side." (Public opinion polls showed that 65 percent of Americans backed the Republic in 1937, a figure that climbed to 76 percent by 1938.) In response, ALB veterans wrote editorials asking whether Reagan would have preferred that they fight for Hitler's ally, and VALB donated cash and ambulances to the Nicaraguan Sandinista government (Bessie and Prago, 1987: 15, 355). The Reagan administration's involvement in the Iran-Contra scandal became public the same month that the IB marked its 50th anniversary.

Other fallout from the Spanish Civil War was less obviously connected. The November 1946 edition of the *Volunteer for Liberty* featured an article titled "International Brigades Vets Carry On" that provided updates about the accomplishments of veterans since the war. One entry was for "Colonel General Enver Hodza, Chief of Staff, ALBANIA" (FBI File—VALB, File 20, ALBA, Tamiment Library, New York University). Hoxha was, in fact, the Stalinist dictator of his country by this point and would remain so until his death in 1985.

In the early 1980s, as Communism waned, Hoxha reversed himself on the question of nationalism and promoted over radio broadcasts heard in Yugoslavia the idea of a transnational Greater Albania (Hockenos, 2003: 194–195). Slobodan Miloševic, the dictator of Yugoslavia, responded in 1987 to rising Albanian nationalism by launching his own attempt to harness Serb nationalism over the issue of ethnic Albanians in Kosovo. These strategies led to the influx of foreign fighters in the Yugoslav secession wars of the 1990s, as well as to the development of civil conflicts in Kosovo and Macedonia that ultimately attracted diaspora Albanian and Islamist foreign fighters.

Elsewhere, Tel Aviv University reported the acquisition of the documents of 300 IB volunteers from Jewish settlements in Palestine (Joseph Brandt, File 13, ALBA, Tamiment Library, New York University). One American recruit claimed to have served with three Palestinian Jews that the British Mandate government had been so eager to get rid of that it had paid their transportation costs to Spain (Jack Shafran, "Letters from the Trenches," Joseph Brandt,

File 7, ALBA, Tamiment Library, New York University). Jewish Mandate survivors of the Spanish Civil War would return to face the British with the experience not just of fighting in an insurgency, but of a transnational recruitment
effort that changed the balance of forces in an otherwise hopeless conflict.
A decade later, these lessons would be implemented in recruitment throughout the Jewish diaspora for the Israeli War of Independence.

5

The Israeli War of Independence (1947–1949)

IN MID-1948, FARMERS on a kibbutz in the nascent state of Israel rushed to the site of a downed German Messerschmitt, prepared to attack the intruding Egyptian fighter pilot with pitchforks. Instead, they were surprised to hear the panicked flier shouting, "Gefilte fish! Shabbes!" at them in a desperate effort to establish his credentials as a fellow Jew. Despite going largely unheralded by the local population, this American pilot and thousands of other foreign volunteers played what the Israeli government would later acknowledge was a critical role in the War of Independence. Yet—even with easier travel to Israel, fewer legal restrictions against participation, and the far stronger position of the Jewish state—no foreign volunteers appeared during the subsequent 1956 Suez crisis or at the outset of the 1967 Six-Day War (Livingston, 1994: 130–131, 198). Likewise, Minister of Defense Moshe Dayan, "seeking salvation" during the unexpected crisis of the 1973 Yom Kippur War, urged recruiting Jews from abroad, but the government did not implement the plan (Bronner, 2010). Why, then, were foreign fighters unique to Israel's first war?

Many "foreigners" fighting in the Israeli War of Independence were refugees, in some cases literally fresh off the boats that brought them from displaced persons (DP) camps in post–World War II Europe. However, roughly 5,000 with specialized military experience—known by the Hebrew acronym MACHAL—volunteered or were recruited from diverse locales such as South Africa and the United States.[1] As Prime Minister Yitzhak Rabin expressed it, "They were not mercenaries. They were Jewish patriots expecting no reward other than to see the battle through and the State of Israel secure....Some were non-Jews who felt our battle for freedom was theirs too....If we failed to defend ourselves, there would be no survivors, no Israel, no Jewish national future" (Dunkelman, 1976: ix–x).

The Israeli War of Independence was an ethnic conflict waged mostly by secular nationalists who asserted their right to govern territory on behalf of their ethnic group. (This was the case for both the Jewish insurgents working to drive out the British administration and for the Arabs who fought against the new state after its establishment.) As an ethnic conflict in which the foreign fighters were coethnic with local combatants, the transnational insurgencies were both type 1 Diasporans. Although the object for each side was the establishment of its own new sovereign state, by the logic of transnational mobilization, recruiters should be expected to frame the conflict as a threat rather than an opportunity. Recruiters would be expected to work through the institutions of ethnonational identity groups, using the transnational connections of the Diaspora to find a likely target audience.

Although the vast majority of recruits were indeed Diaspora Jews, their contributions as a percentage of their respective national Jewish populations varied dramatically. What explains these variations in participation, and why did Diaspora Jews volunteer in far greater numbers when Israel was struggling to be born than after it had been established as the preeminent regional military power? Why did Jewish efforts in Palestine to utilize foreign recruits succeed while similar Arab efforts largely failed, despite the far closer proximity of recruits, state support for the effort, and what would appear to be a more direct stake in the conflict?

The recruitment of foreign fighters by the Jewish faction began more than two years before the establishment of Israel, at a time when the Haganah group (well before the advent of Israel Defense Forces, or IDF, regular forces) was an underground insurgency fighting both Arabs and the British military that administered the territory under international law. The success of its transnational recruitment efforts, as later acknowledged by the Israeli government, permitted the establishment of the state. The fact that foreign recruitment efforts fell away after statehood reinforces the fact that this effort was unique to the prestate Jewish insurgent faction and that Haganah in Mandate Palestine can properly be described as a transnational insurgency. By the same token, with the establishment of Israel, the Palestinian rebel groups at that point became the insurgency (and this formulation is reflected in my coding of the data). The Palestinian insurgent groups received foreign fighters from various Arab states that fought alongside them inside Israeli lines.

Despite the acclaim of recent Israeli governments, the contribution of foreign volunteers to the struggle for Israeli independence went largely unnoticed for decades for reasons that are discussed in this chapter. My experience in gathering information about foreign fighters in this conflict was strangely reminiscent of the recorded experiences of the participants: Access to source material occurred only because of personal connections to Jewish community officials who suggested avenues of contact; efforts at communication with the veterans' groups succeeded only after a particular influential figure provided an introduction on my behalf. Veterans of South African origin, who provided the largest contingent of wartime volunteers, were also the most communicative to me, and invaluable in providing original memoirs and historical records. Their unique stories provide important insight into the recruitment and mobilization of the global Jewish community—and a transnational Arab counterresponse—that shaped the face of the modern Middle East.

Background to the Conflict

The Israeli War of Independence is generally recognized as having occurred in two stages: a simmering civil conflict between Jews, Arabs, and the British Mandate authorities that erupted on November 30, 1947, with the announcement of the United Nations approval of the partition of Palestine, followed by an interstate conflict between Israeli forces and neighboring Arab states after the British Mandate expired on May 14, 1948, that lasted until the last armistice was signed with Syria on July 20, 1949. The latter also involved Arab rebels fighting an insurgent campaign within Israel. Clearly, however, the seeds of the conflict and of transnational intervention were planted far earlier (Markovitzky, 2007: 2; Rogan and Shlaim, 2001: ix).

Defense or Active Measures?

The League of Nations provided for the establishment of a Jewish Agency to coordinate services for the Yishuv (Jewish community) of Mandate Palestine. One component of the agency, which had originated in response to Arab riots in 1920, was Haganah, literally "The Defense." Although community policing was its literal aim, the violence of the 1936 Arab uprising led to a strategy of preemptive attacks and an accompanying intelligence network. By the end of World War II, Haganah had "developed a sophisticated structure with branches that reached into Europe and North America."[2] However, despite its effectiveness as a small-scale force, Agency Executive Chairman David Ben-Gurion recognized that it could not compete against the invasion by foreign regular armies that he expected after the declaration of statehood (Bercusson, 1984: xiv, 6–10, 21).

Ben-Gurion's view that more than humanitarian aid would be necessary to secure statehood at the end of the mandate was an extreme position within the Jewish Agency and even a minority view within Haganah. He therefore turned to a small group of wealthy donors gathered from across North America to finance efforts to secretly obtain weapons and equipment and to recruit technicians and specialists from abroad. The donor group, which would eventually incorporate as the Sonneborn Institute after convener Rudolf Sonneborn, consisted of highly successful, assimilated Jews who were leery of involvement in a distant conflict.[3] However, at their initial meeting in 1945, Ben-Gurion stressed their common identity based on their shared history and homeland, and key members pressured others with messages of responsibility to Holocaust survivors.

Group members ultimately agreed to raise $18 million and allow free use of their business facilities and, using personal connections, to set up a chain of living room meetings to solicit help from their own acquaintances, outside the framework of established Zionist organizations (Slater, 1970: 21–26, 97). This use of social networks appears to anticipate the strategy employed 60 years later in the United States by Internet-driven presidential campaigns that organized via networking resources such as Meetup and Facebook.

Institutions of Recruitment

Although the preeminent concern was to obtain munitions and heavy equipment, Sonneborn participants and Haganah also recognized that trained specialists with combat experience would be needed to ensure effective use of the matériel in the field. The British policy of denying Palestinian Jews the opportunity of military service, which ended only in 1944, had its desired effect of leaving Haganah without the capacity to develop into a professional force. The Jewish Agency quickly seized on the idea of obtaining the assistance of foreign military experts, but it was feared that non-Jewish advisors would abandon them if pressured by their own governments. After receiving no response from non-Jewish military officials in the United States, Haganah moved to its transnational networks of Zionist organizations to recruit Jewish combat veterans (Milstein, vol. 4, 1998: 221–222).

Teddy Kollek, chief of Haganah in the United States and later the five-term mayor of Jerusalem, incorporated a web of dummy corporations headquartered in New York City to acquire matériel and recruits. One of these companies, Materials for Palestine, was responsible for securing war supplies; Land and Labor for Palestine (LLP) ran summer training camps that ostensibly prepared youth for agricultural life on a kibbutz.[4] Quickly, LLP opened branch recruiting offices in eight cities and worked off purloined World War

II chaplaincy records to get the name of every Jewish veteran in the United States and Canada.[5]

Steve Schwartz, charged with the critical mission of recruiting fellow pilots for cargo runs, took sacks filled with $200 in nickels to use in Times Square pay phones, where he called every name that looked Jewish in the U.S. Army Air Force register of reservists, made vague offers of "jobs in aviation" in Palestine, and took information from any reservist who sounded interested. Phone calls were made in the morning, interviews were held that same afternoon, and navigation clinics for newer fliers were conducted that very evening.[6] During interviews, Schwartz would tell recruits: "The salaries were poor…long hours…might be dangerous" (Milstein, 1998: 223; Slater, 1970: 181, 211, 229–230).

Aliyah Bet

After pilots, the experts most immediately in demand prior to the termination of the British Mandate were experienced merchant marines who could run refugee ships past the British blockade. Through Aliyah Bet (an acronym for "illegal immigration"), beginning in 1945, "more than 32,000 immigrants, almost 50 percent of the refugees who sailed from post-Nazi Europe for Palestine…traveled on vessels purchased in the United States and manned by American volunteer sailors" in contravention of British authority. However, as one American seaman justified their actions to a journalist who accompanied one of their voyages, "If these ships were illegal, so was the Boston Tea Party." The goal of Aliyah Bet was both humanitarian (the rescue of Holocaust survivors) and strategic, bolstering the Jewish population of Palestine to increase legitimacy and establish a defensive army.

Aliyah Bet volunteers were paid only "pocket money for cigarettes and sundries," although many had been unemployed anyway before joining. Non-Jewish captains were hired only to sail the ships to Europe, where Jewish crews typically took over, although some gentiles elected to remain on for the duration. Although most volunteers were World War II veterans, and Aliyah Bet veterans claim only about 10 percent of volunteers were accepted for service, many among the first crews actually had no nautical experience but had been members of Zionist youth groups.

One volunteer who was recruited at a Zionist youth convention during the 1945 Christmas holidays ultimately made five voyages despite multiple arrests. Recruits "were warned the job could be dangerous, and…you turned over your passport to Haganah and agreed not to tell anyone where you had

gone. Your family could write to you through a mailing address in New York"
(Hochstein and Greenfield, 1987: xvii, 22, 27, 39–42, 55).

Transnational Recruitment

Despite the importance of harnessing the U.S. postwar capacity for producing
military goods and funding, the proportion of American Jews who ultimately
volunteered to fight for Israel's independence was quite low, compared with
involvement by Jewish communities elsewhere. The stringent enforcement
during this time period of American laws barring participation in foreign
armed conflicts was a major cause. However, governments in a number of the
more than 50 other countries from which volunteers were ultimately recruited
chose to look the other way or even offer tacit support. In Canada, despite its
status in the British Commonwealth, the law did not prohibit recruitment by
Haganah, even for the purpose of fighting British occupying forces.

In November 1947, two former Canadian army buddies, who were at
the time law students in Halifax and Vancouver, began recruitment efforts
on their respective campuses, and in Montreal, a committee of five World
War II veterans organized to recruit and also to purchase weapons, which
was not legal and attracted law enforcement attention. Despite this, a second
recruiting organization opened in Toronto, followed by other major cities.
Informational meetings were held for large groups of veterans in community
locations such as synagogues, where they were openly encouraged to fight in
Palestine, and anyone who was interested was asked to stay after the meeting[7]
(Weiss and Weiss, 1998: 68–74).

Recruitment efforts quickly spread to Latin America, Australasia, and
Europe, with local laws and governments' political positions on Palestine
determining the degree of openness possible in recruiting efforts. In 1947,
Haganah set up recruitment operations in Scandinavia, including military
training camps in Denmark and Sweden. A physical education teacher came
from Palestine to Finland and recruited 28 Jews, including four women, all of
whom were able to communicate in Yiddish (Kafka, 2001: 5–6). In France,
where 20 percent of the Maquis in the French underground during World War
II had been Jews, the French government was generally helpful to Haganah
and allowed an area outside Marseilles to be used as a training and staging
ground for volunteers on their way to Palestine (Slater, 1970: 265).

However, the largest single national group among the recruits was South
African, approximately 800 volunteers. This figure represented roughly 1
percent of their entire Jewish community, a ratio 3 times higher than among

Britons and 50 times higher than among Americans. The high rate of service is attributed by South African veterans of the conflict to their existing tradition of a volunteer national military force during the first half of the twentieth century and to racial polarization making identity more salient than among other communities that had not directly experienced the Holocaust. By November 1948, when volunteers were no longer required, nearly 2,200 South Africans were still in training to go to Israel. The South African League for Haganah extended recruitment efforts to the Jewish communities in Kenya, Rhodesia, and the Belgian Congo as well (Heckelman, 1974: 241–243; Woolf, 2002: 6–7).

Certainly, the South African government's benign neglect of recruitment and mobilization was also a factor. Despite its avowed anti-Semitism, the new Nationalist Party regime was eager to humiliate the British as they withdrew from their historic position of influence in the Middle East. Military training camps for volunteers operated without any need for cover, and, at mass rallies in Johannesburg, recruiters distributed enlistment forms to potential volunteers requesting names, addresses, and details of war service (Bercusson, 1984: 42).

Rival Efforts

Yet Haganah did not have a monopoly on recruitment. In South Africa, there were three main recruiting organizations. The official South African League for the Haganah, the flamboyant Hebrew Legion which turned out to be a scam, and the South African wing of the Irgun, which had operated in complete secrecy for 12 months, starting about mid-1947. [Many], who had no Zionist movement background, were early recruits of the Hebrew Legion. When it broke up, the disillusioned volunteers were mostly absorbed by the Irgun, and some by the South African League for the Haganah. (Woolf, 2002: 6–7)

Irgun was a militant offshoot of Haganah whose members believed that the Jewish Agency needed to take a more confrontational approach with the British authorities to secure statehood. Its preferred tactics were evident in its attempts to secure volunteers for its own ranks. In Winnipeg, for example, Irgun recruited openly, with its youth rifle training group bringing an intervention by the Mounties (Bercusson, 1984: 63–64).

In the United States, Irgun operatives established the American League for a Free Palestine (ALFP) to conduct fund-raising and recruitment operations. Rather than operate clandestinely, ALFP conducted a tremendous public relations campaign, arranging for its board to contain well-known names like Will Rogers Jr. and, as president, U.S. Senator Guy Gillette of Iowa.[8] One of its chief goals was to build its own Aliyah Bet program by purchasing German-built yachts that had been used for smuggling in the Spanish Civil War. The Irgun fleet included a number of vessels purchased in America and registered in Honduras, included the ill-fated *Altalena* (which was destroyed during the final Irgun-Haganah clash in June 1948 by the new IDF) (Hochstein and Greenfield, 1987: 95–101).

The theatricality of the ALFP became literal when it staged its own Broadway play, *A Flag Is Born*, starring Paul Muni and Marlon Brando. The producers explicitly informed the audience that the goal of the show was to raise money for the establishment of a Jewish homeland. Designed to run 4 weeks, the show went on for 10, eventually going on tour, where it made history as the first mainstream play performed before a racially integrated audience in the city of Baltimore (Hochstein and Greenfield, 1987: 95–98). The production raised $1 million for the purchase of the Irgun ship *Abri*, and Monroe Fein, later to captain the *Altalena* on its fateful voyage, reported that he was influenced by the play to take action and therefore volunteered at an ALFP office because it was connected to the play (Weiss and Weiss, 1998: 34, 144–145).

The ALFP followed up by holding a rally at Madison Square Garden on March 29, 1948, where it announced that it was establishing a George Washington Legion, modeled on the Abraham Lincoln Brigade of the Spanish Civil War, and opening an office in New York City to accept recruits. Later that day, the State Department announced that it would refuse to issue passports to anyone seeking to fight in Palestine (Weiss and Weiss, 1998: 74–75), but a report in the next edition of the *New York Times* claimed "three hundred more" had joined the legion overnight. Israel would deny the existence of the George Washington Legion, but American Harold Krausher, who went there as a crewman on the *Altalena*, claimed that 20 on board the ship had come with the legion, with half this number recruited through the publicity campaign and the rest joining through Irgun's worldwide Betar youth group. According to his account, the IDF persuaded the foreign fighters upon arrival to join the regular Israeli military instead (Heckelman, 1974: 78–79).

The success of the ALFP led to the creation of the public relations group Friends of Haganah and its publication, *Haganah Speaks*, to make counterappeals (Bercusson, 1984: 35). More directly, Steve Schwartz scuttled the Irgun plan to get volunteer pilots to bring armed guerrilla forces to Palestine and stole their membership list, obtaining recruits for Haganah in the process

(Slater, 1970: 232). Intrigue aside, Haganah leadership elected to avoid public recruitment activities that would draw the attention of the authorities, instead getting the truly interested to come to closed private recruitment meetings and sending Jewish veterans to personally recruit former comrades.[9]

Framing and Messaging

Who, then, did Haganah target in its recruitment efforts? As noted, some of its tactics were as simple as looking for Jewish-sounding surnames on lists of veterans who had the experience required to build a regular military. But obviously not all Jews contacted volunteered their services, and a number of non-Jews did. Who were the individuals who attended underground recruitment meetings and risked passage to a war zone in a homeland that most had never before seen? Might any evident traits in their backgrounds explain who Haganah targeted and with what appeals?

Target Audience

Heckelman (1974: 195) estimates that the total number of foreign volunteers involved in Aliyah Bet, air operations, and those who entered Israel for military purposes was 1,300 Americans and Canadians, 1,350 Britons, 850 South Africans, 1,000 from continental Europe, and 600 from Latin America. The difficulty in obtaining a more precise figure is less a problem of records than of disputes over who should be counted. "It was only at a late stage of the war [September 1948] that an official definition of the term MACHAL (Mitnadvay Chutz L'aretz, or 'Volunteers from Outside the Land') was decided upon, when the problem of repatriation of volunteers who opted for it became acute." Record-keeping difficulties occurred immediately, as some overseas recruits had not registered as such and "when the census was taken, many had already returned home, and their numbers could only be estimated" (Lorch, 1961: 325). The IDF General Staff defines MACHAL as "those who came to Israel to enlist in the IDF to help establish the state during the period of war, with the intention of returning to their own lands of origin at the end of the war." This definition includes those who manned the Aliyah Bet ships and more than 100 students who arrived on G.I. Bill scholarships to study in Jerusalem but quickly became involved in Haganah activities (Lorch, 1961: 325).

This stands in contrast to the refugees from Arab states, the Maghreb, and DP camps in Europe, many of whom were drafted into arms literally right off the boat. These draftees, known as GACHAL ("Recruitment from Outside

the Land") were placed in infantry positions, often without training or clothing (Heckelman, 1974: 203). Machalniks, as they came to refer to themselves,
resented being paired in units with unprepared GACHAL recruits who
seemed to them to represent liabilities (Bercusson, 1984: 124–125).

Markovitzky (2007: 2) notes that "Mitnadvay" connotes selection for military or technical expertise; Machalniks were "volunteers," not immigrants or
recruits. Smoky Simon, president of the World Machal veterans group, therefore claimed, "Volunteering was the very essence of the Machal story, which
included men and women, Jews and non-Jews, who volunteered to assist
Israel in its War of Independence. These volunteers were not recruited by the
State of Israel" (Simon, correspondence, February 3, 2008).

Transnational Identity: Jews or Zionists?

Nonetheless, many of the volunteers did not initiate their service without
first being contacted by a representative of either the Jewish Agency or a
local Jewish community organization, and this recruitment—or outreach to
volunteers—was often based on the target's prior involvement with Jewish
causes. Before the end of World War II, Zionism had not been a particularly
widespread sentiment among Diaspora Jews in Western nations. While seg-
ments of these communities were active in Jewish organizations that promoted a homeland, many Diaspora Jews attempted instead to assimilate,
fearing a backlash if they appeared to be unpatriotic, and limited their Zionist
activities to small charitable donations. However, the Holocaust raised the
salience of Jewish identity and activated it even among those accustomed to
discrimination: The two largest Zionist groups expanded their membership
from 110,000 in 1939 to 500,000 by 1948 (Bercusson, 1984: 11).

Like most Machalniks, American Jerry Balkin was not religious. But
by his count, he had lost 85 relatives in the Holocaust and was receptive
to recruitment after seeing newsreel footage of British soldiers dragging
refugees off Aliyah Bet ships to return them to DP camps. Colonel David
"Mickey" Marcus, who had served as military governor of Hawaii during
World War II and as a United States Attorney, had not been raised with
either a religious or Zionist perspective beyond his grandmother's contribution of coins every Friday to a Jewish National Fund box in the home. But
after his efforts on behalf of Haganah to find American military advisors
failed, he volunteered his own services, became Israel's first major general,
and eventually led the campaign that ended the siege of Jerusalem (Weiss
and Weiss, 1998: 14–15, 62, 201).

Other Machalniks had more obvious ties to transnational Jewish identity groups. Ben Dunkelman came from a wealthy Toronto family, and his mother had been an active fund-raiser for Zionist causes. However, Dunkelman saw himself as a Canadian first until his Jewish identity was activated by anti-Semitism he encountered while traveling in prewar Europe and by the unwillingness of the navy to allow Jews to serve as officers. When an acquaintance of his mother's, the wife of the president of the Zionist Organization of Canada, introduced him to a Haganah agent, he readily agreed to assume responsibility for recruitment in Toronto (Dunkelman, 1976: 2, 3 13, 56, 155).

Dunkelman (1976: 52, 157) argued that ardent Zionists tended to come from the poorer strata of society, possibly because the dispossessed believed in a cause that could produce a better life elsewhere, and that it is therefore necessary to consider a variety of other reasons to explain most participants. He contended that some among the initial volunteers must have been adventurers but that such individuals probably quickly lost interest upon learning of the minimal level of payment. However, some recruits had prior histories as transnational insurgents, such as Martin Ribikoff, who had flown supplies for the Loyalists in Spain[10] (Weiss and Weiss, 1998: 21).

Then, too, a large contingent of non-Jews volunteered their services to the Zionist cause. Dunkelman (1976: 159) claimed gentile volunteers in Canada outnumbered Jews but that he had orders to recruit only Jews for infantry positions. South African organizer Phil Zuckerman noted that non-Jewish volunteers were more likely to be suspected of being spies. "They came to the office, a mixed lot, sympathizers, bible believers, and adventurers. I gave them forms to fill in, but said frankly their hopes were slight. At the same time, I expressed appreciation for their goodwill" (Katzew, 2003: 299).

Still, dozens of gentiles did make their way into the ranks of MACHAL on the strength of their technical expertise and personal connections. A number of the Christians stated that they wanted to help fulfill the biblical prophecy of the return of the Jews to the Holy Land; others expressed outrage over the Holocaust or "their anger at the British Empire and anti-imperialism in general" (Markovitzky, 2007: 9). Without specific information concerning their individual experiences, it is possible to only speculate whether recruiters used different messaging for recruits who were not ethnically Jewish. There is some evidence that a humanitarian frame was emphasized for gentile foreign fighters in the field (see the Christmas card later in this chapter).

Given the difficulties that even Jewish volunteers without ties to the right organizations or gatekeepers experienced when they attempted to enlist, it is probable that gentile recruits had strong personal ties to Jewish personnel in the organizations and were disposed to identify with their cause. An example was Jesse Slade, a Native American from Oklahoma who had found Jewish acquaintances to be among the few whites who had treated him as an equal. When asked by a journalist why he was fighting, Slade, who wore a cowboy hat into combat, drawled, "Well, ma'am, I reckoned it was the Christian thing to do"[11] (Weiss and Weiss, 1998: 15, 22).

Recruitment Messaging: Live or Die

As Dunkelman noted, the compensation offered to recruits was usually negligible, providing evidence against a mercenary, greed-based model of recruitment. While some pilots, who were critically needed, received offers of up to $600 per month, most volunteers received a promise of two Palestinian pounds, about $6 per month.[12] Funds were usually wired directly home to wives or mothers, as arranged by the recruiter (Bercusson, 1984: 72).

If not greed, then how was grievance over the postwar status of Jews in Mandate Palestine used as a sufficient motivator to recruit service in a war zone, particularly when it entailed the risk of violating antirecruitment laws in the process? The fruits of victory were not a credible promise: In Palestine, Jews were outnumbered, lacked control of key strategic territory, and, until the first truce in 1948, had inferior weaponry despite the best efforts of Haganah (Rogan and Shlaim, 2001: 80). This situation was compounded by British authorities who, despite their aggressive enforcement of the embargo against Palestine, did not intervene to halt arms shipments to Arab states in their sphere of influence until two weeks after the Arab invasion (Bercusson, 1984: xvi).

Instead, recruiters raised the specter of the Holocaust and the possibility of its continuation after an Arab victory against the nascent Jewish state in meetings, through propaganda efforts such as *A Flag Is Born*, and by individual contacts. Slater (1970: 232) claimed, based on memoirs and interviews, that "very few of the volunteers were Zionists," and Heckelman (1974: 55) reported that many said that they had not held strong political views on Palestine but wanted to help Holocaust survivors. Hank Greenspun (1966: 83, 91), when presented with the message by associates that his intervention was required to prevent annihilation, said: "That's all over now, I tried to tell myself. The hell it is! my conscience answered. It's been going on for thousands of years.... We were more than crazy if we kept taking it: We were suicidally stupid." After his recruitment, Greenspun found a direct way to frame the issue of contention and the stakes for those he attempted to recruit: "Are the Jewish people going to live or are they going to die?"

Recruitment Process

Ralph Anspach, an escapee from Nazi Germany who was raised in Zionist youth groups, was sensitive to the treatment of DP camp refugees: "I felt I owed them because I could have been in their place very easily." Anspach contacted LLP, and "they let me know with a wink it wasn't really agricultural labor." He was then sent for a series of medical examinations "to see whether I was capable of picking oranges"[13] (Katz, 1998).

The LLP recruitment effort in North America was coordinated by Major General Wellesley Aron, who had commanded a British Army unit of Palestinian Jews during World War II and traveled to Jewish community meetings to describe the perilous situation in Palestine and the necessity of action (Milstein, 1998: 223). Lou Lenart, a former Marine Corps fighter pilot, attended a meeting in Los Angeles where Aron spoke. He came away from the presentation with the conviction that "we'd won as Americans, and lost as Jews" because of the Holocaust. He offered his services to Aron after the speech and was instructed to drop his résumé at Aron's hotel (Slater, 1970: 231).

Other war veterans with special skills (and, presumably, Jewish surnames or personal connections) literally received cold calls stressing their duty to defend world Jewry. Paul Kaye, who had served in World War II as a naval engineer, received a phone call from "a stranger" asking "Do you want to help your people?" They met that night, and the next day he was on a train to Baltimore to join the crew of the Aliyah Bet ship *Tradewinds*. After his capture by the British, Kaye was repatriated back to the United States, where he joined another Aliyah Bet vessel and eventually fought in the Israeli Navy during the war (Lowenstein, "Phone Call from a Stranger," Machal Museum).

Al Schwimmer, who would play an indispensable role in the war effort by procuring aircraft and pilots as the head of the fictitious Service Airways Corporation, had been a commercial aviator whose route took him to Palestine, where he was approached by a Haganah agent and recruited as a courier. Among the many that Schwimmer recruited were Greenspun, whose cousin was a Schwimmer associate (Greenspun, 1966: 75–76), and Hal Livingston, who received a letter in a blue envelope from an acquaintance telling him to go to New York and contact Service Airways (Slater, 1970: 231).

Livingston considered himself assimilated into American society and had not followed events in Palestine closely, but "he never had to sell me" despite being warned of the risks of combat missions. He then became a recruiter himself, combing a stolen list of New York Air National Guard rosters to search for Jewish surnames. Livingston recalled:

> I would telephone the selectee, vaguely query him concerning his interest in a flying job.... If he expressed interest I invited him to visit the Service Airways office. Whether this technique actually recruited anyone, I do not recall, but somehow we were finding more and more candidates. Friends of friends, or they had heard of the outfit, or had been referred by other Zionist groups. (Livingston, 1994: 15–19).

However, the recruiters may have also have been vague about the extent of their involvement with military activity. Just before American pilots were sent to Panama, where the regime accepted a payoff to register Service Airways aircraft, Schwimmer told them, "You are all now members of Haganah." Some reacted with misgiving, apparently having expected only a job (Slater, 1970: 234).

As in the Spanish Civil War, the pilots were more likely to receive promises of greater pay and benefits than the average recruit. Joe Warner, later to serve as president of the American Veterans of Israel, recounts that he was not offered pay or incentives "of any kind." A Canadian veteran who had followed events in Palestine closely, Warner said, "I was contacted by one of the 'recruiters' that I had known for quite some time. We were told honestly about the lack of arms and ammunition by the Jews in Palestine, but for some reason that I cannot truly explain, it just convinced me even more to make that journey." Gordon Mandelzweig similarly stated that he "was a member of the South African Jewish Ex-Service League and active in Zionist affairs" who was offered only free passage to Palestine but not salary or benefits for his service (Questionnaire, April 23, 2008).

Other Machalniks came to the cause by differing routes. John Harris, a veteran of the British RAF, developed an interest in Zionism after visiting DP camps and asked around until he connected with Haganah representatives (Questionnaire, April 24, 2008). Joe Woolf, who had immigrated to South Africa from Lithuania as a small child, was not active in Zionist groups, so "my awareness of the situation was delayed until I saw an advertisement in our local newspaper calling for Jews to join the Hebrew Legion" (Questionnaire, May 17, 2008). Another South African, David "Migdal" Teperson, who would eventually become a colonel and fight in every subsequent Israeli war for decades, "only knew what I saw on the news" and made his own way to Jerusalem (Questionnaire, April 23, 2008). Larry Raab, a 20-year-old World War II bomber pilot, had to make several trips to the Philadelphia office of LLP before convincing them to send him to main office in New York[14] (Slater, 1970: 232).

Norman Spiro (in an unpublished memoir) stated that he "was privileged to be chosen as Machal volunteer, having had no previous military training, probably for having been active in Zionist youth movements," and trained at a farm outside Cape Town. David Susman, future head of the South African Woolworths conglomerate, watched unfolding events in Palestine with "growing trepidation" and risked a confrontation with his father to go after discovering:

> A friend of ours, Leo Kowarsky, was secretly recruiting volunteers with some military or technical skills to help Israel stem the invasion. The call was mainly for pilots and doctors, but our first hand experience of infantry combat, said Jeff, would surely be of inestimable value to the new Israeli Army. All we had to do was to persuade Kow that Israel would be doomed without us. With some misgivings on his side, and much importuning on ours, he agreed to include us. We were to join a covert mustering base on a farm outside Johannesburg to help train and organize other volunteers, whilst awaiting precious space on a flight to Israel. (Susman, 2004: chapter 4, p. 1)

Some Machalniks were recruited in Palestine, where they had made their own way as students. During the 1947–48 academic year, 110 Americans used their new G.I. Bill benefits to study at Hebrew University and at Technion. They were greeted particularly warmly by the Jewish Agency, which hoped that if they were happy, they would persuade others to join them (Weiss and Weiss, 1998: 57).

Zipporah Porath, while eating at a student hangout, received a note from a stranger asking her to go to a meeting so that she could help with the defense of Jerusalem. She was interviewed by a tribunal and sworn into Haganah (Markovitzky, 2007: 8). Daniel Spicehandler (1950: 36, 44), who wrote in his memoir of "jealousy at seeing younger, less developed nations become independent while we lay prostrate under the bull's hoof," went to Jerusalem as a student and was recruited into Haganah in an interview conducted from behind a curtain so that he could not see the faces of his interlocutors. They, however, apparently had a thorough file on his Zionist activities and military experience.

When British fascists marched through London's Jewish districts in 1939, Esther Cailingold, who had been "beset by confusion over mixed loyalties to her British and Jewish heritages," noticed that the fascists were supported by the elite "Cliveden set" of English society. This experience and her subsequent volunteer work with Holocaust survivors convinced her to go to Jerusalem to train to be a teacher. While sitting in one of her classes, she was passed a recruitment note by Haganah (Cailingold, 2000: 16–17, 37).

David Gutmann, a merchant marine, saw an ALFP ad in the *New York Times* criticizing British immigration policy. Angered by the Holocaust, the British, and his lack of regular military veteran's benefits, Gutmann responded to the ad to sign on as a crewman on one of Irgun's illegal immigration vessels. At his interview, he was warned, "You know, you could go to jail for this. Are you prepared to spend a year in jail?" Gutmann eventually grew disillusioned with Irgun's penchant for dramatic but costly gestures of defiance and switched sides via LLP to work on the Haganah vessel *Paducah* (Weiss and Weiss, 1998: 24–28, 37).

Mobilization and Deployment: "Join Our Unit, Join Our Unit!"

By the time of partition, LLP had developed an efficient recruitment and screening process that simultaneously relied on secrecy and networking. Speakers at public meetings followed a circumspect script from which they expressed the need for volunteers:

> The struggle in Palestine needs manpower. Struggle doesn't necessarily mean fighting. Labor to provide food and other necessities is not less important. The aims and objectives of Land and Labor for Palestine are to encourage and assist individuals interested in strengthening and developing the Jewish Homeland by providing technical and agricultural skills. Land and Labor for Palestine is the official body deputed to advise individuals as to the needs of Palestine and the procedure recommended.... The need is for people of integrity with an urgent desire to assist, to the utmost of their capacity, for the duration of the present emergency in Palestine. Volunteers are needed who can adjust themselves to a new environment, rugged living conditions, and who are ready to do any kind of hard labor.... The minimum stay required is two years, or the emergency to be determined by the Palestinian authorities....

The speakers were directed to offer a "cold, factual presentation" and that "it should be made clear to the audiences that LLP is operating as a perfectly legal organization." Application blanks were distributed to audiences, and speakers were to report on who had been addressed, including "age level, response, and recommendation." Aron, spearheading the recruitment of insurgents who would face his old comrades in arms, ordered that no press releases or printed material be disseminated, but that word should spread along social channels "by chain reaction" (Slater, 1970: 211–212). Indeed, if volunteers sought to offer their services unsolicited, they were frequently denied or stonewalled for security purposes (Bercusson, 1984: 56).

Ultimately, LLP was advised by American military experts, including members of General Eisenhower's staff, who asked the first cut of applicants to fill out "personnel placement questionnaires" with questions such as "Do you expect to make any financial gain in this project?" and "Are you prepared to do any kind of job that may be required of you, even though it may involve hard, dirty work?" In some cities, the medical exam included a session with a psychiatrist. Usually, only experienced military specialists between the ages of 18 and 35 were accepted (Slater: 1970: 212–213) because, as Dunkelman (1976: 156) was told by his superiors, "We have more men than guns." However, Livingston (1994: xiv), who would later write a memoir critical of the treatment of Machalniks by the Israeli military, claimed, "They took anyone—for excitement, for money. 'If you want to write a book, if you're running from the police. If you want to get away from your wife. If you want to prove the Jews can fight.'"

There were initially no fixed criteria for recruits, and decisions rested with the judgment of interviewers who met afterward to vote, so recruits were not told whether they were rejected or accepted while there (Slater, 1970: 212). Joe Warner noted that "many possible recruits who attended the early meetings did not show up after the second or third time. Possibly the facts on the ground in Palestine (Israel) were a factor in them declining to go any further" (Questionnaire, April 23, 2008). In January 1948, the Jewish Agency Executive in Jerusalem established the Committee for Overseas Mobilization, which provided recruitment guidelines to Zionist organizations that included standards of age, physical condition, family status, and a two-year commitment (Bercusson, 1984: 53).

In the end, LLP sent about a quarter of the North American volunteers (Markovitzky, 2007:15). Personnel worked diligently to maintain plausible deniability that the organization was not violating the U.S. Criminal Code by recruiting; it was merely supplying information. All recruits were interviewed at the Hotel Breslin in Manhattan, questioned about their motives, "and told in no uncertain terms what they were getting themselves into." Medical and psychological tests were administered, as were passports. Unless recruits had skills in critical supply, they went to Palestine by ship, either directly or via France (Bercusson, 1984: 57–58).

Like International Brigade volunteers in Manhattan a decade earlier, recruits bought their own uniforms and supplies at military surplus stores (Livingston, 1994: 21). However, unlike the Comintern, Haganah did not front a travel agency among the many dummy corporations it maintained. Accepted applicants would request a passport at the State Department office, often with coaching to create a credible story of travel to Western Europe when passport applications for travel to Palestine began to be rejected. Later, when applications by any military-age American with a Jewish surname came under special scrutiny, 40 dummy corporations—one for each applicant— offered letterhead assertions of job offers abroad.

Once recruits had their tickets, they went to a LLP training camp outside Peekskill, New York, "across the Hudson River from West Point."[15] The camp was referred to as "the Seminar," and trainees received lessons in Hebrew, Zionist history, and military exercises until transport was available to take them to Israel (Slater, 1970: 213–215). This seclusion before departure was no doubt in part because many parents did not want their children to go and resorted to begging, bribery, or even reporting them to the police to prevent their departure[16] (Weiss and Weiss, 1998: 240). Although, to be sure, a number of strong Zionist families were proud, most parents reacted negatively, and many wrote letters asking their children to come home (Bercusson, 1984: 64).

"Altogether, more than 1,500 men and women would go to Palestine from the United States and Canada to fight with the various units of the Jewish army." Most left from New York on converted Victory ships for France. In Le Havre, they were met by a Haganah agent carrying a copy of *A Farewell to Arms*, who put them on a train to Paris and French Haganah headquarters. Then they went by train to Marseilles, waited and trained at a DP camp, and went on to Haifa when there was space on illegal immigrant ships (Slater, 1970: 216–217). "Several dozen" of the first overseas volunteers arrived in February 1948 (Markovitsky, 2007: 16).

Local Zionist Federations were supposed to send ahead lists of names and information, but many did not, and new arrivals were "wandering aimlessly about... it was totally chaotic." New arrivals were overwhelmed when "five or six commanders of various ranks and specializations would approach them to get them to join their outfit with whatever presumed skills they had" (Susman, 2004: chapter 5, p. 1). Ralph Anspach recalled, "You had different people saying, 'Join our unit. Join our unit.' It was totally disorganized" (Katz, 1998).

Despite this confusion, the foreign volunteers quickly made their mark by employing skills and deploying weaponry hitherto unseen in the theater of conflict. For example, Machalniks constituted 97 percent of the Israeli Air Force (David Teperson correspondence, October 10, 2007), and Canadian volunteers were responsible for a third of the Arab planes downed (Dunkelman, 1976: 159). On the 50th anniversary of the War of Independence, Prime Minister Benjamin Netanyahu wrote: "Their contribution was crucial and effective. They brought with them World War II experience, Western efficiency, exemplary dedication and infinite courage... the secret of our survival lies in the fervor of our faith and in the feeling of oneness which unifies our people in times of crisis" (Weiss and Weiss, 1998: 5).

The Arab Response

The effectiveness of MACHAL in building a modern army capable of employing World War II military tactics and weapons alarmed Arab leaders, who soon decided to develop a transnational force of trained soldiers to match the Israeli success. But if divisions between the Zionist factions had led to internecine conflict, the divergent and self-interested goals of the Arab governments and factions ultimately sabotaged their most effective paramilitary organization. Vatikiotis (1967: 2) noted, "One hardly expects [unity] to be developed—or even to exist... in regions where many sovereign states have emerged, or were deliberately created, in geographical contiguity to one another, amidst what their inhabitants consider to be one ummah." Although it would later serve as inspiration for a subsequent generation of mujahidin, the Arab Liberation Army (ALA)—also known as the Army of Salvation—at the time of its fielding instead served as an illustration of how the *ummah* was hobbled by the rulers of Arab states.

Background: Arab Political Leadership

The deadly 1936 riots by Palestinian Arabs led Mandate officials to insist that their local leadership establish a coordinating counterpart to the Jewish Agency (Lorch, 1961: 37). The resulting Higher Arab Committee (HAC) consisted of five local political parties under the presidency of the mufti of Jerusalem, the supreme Palestinian religious leader, who subsequently defected to Nazi Germany (Levenberg, 1993: 7–8). Without clear Palestinian leadership to resist the establishment of Israel, Arab leaders elsewhere took it upon themselves to attempt to organize a pan-Arab opposition.

Iraqi politicians formed the Palestinian Defense Committee to pressure their government to intervene. In a telegram sent to the HAC, the committee proclaimed: "[Our] aim is to adopt all possible means to preserve the Arabism of Palestine. The tranquility of the Islamic world depends on keeping Palestine an Arab country." A May 1946 meeting of the Arab League declared Palestine to be "an Arab country and it was the duty of other Arab countries to see that Arab status was maintained." The Syrian delegate made an impassioned appeal "to all Arabs to die for the beloved Arab land of Palestine" (Levenberg, 1993: 41, 43).

Just as the Israelis did, Palestinians and their supporters in the region framed the conflict in ethnonationalist rather than religious terms, with a call to defend Arab lands rather than Muslim holy sites. Even the mufti, then harbored by Syria and largely shut out of preparations for a transnational military force by the Arab League, adopted this frame after succeeding in installing his supporters in the leadership of another political body, the Higher Arab Executive (HAE). The HAE sent fund-raising materials to Christian countries that emphasized that theirs was a nationalist effort, not the seizure of holy sites by Muslims (Landis in Rogan and Shlaim, 2001: 99, 104).

However, when an Arab League conference held in Lebanon during October 1947 established the Jaysh al-Inqaz al-'Arabi (ALA), Palestinian Arabs viewed the appointment as field commander of the mufti's bitter rival, Fawzi al Qawuqji of Lebanon, as an attempt to undermine the Palestinian influence on the force (Elpeleg, 1993: 86). In December, the Arab League voted to supply volunteers for the ALA by national allocations: 500 Palestinians, 200 Transjordanians, 500 Syrians, 500 Iraqis, 500 Saudis, 300 Lebanese, and 500 Egyptians (Levenberg, 1993: 189). It also offered to contribute 2 million pounds in funding but ultimately provided only 10 percent of that amount and no military equipment (Collins, 1972: 161).

Recruitment was largely financed by the HAC, with fund-raising conducted in the United States in cities including Washington, D.C., and Chicago (Schechtman, 1965: 221). Syria offered to host the volunteer force as it was not militarily prepared for the conflict and saw the ALA as an opportunity to control events within Palestine and to serve as a counterweight to Transjordan's strong Arab Legion. Landis (in Rogan and Shlaim, 2001: 193–194) argues that, at least so far as Syria was concerned, the ALA was not intended to secure victory, but to forestall defeat and mitigate its consequences. Lorch (1961: 42,

80) adds that Damascus's real intent was to use the ALA to defend the Syrian frontier against Transjordanian incursions, rather than to liberate Palestinian Arabs. Perhaps because of these strategic interests, Syria, along with Iraq, was most faithful to its Arab League quota.

Recruiting the Army of Salvation

With the military leadership in place, the effort to mobilize a transnational Arab force quickly followed. Recruitment centers opened in Damascus and Aleppo on December 6, and Qawuqji opened a training camp at the former British base at Qatana, 10 miles outside Damascus. Like the Jewish Agency, the Syrian government placed weapons orders with Belgian and Czechoslovakian arms companies (Levenberg, 1993: 190). Approximately 600 Syrian regular army officers were assigned to the unit for logistics and training purposes, but fighting the Israelis was to be the work of the volunteer force (Lorch, 1961: 263).

A flow of Palestinians had begun arriving in November, with Jewish intelligence estimating 600 in training by January 1948, most of them veterans of the British Army. Recruits were "carefully selected by members of the National Committee and the Arab Youth Organization," paid during training by the HAE, and "encouraged to return to Palestine" after completing their training (Levenberg, 1993: 191–192).

In the wider Arab world, recruitment appeals for the ALA appeared "on the radio, by enormous newspaper ads, with fiery speeches in mosques and coffee houses…those calls promised to volunteers the not inconsiderable sum of 60 Syrian pounds a month for private soldiers and Syrian Army pay scales for non-coms and officers.[17] Buses brought volunteers to Damascus, and they rode through the city with patriotic slogans painted on trucks, singing and shooting." Volunteers came in groups with names such as the "Lions of Aleppo" and the "Falcons of Basra." These parties, with their nationalist rather than sectarian slogans, indicated that recruits accepted the frame of the conflict as an ethnic one of Jews against Arabs rather than a religious one of Jews against Muslims.

The recruits were a mix of classes and education levels: "Syrian Baathist politicians, Egyptian Muslim Brothers, Iraqis fleeing their new regime, Yugoslav Muslims sentenced to death by Tito for collaboration, escaped German POWs." As with efforts to organize newly arrived Jewish volunteers, the result was chaotic. Sir John Baggot Glubb (or "Glubb Pasha," the British commander of the Transjordanian Arab Legion) described the scene at Qatana as "a madhouse" (Collins, 1972: 160–162).

Other Foreign Fighters on the Arab Side

While Glubb was serving as a regular military officer in a position remaining as a legacy of British rule, some of his countrymen were attempting to reach the theater of conflict for less apparent reasons. In January 1948, the London office of the Palestinian Arab political mission announced it had "applications from over four thousand Britons" seeking to volunteer on the Arab side. The public position of the office was that it would not encourage them and most would probably not receive visas, but "there is no reason they cannot enter Arab states for any other bona fide purposes" (Slater, 1970: 215).

Meanwhile, four divisions of the Polish Army, having fled the German war machine through the Soviet Union and eventually down to Palestine, had become involved in the contentious local politics. A number of officers trained Arab armies and militias in drilling, bomb making, and espionage, and the head of the Polish organization in Jerusalem was arrested after publishing circulars calling for Poles to volunteer for Polish-Arab forces to fight the Jews. Ironically, many Arabs mistrusted the Poles, whom they imagined to be Jews posing as Christians. This misperception was not aided by Poland's vote in the United Nations for partition (Deckel, 1959: 300–308).

Effectiveness in Combat and Difficulties in Command

By the end of January 1948, 3,800 foreign (including irregular Syrian) recruits were in training in Syria, with many having already slipped into Palestine. The Arab League's stated goal was 16,000 recruits, but the effective fighting force was probably never more than 5,000. Tensions between Syria and Transjordan contributed to some of the organizational difficulties, with most ALA forces stationed defensively "in Arab districts [Amman] wanted to annex." Additionally, the mufti's officers concluded that the ALA's real mission was "to wreck the organized resistance of the [mufti's local militias, the] Jihad Muqaddas" (Landis in Rogan and Shlaim, 2001: 195–198). In response, the mufti apparently sent agents to the training camps at Qatana to encourage recruits to desert and join his forces instead (Elpeleg, 1993: 86).

The first military units of the ALA, dressed in surplus American and British uniforms and led by a German officer, infiltrated Palestine on January 9, 1948. "Their discipline and cohesion [were] far superior to anything hitherto seen among the Arabs." The 1st Yarmuk unit, 700 Syrians commanded by an Iraqi major, attacked on January 20, with a second, similarly composed group attacking nine days later.[18] The introduction of the ALA to the battlefield resulted in a new escalation of the conflict, with the Yishuv proclaiming that the failure of the British to prevent these incursions necessitated the acquisition of still more foreign armaments for defense (Levenberg, 1993: 193–194).

On February 16, an ALA force of 300 to 500 made a large-scale attack on the Jewish settlement of Tirat-Zvi near Nablus. Although reported in the Arab press as a victory, the assault was repelled with nearly 30 percent casualties; "it caused anger and frustration among the volunteers, and as a result of this some of them returned to their countries." Part of the difficulty, and perhaps a deliberate one given the discord, came when nine carloads of Syrian volunteers were turned back by Transjordanian authorities and had to ford the Jordan River to join the attack. The British Office noted sardonically that "should their next attempt meet with similar results, there is little doubt that many of these noble strugglers will consider it expedient to return home and mind their own affairs" (Levenberg, 1993: 198–199).

By March 1948, roughly 6,000 ALA fighters had arrived in Palestine, a peak figure that never reached the target number. "In fact, by that time, recruitment had almost stopped." Worsening internal divisions, chiefly involving the mufti's Palestinian faction, had diverted the mission of the ALA. The main concentrations of forces were not sent to battle for control of major towns, but groups of 200 to 300 were used to establish control over Arab areas and make guerrilla attacks in Jerusalem (Levenberg, 1993: 200–201).

Arab Reaction to the ALA

This defensive posture was in part a reaction to King Abdullah of Transjordan, who planned to use his Arab Legion to bring the Samaria region of the West Bank under his political control. The mufti, aware of this objective, ordered Palestinians to stockpile weapons to use against Arab invaders and fomented mistrust of Arab foreign fighters among the Palestinian Arab populace (Levenberg, 1993: 192). The Jihad Muqaddas often engaged in clashes with the ALA and Transjordanian forces, in part because of the propaganda campaign by the HAE to resist foreign Arab occupation. The mufti at the time claimed that the ALA treated the local Palestinian population cruelly, and his warnings led to a mass exodus from Jaffa by Arab civilians fleeing robbery and murder at the hands of their purported liberators (Elpeleg, 1993: 96–98). Indeed, as Glubb Pasha reported, "As their moral enthusiasm waned, the Arab Liberation Army became more interested in looting—often from the Arabs of Palestine" (Schechtman, 1965: 228).

The Muslim Brotherhood

While the ALA operated as a secular pan-Arab force, a key Islamist group also attempted to add a distinct contribution to the effort. The Muslim Brotherhood, founded by Hassan al Banna in Egypt in 1928, had already called unsuccessfully for volunteers to Palestine during the 1936 Arab revolt. In October 1947, the Brotherhood announced the necessity of saving Palestine by force, urged all Arab states to open recruitment offices, and offered 10,000 fighters as the first detachment of the ALA. Instead, although al Banna claimed a force of 2,000 brothers entered Palestine, the evidence indicates that a small raiding party went out against Jewish forces and—after the Egyptian government refused at the last minute to provide military training—it broke under fire and fled.

Cairo refused to train the Brothers because it was aware that al Banna hoped that combat experience gained in Palestine would eventually be employed against the government at home. However, after about 100 Brothers infiltrated Palestine while posing as members of a survey expedition of the Sinai, Egypt reversed its policy and announced that it would open two recruitment centers and train and assist all volunteers who wished to go. This assistance came in the form of sending 200 recruits on a boat to Haifa, where they were apparently surprised that they were refused permission to land and forced to return home (Levenberg, 1993: 167, 173–178). Given the extraordinary clumsiness of this effort and the qualms of the Egyptian government, it seems likely that Cairo had hoped to rid itself of a number of troublemakers.

The First Failure of Pan-Arabism

The Egyptian maneuvers, the intrigues of the Palestinian factions, and the self-serving policies of Syria, Transjordan, and the various states that withheld their pledges to the ALA ensured that the supposedly pan-Arab transnational insurgency would never match its early promise. It apparently also suffered from the divergent goals of its own commander. Qawuqji held a bitter grudge against the mufti, who had arranged for him to be imprisoned by the Nazi regime while both were refugees in Germany, and told his contacts in Israeli intelligence that he hoped that they would show up the mufti. He reportedly even offered in April 1948 to refrain from further attacks against the Jews if he were permitted one military victory to establish his credentials. No such offer was accepted, but Jewish intelligence came away from the meeting with the distinct impression that the ALA would not intervene to protect the mufti's forces in battle.[19] Indeed, three days later, ALA forces in the vicinity failed to come to the aid of the mufti's forces at Ramla as they were decimated by the Israelis (Rogan and Shlaim, 2001: 85–86).

By the anniversary of its creation, ALA force levels dropped to approximately 2,200, with many Iraqi volunteers leaving to join their own army as it entered the conflict. By the time of the first United Nations–sponsored truce in June 1948, the ALA was not a significant military force, but its position along interior lines allowed it to fight in conjunction with regular Arab military forces (Lorch, 1961: 263). In October 1948, the IDF launched Operation Hiram, which expelled the ALA from the Galilee and closed the border with Lebanon where infiltrations originated (Rogan and Shlaim, 2001: x).

Experience in the Field: "How to Get Along"

Besides Operation Hiram, Machalniks participated in key battles on every front of the war for Israel. Unlike the International Brigades in the Spanish Civil War, MACHAL was not developed for its propaganda effect, but to place experts where they were most needed with untrained insurgents and later fledgling regular troops. The IDF therefore deliberately scattered Machalniks throughout different units. The units that benefited most from foreign experts were medical, armor and "[they] made their greatest contribution to the Haganah's Air Service and its reincarnation as the Israeli Air Force" (Bercusson, 1984: xviii).

Babel

However, along with their unique contributions came special difficulties in coordination:

> In the beginning, the training was a nightmare. My platoon was a polyglot group of disparate characters and varied ages. None of them had combat experience, and most had only ever seen a weapon when looking into the barrel of a concentration camp guard's rifle.... I had in my unit, from time to time, Bulgarians, Poles, Costa Ricans and refugees from the Displaced Persons camps of Europe, in addition to Americans, Canadians, British, and of course South Africans. The most common language was Yiddish, which I barely understood. It was surprising, however, how quickly we came to understand each other whilst under fire. (Susman, 2004: chapter 5, pp. 3–4)

Still, difficulties in integration persisted for two reasons. The most prosaic was the linguistic communication barrier. Except for pilots, who were permitted to speak English, all recruits were expected to speak Hebrew in their integrated units (Weiss and Weiss, 1998: 22–23). David Shachar, a Polish Jew from France, was one of the few who could translate in his mixed unit of MACHAL and GACHAL troops and officers from Palmach (Haganah regular forces) who had no common language between them (Shachar, 2002: 2).

In the Armored Corps, there were "Russian" and "English" tank companies organized by operating language. Both were under the command of a Pole who spoke only Polish and Russian and whose operations officer spoke only Yiddish and Hebrew. Two interpreters were employed in an attempt to make this situation work, but, after the Russian company never reached the field in a key battle because of communication difficulties, the Polish commander was relieved of his duties. Perhaps the most unfortunate consequence of the linguistic problems was that General Mickey Marcus was shot and killed by his own sentry within hours of the end of the war when he failed to recognize a command to halt (Slater, 1970: 163).

The second concern was the persistence of nationalism among the Diaspora volunteers. Many wanted to serve in mixed brigades and viewed the common use of Hebrew as the fulfillment of the Zionist dream, but this sentiment was hardly universal. French and North African volunteers insisted on their own unit, but when they received it, they also received lower pay and less equipment. Senior officers in the newly established IDF complained that the battalion functioned poorly and included criminals.[20] Its commander, Teddy Eitan, eventually winnowed it to the crack Commando Français, which continued to function as a Francophone outfit for the duration of the war (Bercusson, 1984: 184, 185).

When the Canadian contingent was dispersed to different units, recruits complained "bitterly" about the "breach of confidence," having been assured that they could serve alongside their countrymen. Morale problems grew so bad in the 72nd Battalion that the North Americans were given a stern pep talk by a gentile on leave from the British army, who told them that they needed to consider themselves privileged "to defend their country again after 2,000 years of dispersion" (Dunkelman, 1976: 227, 311).

Many volunteers reported feeling unappreciated, particularly because of the general policy that an Israeli always had to be the commanding officer, even if he lacked specialized experience (Weiss and Weiss, 1998: 22–23). Machalniks were scattered through different units, with the largest concentrations in the Medical Corps and the Mixed 7th Brigade (approximately

300), which included the 72nd "Anglo-Saxon" Battalion (Heckelman, 1974: 161–162). Company B of the 72nd was "the only unit in the Israeli army made up totally of English speaking volunteers" (Lowenstein, 2006).

Anglo-Saxonim: Madmen from Outside

Overall, morale problems appeared to be most common and most serious among volunteers from English-speaking countries, who were universally termed with the Hebrew plural "Anglo-Saxonim." English speakers tended to have little fluency in Hebrew, such as the downed pilot mentioned at the beginning of this chapter, and this linguistic barrier served to increase their isolation and sense of distance from Palestinian Jews. When word of the tension began to trickle back home and possibly impact recruitment, the Canadian Jewish community sent representatives to Israel to investigate complaints and suggested increased R&R (Bercusson, 1984: 196, 197).

Anglo-Saxon was generally regarded as a positive status term, although one volunteer commented, "throughout my life I've been called a dirty Jew, and now, in Israel, suddenly I'm an Anglo-Saxon!" The Anglo-Saxonim, given the higher standards of living in their home countries, were more apt to complain about conditions in Israel, and many Israelis likewise could not understand why Western Jews chose to leave the comfort of their everyday lives to join their struggle. Some wags, substituting the Yiddish word for "lunatic" in the place of "volunteer" in the MACHAL acronym, claimed the organization really represented "Madmen from Outside the Land of Israel." Some Israelis also joked that the Anglo-Saxonim spent hours primping in front of the mirror before combat. Reportedly, brawls in pubs between Haganah and Irgun supporters ended when both factions united to fight Americans (Livingston, 1994: xii–xiii, 162). By other accounts, English-speaking volunteers received more gratitude from the Israeli populace than other foreigners (Joe Warner, Questionnaire, April 23, 2008).

> To the [Israelis on Aliyah Bet missions] indoctrinated to austerity in Socialist youth movements and hardened by underground conflict with the British and Arabs, the freewheeling Americans were an unfamiliar element. They sometimes seemed naïve, undisciplined, uncontrollable.... To [the Americans,] the determined [Israelis] seemed arrogant, narrow-minded, overly secretive and conspiratorial.... [However, an Israeli intelligence operative] noted the willingness of the Americans

to undertake seemingly impossible assignments. He doubted that hired crews would have done the same. (Hochstein and Greenfield, 1987: 32–34)

For all of the vital contributions Machalniks were making to the Israeli war effort, the different perspectives ultimately created operational difficulties as insubordination increased. Many foreign fighters expected Western operating standards and recognition of their special contributions (Lorch, 1961: 325), but many Israelis did not believe it necessary to treat the outsiders any differently, particularly as many assumed all of the Machalniks would eventually become Israelis anyway. Bercusson (1984: 215, 228) sums up the source of the disappointment of the disgruntled Machalniks: Israelis could not live up to the idealized vision of them held by the Anglo Saxonim. Ironically, Milstein (1998: vol. 4, 224) claims also that "Yishuv residents treated the GACHAL soldiers, who came from countries in distress, differently than the MACHAL recruits, who hailed from affluent nations. Many former GACHAL fighters recall open displays of scorn and snobbery."

Efforts to Integrate Machalniks

Disagreements between the foreign specialists and the IDF leadership continued over issues ranging from combat tactics to benefits. In the Anglo-Saxon Brigade, protests and even refusals to follow orders led the command to consider dispersing or limiting all foreign volunteers (Bercusson, 1984: 212). Something had to be done.

> The IDF Manpower Branch, in September 1948, set up a special department to deal with overseas volunteers. It was at this time that the group's name was officially designated as MACHAL.... It focused on publishing newspapers and informational material for MACHAL in several languages (mainly English and French). The department endeavored to provide social and welfare assistance to overseas volunteers, distributed pocket money, dealt with difficulties encountered in their military units, their personal problems, and much more. It also set up a club in Tel Aviv, on Hayarkon Street, where volunteers could meet during furloughs. (Markovitzky, 2007: 19)

As part of this effort, the IDF issued *Frontline*, a military newspaper for English speakers published by the former editor of *Stars and Stripes*. At another point, it printed a leaflet "To Christian Volunteers," wishing them Christmas greetings from the military chief of staff and reinforcing the recruitment frame by informing them: "You are part of a noble tradition of men who have volunteered to fight for justice and righteousness, which know no national boundaries." Another publication for Anglo-Saxonim was a guidebook titled *How to Get Along* (Weiss and Weiss, 1998: Photo section, p. 3). The cartoon cover of this pamphlet showed a smiling young man holding several suitcases, possibly a reflection of the stereotypes of highfalutin Americans.

Still, the IDF and Haganah soon discovered that the cost of MACHAL, particularly in the outlay of foreign currency, was prohibitive. Disciplinary and assimilation problems compounded these concerns, resulting in a gradual tightening of restrictions on Machalnik applications. "By the end of the War of Independence only a trickle of Machalniks was being accepted to the IDF, mainly specialists in specific fields, selected according to need" (Markovitzky, 2007: 19–20).

The peak concentration of foreign volunteers occurred in spring and early summer 1948, immediately following the declaration of statehood, after which numbers began to decline as volunteers returned home when their terms of service ended. By the end of the summer, the emphasis of recruitment shifted from specialists to military instructors who would contribute lasting capacity to the new regular army[21] (Mardor, 1959: 238).

Outcome and Legacy

The declaration of the State of Israel on May 14, 1948, ended the civil conflict in the Mandate and left the Israelis free to establish an open regular military, albeit one that still relied on a dwindling flow of outside advisors. After Israel's victories, culminating in the armistice with Syria on July 20, 1949, the interstate phase of the war ended, too.

Israeli Recognition of MACHAL

Despite offers of financial assistance such as loans to start businesses and Hebrew lessons, fewer than 10 percent of Machalniks stayed after the war in the homeland they had fought to secure (Weiss and Weiss, 1998: 22, 267). Among the enthusiastic South African contingent, only 20 to 30 percent of Machalniks stayed to settle or returned later. Hymie Josman, who observed, "I returned to South Africa and often wondered how it was that I was prepared to die for Israel, but not live in it," eventually relocated there in the 1960s (Katzew: 2003: 279). Still, like the victorious foreign fighters in Texas more than a century earlier, many volunteers simply went home after having won the war.

A number of others would not return home: 119 overseas volunteers lost their lives in Israel's struggle for independence, including nine gentiles and four women. Among Israeli pilots, 19 of 33 killed in action were Machalniks, as had been six of seven prisoners of war. Clearly, the volunteers had placed themselves in positions of peril rather than simply collecting paychecks. But it would not be until 1993 that a monument to them would be erected in Israel with private funds (Markovitzky, 2007: 27, 41).

The Israeli government downplayed the MACHAL contribution for a variety of reasons, including avoiding divisive concepts such as describing portions of the Jewish people as foreign, an unwillingness to admit dependency on outsiders because of local pride, and fear that enemies would discern a reliance on volunteers who had departed. Plans to honor MACHAL on Independence Day in 1965 were canceled until 1968, when the state was in a stronger position (Heckelman, 1974: xx–xxi).

Over time, however, there has been greater recognition by Israel of the MACHAL legacy, including commemorative postage stamps in 1997. An IDF-sanctioned successor organization, Mahal 2000, was established in 1988 to recruit Diaspora Jews for two-year terms in the IDF (Markovitzky, 2007: 1–2). After 10 years, "over a thousand young people from more than 40 countries" had joined (Israel Ministry of Foreign Affairs, 1999). And in May 2008, on the 60th anniversary of Israel's independence, surviving Machalniks were honored by the government at a reunion in Tel Aviv.

Evaluation

The data from this case supported both hypotheses: Recruiters targeted the Jewish Diaspora as the pool of potential volunteers most likely to be responsive and exploited various ethnic institutions such as charities and chaplaincy records to find names to contact beyond personal acquaintances. A number of non-Jewish recruits also joined; nearly all had specialized skills and had been recruited by Jewish acquaintances. On the Arab side, the evidence suggests that mobilization occurred at the local and municipal level through government and community institutions. The second hypothesis on defensive mobilization is also mostly supported: What could have been portrayed as an opportunity to reap the material benefits of service to a new state was instead represented as a battle for survival (on both sides). That the overwhelming majority of victorious Jewish recruits simply returned home despite generous offers of resettlement assistance indicates that they were fulfilling a sense of obligation to their community and were primarily interested in eliminating a threat rather than material reward.

Elsewhere

"No longer needed, the American underground quietly disappeared.... Schwimmer Aviation and Service Airways continued only on paper.... [LLP] closed down its offices even before most of the hundreds of volunteers it had dispatched to Israel had returned." Materials for Palestine changed its name to Materials for Israel and supplied immigrants with basic goods until 1955, the same year that the Sonneborn Institute finally disbanded, its members deciding that their decade of activity had accomplished its goal. The movement's "records were destroyed, only scattered fragments surviving in the bottom drawers of law-office files, in the basements and attics of some of the participants' homes.... The published histories of the Israeli struggle for nationhood would barely mention the American underground" (Slater, 1970: 320–321).

But the story was not yet over for all of its participants. In 1950, the U.S. government issued nine indictments for violations of the Neutrality Act in the supply of aircraft to Israel. Ultimately, three convictions resulted. Al Schwimmer and Hank Greenspun received suspended jail sentences and fines of $10,000, which Greenspun related were quickly paid by benefactors (Livingston, 1994: 256).

Greenspun received a presidential pardon in 1961 and went on to become a fixture in Las Vegas politics; Schwimmer received one as well in 2000. The only individual to be imprisoned was Charlie Winters—a Protestant businessman who had provided three surplus B-17 aircraft and helped fly them to the Haganah air base at Zatec, Czechoslovakia—who pleaded guilty in 1949 and received 18 months in jail. In 2008, Winters received only the second posthumous presidential pardon in American history (News Agencies, 2008).

Another development was the legacy of the Arab Liberation Army. In the short term, "its failure resulted in the galvanizing Pan-Arab agenda in the following decade," built on the desire to develop an effective capacity for collective action (Rogan and Shlaim, 2001: 6). Pan-Arabism, however, would not become an effective international force, and it was soon superseded as the leading ideology among dissidents by fundamentalist Islam. Among the Islamist theorists and activists was Abdullah Azzam, who named the intervention by the ALA and the Muslim Brothers as his source of inspiration for organizing transnational recruitment to drive the Soviet Army from Afghanistan.

6

Afghanistan (1978–1992) and Beyond

SHEIKH ABDULLAH AZZAM, the Palestinian militant who had settled in Pakistan and organized foreign fighters to help drive Soviet forces from Afghanistan, savored the withdrawal of the Red Army in February 1989 as proof of the success of his model of transnational activism. Nine months later, he was killed by a car bomb, and the movement he initiated was left in the hands of his colleagues and rivals, Osama bin Laden of Saudi Arabia and Ayman al-Zawahiri of Egypt. Shortly thereafter, the former successfully organized Arab Afghan veterans as the foundation ("al Qaeda" in Arabic) of a new and permanent network of foreign fighters globally active within and across a variety of disparate civil conflicts (Wright, 2006: 130, 149).

The Afghanistan War represents type 2 transnational insurgencies, in which outsiders join the civil war as Liberationists on behalf of an ethnic group with which they share some connection, although they do not share ties of ethnicity. In this case, the evidence should indicate that recruitment occurred through networks of the (religious) institutions that Afghan mujahidin shared with Arabs. The messaging would portray the Afghans as a distinct ethnic group under threat. In this case, the insurgents also diffused into a number of other civil conflicts, but the same frame that was used successfully in Afghanistan would be expected to hold.

The outcome for the transnational insurgents of the Afghanistan War differed from those in previous instances in which, with rare individual exceptions, both victorious and vanquished foreign fighters settled down to apparently average daily lives in their home or adopted countries. The Arab Afghans—a group joined by South Asians, Malays, Africans, and some Westerners, roughly 4,000 in all—whose surviving leaders remained active in transnational insurgency 30 years after their work began, instead continued to expand their activities and trained successors to fight in other conflicts. Al Qaeda and related jihadist groups are now ubiquitous, engaging in terrorism and international crime in areas where they are not participating in civil wars.

In this chapter, I examine the Afghanistan War to determine why the foreign fighters persisted in their activities beyond the accomplishment of their stated goals. The recruitment messaging of threat to fellow Muslims by atheist Soviet imperialism is an obvious frame, quite similar to the message of threat to Catholicism by Soviet Communism employed by the Nationalists in the Spanish Civil War. But whereas those victorious foreign insurgents returned to their home countries rather than launching assaults against Communist or secular regimes elsewhere, the mujahidin branched out to other states, beginning with completely unfamiliar territory in Bosnia. When the adversary is defeated, it would be logical to assume that the perceived threat has been removed and that the existing recruitment messaging would no longer prove effective. What factors are responsible for this variation in the case of Afghanistan? Why did the defeat of the adversary not remove the perception of threat? Would the adoption of different policies by Afghanistan or the home states of the foreign fighters have resulted in a different outcome?

In approaching these questions, I encountered a wide array of post-9/11 literature on the rise of militant neofundamentalist Islam, but surprisingly little scholarship is available on the initial recruitment of foreign jihadists to Afghanistan, with most of the few Western accounts written at a time when "al Qaeda" would not have been recognized by word processor spell check programs. Russian military analyses of the defeat neglect to differentiate between Afghan and foreign insurgents. In the Arab-language press, only two memoirs have been published by Arab Afghans.[1] For primary source material, I have therefore relied on the files of Thomas Hegghammer, who has produced the most authoritative account available of the life and operations of Abdullah Azzam and who was kind enough to share his audio and video files, as well as his full collection of reproductions of Azzam's recruitment magazines published during the 1980s and archived at the Islamic University of Medina.[2] In this chapter, I present these data as emblematic of the common approach used by recruiters to transnationalize insurgencies, particularly in type 2 cases, and then examine how the insurgency transformed and exported itself once the threat used to mobilize volunteers had disappeared.

Background to the Conflict

What would become the present state of Afghanistan was established in 1747, when Pashtun tribal leader Ahmad Shah Durrani was elected leader by a *lloya jirga* (pantribal council meeting) following the assassination of the ruling Persian king. Durrani's mountainous kingdom was written off as essentially ungovernable by the Russian and British empires during their Great Game for control of Central Asia and left as a buffer state between them. The artificial borders imposed by the imperial powers left a fragmented nation, with many Pashtuns in India (now Pakistan) and minority groups such as the Shiite Hazara tribe in the central highlands (Overby, 1993: 7, 9). In the 1920s and 1930s, forced collectivization efforts in the Soviet Union led many Uzbeks and Tajiks to flee across the Amu Dar'ya (Oxus River), adding to the minority populations and further increasing the cleavages within Afghan society (United States Senate Committee on Foreign Relations, 1984: 4).

After World War II, the Afghan monarchy felt pressure from the cosmopolitan upper class to modernize, and the United States and the Soviet Union competed to provide development projects in the 1950s, with the Kabul regime eventually developing closer ties with Moscow as a supposed better exemplar of modernization. Along with efforts at economic development came attempts to expand education and limit tribal and traditional religious authority, policies that enjoyed limited success but were quite effective in mobilizing an opposition. Proreform student Communist groups such as Khalq ("Masses") and its more moderate splinter Parcham ("Banner") battled radical Islamists in the streets during the 1960s, with the latter's rallying cry "Islam is in danger!" (Overby, 1993: 17, 31, 36, 54).

Mohammed Zahir Shah, the last king of Afghanistan, supported the modernizers and imprisoned their fundamentalist opponents until, while out of the country for an eye examination in 1973, he was overthrown by his brother-in-law Mohammed Daoud, who proclaimed himself president (Overby, 1993: 55). Daoud continued modernization efforts and initially enjoyed the support of the Marxist factions, prompting armed Islamist groups to form in response. By the time of the Soviet invasion nearly six years later, many of the traditionalist warlords had developed their own party apparatuses to resist Soviet-style collectivization (Sinno, 2008: 126).

These party leaders were targets for assassination by the Daoud regime, and many future leaders of the Afghan mujahidin found shelter in Pakistan, where President Ali Bhutto viewed them as useful in providing an Islamist counterappeal to Daoud's attempts to waken Pashtun separatism in Pakistan. With Islamist opposition rising, the feckless Daoud was overthrown by a coalition of the Communist factions supported by the army on April 27, 1978 (Westad, 2005: 300–302).

The new government, led by the People's Democratic Party of Afghanistan (PDPA), accelerated land seizures and openly aligned with the Soviet Union. But the regime failed to consolidate power and built traditionalist resentment over policies such as increased literacy, women's rights, and land reform, which it proposed but proved incapable of implementing. Open rebellion began in the Hazara region in late 1978 and spread to the Pashtun population by spring 1979 (Chaliand, 1981: 48–49). That March, a four-day battle against mujahidin returning from Pakistan left 5,000 dead in Herat after Soviet pilots bombed the city in response to PDPA appeals for aid (Westad, 2005: 304–308).

As the increasingly embattled leadership in Kabul asked for more intervention from Moscow, the Kremlin decided to replace the weak Afghan government and prevent the loss of a neighboring ally to an Islamic revolution of the type that had just occurred in Iran.[3] On December 27, 1979, at the urging of KGB Chief Yuri Andropov and Defense Minister Dmitriy Ustinov, both jockeying for a position as future Kremlin chief, Soviet Special Forces assassinated President Amin and his inner circle and installed as president Parcham faction leader Babrak Karmal, who they hoped would have better success with his more cautious approach to modernization. This action marked the launch of Operation Agat, which President Leonid Brezhnev understood to be a limited intervention to provide security while the new government consolidated power, "over in a few weeks' time." Instead, the Soviet presence invigorated the resistance movement, expanded the conflict, and led to the deployment of peak numbers of 100,000 Soviet troops in Afghanistan, with more than half a million serving there throughout the 1980s (Westad, 2005: 316–318).

Institutions of Recruitment

Prior to the mass Soviet intervention, the insurgency had been fading, with recruitment efforts suffering in the wake of the Herat offensive. Initially, the dominant Afghan opposition to the Soviets consisted of monarchists and clan-based groups. However, the large-scale Soviet military presence, designed in part to prevent cross-border rebel attacks, drove local opposition leaders who had resisted cooperating with Islamists to ally with them because the latter were able to maintain their Pakistan-sponsored weapons supply channels. Additionally, Pakistan required all of the millions of Afghan refugees to register with one of the recognized Islamist parties, which directly distributed humanitarian supplies.[4] These parties, in turn, successfully reframed the war as one for an uncorrupted Islamic society rather than a question of who controlled the government. Although the transnational Islamist frame drew outside support and foreign advisors, commanders enjoying new levels of popular support for leading the defense against foreign invasion tried to keep them out of Afghanistan to avoid controversy with the local population. Foreigners interested in aiding the Afghans were therefore obliged to set up operations in Pakistani border towns (Westad, 2005: 326–327, 348).

Initial State Responses

Partly as a result of Islamabad's direct support for the most Islamist of the resistance parties, the Afghan civil conflict had now given way to a transnational religious mission to drive the secularizing Soviet force from Muslim lands. As one Pakistani Interservices Intelligence (ISI) official who served as liaison to the Afghan resistance noted, "Operations were also directed against the communist Afghan Army, but I emphasize that my main enemy was the USSR. It was the invader. Without its massive presence the conflict would have been over long before I took up my post in October 1983" (Yousaf and Adkin, 1992: 2).

Although the Soviets had already begun looking for an exit strategy by March 1980, the Red Army quickly succumbed to mission creep, moving outside the major population centers to secure borders and highways, and protecting secondary targets such as schools, which provided compulsory education for women, and where teachers had become targets. The United States had sensed the opportunity to turn Afghanistan into a Soviet Vietnam and had secretly begun supplying the insurgents during the Soviet buildup in the latter half of 1979 in the hopes of luring Moscow in by provocation. In February 1980, National Security Advisor Zbigniew Brzezinski visited Saudi Arabia to secure matching funds for the effort, and Washington soon partnered with a variety of other governments in providing armaments and training to both Afghan and foreign mujahidin (Westad, 2005: 329, 351).

The Carter administration had previously cut aid to Pakistan due to the seizure of power by General Mohammed Zia ul-Haq and had fiercely criticized his human rights record. Establishing intervention required not only making amends with Zia by agreeing to let the ISI distribute all donated weapons, which it gave to its favored Islamist parties, but also reframing the conflict as a struggle worthy of American support. President Carter, and soon thereafter President Reagan, referred to the mujahidin as "freedom fighters," and the CIA placed stories in newspapers describing the killing of civilians and underwrote books profiling the heroic insurgents.[5]

This support was ultimately exceeded by Congress, where staunch anti-Communist Representative Charlie Wilson of Texas shepherded escalating levels of aid to the mujahidin. Wilson, who would later deny responsibility for the rise of al Qaeda and doubtless did not see the historical connections, was ironically drawn to the situation in Afghanistan through the mythologizing of past foreign fighter insurgencies: He claimed that he had initially become active in Middle Eastern affairs after reading Leon Uris's *Exodus*, a fictionalized account of Aliyah Bet and Haganah operations later made into an Oscar-winning Paul Newman film, and reported that when he learned of Afghan mujahidin fighting the Soviets he instantly equated them with Travis defending the Alamo (Crile, 2003: 15, 16, 19, 30).

Thus the United States provided not only money and arms to the Afghan rebels but also eventually training. Specialized combat training occurred globally, with the Soviet Army General Staff noting at least 78 training centers in Pakistan, 11 in Iran, 7 in Egypt, and possibly 6 in China, staffed by instructors from the United States, Japan, France, Saudi Arabia, the United Kingdom, and Egypt. Some of this activity was sponsored through fund-raising by private organizations supported by the CIA that operated in the United States, including the Federation of American-Afghan Actions, Southern California Aid to Afghan Refugees, and the Society for a Free Afghanistan (Grau, Gress, et al., 2002: 60–61).

Iran, keen to export its Islamic revolution, trained perhaps the first transnational volunteer force sent to Afghanistan. In suburban Tehran, Manzarieh Park served as a training ground for 175 paramilitary cadets in February 1981, including 9 Afghans and 14 Arabs from various countries. At one point, the group commander was a Palestinian. On July 30, 1981, the first class of 100 graduates was sent forth, some to Lebanon and others to Afghan Baluchistan (Cooley, 1999: 102).

Despite the covert support by a number of Arab governments for the U.S.-Pakistani operation, tangible public support by leaders in the Muslim world was not initially forthcoming. The Organization of the Islamic Conference, for example, consistently refused to seat the Afghan mujahidin during the war. Meanwhile, the Pakistani regime gave material aid to neofundamentalist Islamic parties that rejected the concept of national borders and viewed all Muslim lands as one territory, a message too close to the Islamist oppositions that threatened the rulers of Arab states (Overby, 1993: 124). Indeed, the well-armed Afghan neofundamentalists garnered the most prestige and military success. They were well positioned to accept support from like-minded militants who recruited volunteers by promulgating the idea that their governments were failing to tackle the Soviet invasion and that it was therefore the responsibility of individual Muslims to wage jihad.[6]

Recruitment by Nonstate Transnational Organizations

Probably the most notable member of this category, and the individual most responsible for recruiting a transnational mujahidin force into the conflict, was Abdullah Azzam, a scholar of Islamic jurisprudence born in West Bank Transjordan in 1941 and recruited in the mid-1950s by a teacher to join the local branch of the Muslim Brothers. Although he served with the Jordanian fedayeen irregulars during the Six-Day War, Azzam grew disillusioned with the secular Palestine Liberation Organization and launched a career in academia, during which he gave influential and widely distributed lectures outlining his philosophy of the need to retake control of Muslim lands. Because of his connections with the Muslim Brothers, he was repressed or expelled by the governments of Jordan, Egypt, and Saudi Arabia, where he served on the faculty of Abdullah Aziz University, where accounts differ as to whether he had Osama bin Laden as a student. With the Saudi crackdown on militants in the wake of the 1979 seizure of the Grand Mosque by armed Islamists, Azzam took a position at Islamic University in Islamabad just in time for the Soviet invasion of Afghanistan. He soon relocated to Peshawar, capital of Pakistan's Northwest Frontier Province (now Khyber Pakhtunkhwa) on the Afghan border, to teach at its university and work in support of the mujahidin[7] (Hegghammer, in Kepel and Milelli, 2008: 82–89).

Members of the Muslim Brotherhood had volunteered to fight during the Israeli War of Independence. Although their private contributions were ineffective, as described in the previous chapter, those who enlisted with regular Egyptian forces penetrated as far as the outskirts of Jerusalem (Schweitzer and Shay, 2003: 14). As the Afghan conflict escalated, Azzam grew frustrated that by 1984 only "ten or twenty men" had come from the outside to fight, and he called on the Brothers to send mujahidin. When the leadership demurred, preferring to send weapons and humanitarian aid, Azzam publicly broke with the group. Although he would use his connections to Brothers to deliver recruitment sermons, he set out to attract his own volunteer force dedicated to his territorial view of Islam and the need to repel infidels from its historic lands (Hegghammer, in Kepel and Milelli, 2008: 94, 95, 99).

Although a few other Islamist activists worked to recruit transnational volunteers, some in efforts that predated Azzam's, they met with meager success (Hegghammer, 2010: 86). Likewise, a number of transnational charitable organizations in Peshawar, including the Muslim World League and the Red Crescent, were already providing supplies and assistance to the Afghani mujahidin, using millions of dollars raised in wealthy Arab oil states, and many employees of these groups were affiliated with the Muslim Brotherhood. But there was little central planning among these groups due to fragmentation and antagonism both among and between donor states and Afghan Islamist parties. Azzam used his direct connections to Wahhabi Saudi donors to fund his own organization, the Makhtab al-Khadamat (MAK or "Services Bureau"), and published recruitment and fund-raising magazines such as *al Jihad* and *al Bunian-I Makhus* (Dorronsoro, 2005: 133). It operated differently than the other groups, establishing a hostel and a registry of volunteers for deployment to Afghanistan. After bin Laden arrived in Pakistan to serve as a financier to jihad, it also established parallel community institutions for its members and their families, including mosques, schools, and newspapers (Wright, 2006: 103–105).

Bin Laden claimed that his association with Afghanistan began in 1980, when he went to Peshawar to see the humanitarian situation. He met a number of influential party leaders and then returned to Saudi Arabia to raise money and elite support. In 1984, he moved to Peshawar to set up Beit ul-Ansar ("the House of Supporters") at roughly the same time Azzam started MAK (Gutman, 2008: 14).

Message Dissemination

Azzam's ambitions were not limited to the guesthouses of Peshawar. While he networked with contacts among the Muslim Brothers in major Islamic institutions to find support, he also developed a strategy for recruitment throughout the transnational Muslim world, which Islamists view as a single communal *ummah*. As MAK distributed its magazines and a number of recorded Azzam sermons globally, its leaders also undertook speaking trips throughout the world, including "dozens of American cities" (Hegghammer, in Kepel and Milelli, 2008: 94, 95, 99).

In his book *The Lofty Mountain*, Azzam (1988: 53) notes that his colleague Sheikh Tameem al-Adnani had urged jihad for Afghanistan in American metropolises including San Francisco, Orlando, and Tucson. Elsewhere, in a letter *To the Young Muslims of the United States*, Azzam declares that he enjoyed one of his own American visits, particularly appreciating "Help Free Afghanistan" T-shirts sold to raise funds for the mujahidin and a bake sale where the proceeds also went for jihad. He notes as well a New York mosque that "opened an office to serve the Afghan jihad, hired a lawyer, and received permission from the authorities; then they sent fighters to Afghanistan, paying for their tickets and obtaining visas for them from the embassy in New York. In this manner, we received seven groups of volunteers without spending any money." He concludes, however, by publicizing an account for donations that he opened at Independence Savings Bank in New York (Azzam, translated by Hegghammer, in Kepel and Milelli, 2008: 137–138).

Al Jihad magazine was eventually sold in 50 countries, from Sweden to Brazil and from Portugal to Hong Kong, with a peak circulation of 70,000 copies per issue. In the United States alone, the magazine had 52 distribution centers, mostly in cities with sizable Muslim populations and the potential for reaching well-off American donors (Bergen, 2006: 33–36). Although recruitment material was disseminated in North America, MAK efforts focused primarily on Muslim countries, particularly Saudi Arabia and the Gulf states, where *Al Jihad* was distributed by both state and private channels. In another magazine, *Al Mujahid*, Azzam shifted the focus from the casus belli to coverage of Afghan, and later foreign, insurgents, offering statistics and detailed biographies of those killed in action (Zaidan, 1999: 39, 45).

Indeed, this coverage, while insisting on the importance of saving Afghanistan from atheist infidel domination, makes it clear that this is only one front in a larger conflict, one that required the creation of an educated liberationist cadre for a global reconquest of Muslim lands. As a rationale for serving in such a vanguard, in addition to self-preservation and defending the *ummah*, Azzam also encouraged religious martyrdom in a manner new to Sunni militants (Hegghammer, in Kepel and Milelli, 2008: 100–101).

Framing and Messaging

Recruiters during earlier conflicts, such as the Spanish Civil War, had needed to prime their audiences before pitching participation by describing the significance of the conflict, its effects on the local population, and how it also impacted the target audience. Azzam and his associates, operating in the mid-1980s, were able to travel internationally and select venues in sympathetic mosques and community gatherings in the West and Middle East, where audiences had been exposed to years of television coverage of Muslim mujahidin battling invading Soviets and their Communist allies. Recordings of speeches and printed recruitment material focused instead on reinforcing the message of religious and communitarian responsibility to intervene and on overcoming the constraints of self-interest.

In *A Message to Every Youth*, Azzam (pp. 12–14) notes that "so-called rational thinking…says to the person 'do not exert yourself and do not sacrifice.'" He claims that during the world wars, the United States and the United Kingdom relied on their youngest soldiers to carry out the most dangerous operations, and that Japan similarly selected kamikaze pilots because "they were prepared to do anything and they do not stand for a long time to think." The tract concludes by exhorting readers to take advantage of the free time afforded them by their university holidays to follow the path of true Islam. An article in *Al Jihad* similarly "remind[s] you that the Afghan Jihad is a necessity for the Muslims, even if the number of Russian enemies and others are double your number." Satisfying this requirement would lead to "relief from your earthly chains" (Bergen, 2006: 32–33).

Rationale for Fighting: Religious Bonds and Martyrdom

In *Join the Caravan*, Azzam (1987: 12, 16, 22, 24, 25) describes Afghanistan as merely one front in a larger war against Muslims, in which fighting is necessary so "that unbelievers do not dominate." In this frame, Muslims in many countries are living in subjugation, with "Muslim women being taken captive in every land," and "they cannot repel attacks on their lives, honor, and properties." Echoing the Zionist claim that a homeland was necessary for self-preservation, Azzam argues: "Establishment of the [uncompromised] Muslim community on an area of land is a necessity, as vital as water and air. This homeland will not come about without an organized Islamic movement.… The Islamic State will be born, but birth cannot be accomplished without labor, and with labor there is pain."[8]

Azzam focuses on the transnational nature of this imperative in *The Defense of Muslim Territories: The First Individual Duty*, in which he argues that jihad is the obligation not only of residents of Muslim lands that are attacked but also

> If there are too few of them, or if they are incapable or reticent, then this duty is incumbent upon those who are nearby, and so on until it spreads throughout the world. In such a situation, a husband's permission is not required for his wife to fight; nor is the father's permission necessary for the son, or the creditor's for his debtor.

Any sins by past generations in letting historical Muslim lands fall were not as grave as "the sin our generation has committed in neglecting contemporary issues like Afghanistan, Palestine, the Philippines, Kashmir, Lebanon, Chad, and Eritrea." While averring that mujahidin should begin their struggle with Palestine if possible, he presses the case that the majority should focus their efforts on Afghanistan, where the battle was raging full force, the insurgents were clearly governed by Islamic principles, and "over three hundred thousand kilometers of open borders" with the tribal regions in Pakistan permitted far easier entry.[9]

He insists that more than charitable donations are required; rather, combatants and "preachers most of all" are needed as foreign fighters. In "The Solid Base" ("Al-Qaeda al-Sulbah"), which appeared in the April 1988 issue of *Al Jihad* magazine, Azzam argued that this struggle would be best realized through the efforts of a cadre with proper religious and military training because "without a profound education, which provides the safety valve for the long march, the enormous sacrifices and disproportionate costs it exacts cause boredom and disrepair in time" (Hegghammer, translator, in Kepel and Milelli, 2008: 107–108, 112, 142).

While mujahidin from throughout the single transnational *ummah* are tasked with the mission of defending Islamic lands, Azzam distinguishes Afghans as ethnically separate from the Arab recruits, casting participation in Afghanistan as an effort to liberate a distinct Muslim people:

> They no longer have the arrows to shoot; their quivers are empty. During this long period the Afghans hoped their Muslim brothers would come forth in their thousands, that their brothers in Islam would march to their aid, but until today the Muslims have not answered the call, as if they could not hear the mothers crying for their sons, the virgins screaming, the orphans sighing, and the elderly groaning. Many fine people felt it was enough to send their leftovers by way of assistance. The situation is more serious than that, however. Islam and Muslims in Afghanistan live in anguish and must face a grave peril....
>
> Afghans are like other human beings, with their ignorance and defects, so we must not expect to find perfection in them. The difference between the Afghans and the others, however, is that the Afghans have refused to stand by and watch as their religion is dishonored, and they have paid the price for this resolve with bloodbaths and piles of corpses....
>
> The Afghan people are ignorant, educated in the Hanafi school [of religious jurisprudence] alone...the Afghans are a valiant people, virile and proud, without ruse or flattery in their nature....By abandoning

some ways of praying, at the beginning of your stay among them, you will be able to affect them, guide them, and eventually educate them, in order to reform their religion and their way of life.[10] (Hegghammer, translator, in Kepel and Milelli, 2008: 120, 123, 124)

Elsewhere, Azzam acknowledged the difficulty of the life of a foreign mujahid, fighting in the mountains "in ignominy and wilderness...among people whose language you do not understand." Rather than material gain, in a memorial to Yahya Senyor,[11] distributed as a recruitment audio recording titled "Words of Gold" (Azzam, 1985), the emphasis is on hardship. Senyor, described as dying without any money, is reported to have written home stating, "I will never return to you, and if I visit you, then I won't visit you before six months. Everything in my place here is difficult, the cold is bitter, and the heat in the morning is killing, the food is insipid, the mountains are nauseous, and everything is strange to me, but I am at the peak of happiness...because I feel that I am performing an obligation."

In the same sermon, Azzam references a sura from the Koran describing the difficult necessity of jihad. He notes that "leaving behind the house and children...[is] a tough and heavy operation on the human self.... The case of migration is difficult. It is—it is really tough.... I saw it myself in those Chechens and Shirkats who ran from the hell of Communism and czarism before...[and] had to work diligently and struggle [their] whole day to get the price of a loaf."

Nonetheless, Azzam proclaimed, unconsciously echoing the calls for volunteers in Texas 150 years earlier, recruits must step forward, or "Who is it who will protect the honor of our sisters in Afghanistan? Who is there for her?... Where is the chivalry? Where is the manhood if we lose the religion?" Additionally, he references orphans calling for assistance as well.

In *The Scales of Allah* (pp. 13–14), Azzam offers anecdotes to demonstrate that, despite the lack of material goods or social status available to foreign fighters, their sacrifices will still be rewarded: The bodies of a number of those killed in battle reportedly emanated perfume for a week after their deaths in an indication of their ascension to the divine. As additional evidence of Allah's blessing, other foreign fighters miraculously survived attacks that killed local insurgents (who presumably suffered because of their imperfect religious education). "It is not strange that five mortar rounds are shot over a single trench containing three brothers: The Arab survives, the Afghan falls a martyr into the arms of the Arab."

Alternative Motivators

In other lectures (collected and distributed as *Martyrs: The Building Blocks of Nations*), Azzam claimed that the sins of martyrs were forgiven at the shedding of their first blood. Wright (2006: 106–107) argued: "It was death, not victory, that summoned many young Arabs to Peshawar. Martyrdom was the product that Azzam sold in the books, tracts, videos and cassette tapes that circulated in mosques and Arabic-language bookstores," and the appeal of this "death cult" lay in the lack of economic opportunities in the Muslim world.

Despite Azzam's declarations to potential recruits about poverty and jihad, there is evidence that at least some recruits responded to monetary incentives:

> Paid agents rounded up prospects, pocketing half of the money—typically, several hundred dollars—that the recruits received when they signed up. Young Muslim pilgrims were particular targets. To get them to the front, agents promised them jobs with aid organizations that never materialized. Fugitives from Algeria and Egypt slipped into the country and were provided with false papers by Saudi intelligence.

The Bin Laden Group construction office in Cairo was known as pipeline for those interested in going to Afghanistan (Wright, 2006: 97), with Osama bin Laden reportedly offering $300 a month to recruits to cover the costs of their participation (Coll, 2004: 155).

Target Audience

Hafez (2009: 76) also argues that some recruits were unemployed Muslim Brothers or North African guest workers traveling for work rather than jihad. Likewise, many foreign fighters were students who came only during university holidays and never participated in combat, but the rebel commanders still portrayed them as heroes to maintain donations from the Gulf states. However, projihad analysts also stated: "Most of the Arab youth [come] for training and participation for the limited time period [before they] return to their countries, because they are students or clerks, and have to go to work. Many come during summer vacations or long holidays" (Zaidan, 1999: 13).

Whether these students were genuinely motivated idealists or simply looking for adventure between study terms is less clear. Wright (2006: 97) gives the benefit of the doubt to those who answered the call of Azzam and his spreading network of supporters: "Afghanistan meant little to [the recruits], but the faith of the Afghan people meant a great deal. They were drawing a line against the retreat of their religion, which was God's last word and the only hope of human salvation." Conboy (2006: 40–41) claims that some sought adventure, others martyrdom, and still others were "certifiable psychopaths." Hafez (2009: 75) describes the first recruits as young men in their early 20s—with Saudis, Kuwaitis, and Yemenis the largest national contingents—who went to Afghanistan for five common reasons: religious fulfillment, employment opportunities, adventure, a safe haven, or military training.

Infidels for the Cause

As with previous transnational insurgencies, foreign fighters joined who were not directly targeted by the recruitment framing but who nonetheless perceived the distant conflict to be relevant to their own interests. A small but noticeable number of non-Muslims went to Afghanistan to defeat the Soviet Union, and they were essentially staunch anti-Communists, like many of the foreign volunteers who served with the Nationalists in Spain half a century earlier.

Despite its relative inaccessibility, private Westerners had been involved in Afghan intrigues for centuries: Josiah Harlan, a Pennsylvania Quaker, arrived in Kabul in 1824 and switched his military services between incumbent and exiled rulers, at one point even proclaiming himself prince of Ghor province and inspiring Rudyard Kipling's "The Man Who Would Be King." Harlan met a number of European mercenaries and unemployed soldiers of the Napoleonic Wars who had already arrived and even recorded discovering the grave of an English artillery officer who served the governor of Kabul in 1666 (MacIntyre, 2004: 5, 119).

By the 1980s, the forces of globalization permitted the journey to be undertaken in jet aircraft, the mode of transportation used by most Arab mujahidin, and determined Westerners arrived via Pakistan as well. Charles Fawcett had not only starred in action movies but also had reportedly fought with the Abraham Lincoln Battalion in Spain, in the 1947 Greek Civil War, and in the Belgian Congo in the 1960s. Recruited by his friend Joanne Herring, the wealthy Texas conservative who introduced Charlie Wilson to the Pakistani ISI, to film a promujahidin propaganda film to influence policy makers, Fawcett decided to actually join the fight and teach the rebels tactics he had learned in the French Foreign Legion. Vaughn Forest, an aide to Florida Republican Representative Bill McCollum, violated regulations on federal employee conduct to travel to Afghanistan to fight as well (Crile, 2003: 72, 388).

Paul Overby reported that he was working in an Oregon steel mill, suffering guilt for not having served in Vietnam. Disillusioned with union colleagues on "the extreme left," he realized that he wanted to see Marxism fail in person. He sought out academic experts on Afghanistan and took advantage of their "web of connections" to meet Tahir, "the political representative of the mujahidin in Oregon," with whom he trained for mountain trekking and operating an AK-47. When he ultimately arrived in the conflict zone, he soon met an East German volunteer, a former political prisoner who had gone to Pakistan in 1985 and was still fighting Communists two and a half years later. Overby learned of a Polish anti-Communist foreign fighter who had previously been killed in action. He also met a Muslim African American who came "because this is where the action was" but who did not know any Arabic and was treated derisively by the local mujahidin (Overby, 1993: 2–6, 42, 208).

Mobilization

That some Westerners would identify with the mujahidin and be swept up in their cause is perhaps not surprising, given the scope of the recruitment operation. The CIA encouraged recruitment by Muslim charities and mosques in population centers including Detroit and Los Angeles. In Brooklyn, supporters established a fund-raising organization called the Al-Kifah Refugee Center, whose members called it Al-Jihad, which was bankrolled directly by Saudi government funds and private donations.[12] Among the Brooklyn Islamic community connected to Al-Kifah was Sheikh Omar Abdel Rahman, the blind cleric convicted of plotting the 1993 World Trade Center bombing, whose sons volunteered through the center to go to Afghanistan. Direct paramilitary training for recruits occurred relatively nearby at the High Rock Gun Club in Naugatuck, Connecticut, and also at CIA facilities near Williamsburg, Virginia.[13] Tablighi Jamaat, a Pakistan-based transnational Islamic charitable organization that spread through university campuses, held a convention on Afghanistan in Chicago in 1988 that attracted more than 6,000 Muslims from around the world and recruited hundreds of mujahidin from North Africa[14] (Cooley, 1999: 83–89, 100).

The governments of various Muslim countries also permitted or actively facilitated recruitment for Afghanistan, hoping to simultaneously gain favor with the United States and domestic legitimacy by supporting Islam, as well as taking the opportunity to unload militants and troublemakers. President Sadat, somewhat ironically invoking their activities in 1948, openly encouraged the Egyptian Muslim Brothers to join the jihad, and the Saudi government subsidized airline tickets to Pakistan by 75 percent for jihadis. "Young Muslims were bombarded with calls to join in jihad against the atheist occupiers. Mainstream and radical clerics alike urged and incited the youths to migrate to Afghanistan to help their Muslim brethren." Arab state media contributed "through coverage of the arenas of jihad, particularly the press interviews that were held with some of the leading mujahidin figures" (Gerges, 2005: 68, 69).

Fawaz Gerges, who interviewed former jihadis as they completed their prison sentences for militant activity in Arab countries, argued that greed was not a sufficient motivator in many cases: "They came from all walks of life and were driven by the plight and predicament of their Afghan counterparts who were seen as struggling against an atheistic enemy. I heard heart-wrenching stories of men who sacrificed their jobs, economic well-being, and comfort and went to Afghanistan to do their 'duty' and partake in what they saw as a sacred struggle." A number of his respondents claimed that their mothers or wives had to sell their jewelry or spend their life savings to purchase the plane tickets to Pakistan. Many claimed that they had not previously been involved in activist groups, but were responding to mass media recruitment (Gerges, 2005: 80, 81).

As noted, the established militant groups were reluctant to divert members away from their local causes of regime change and did not at the time accept Azzam's interpretation that the mission of Islamists should be territorial liberation. In addition to his break from the Egyptian Brothers over this issue in 1984, the Saudi chapter of the Brothers also rejected Afghanistan as a cause for jihad. Therefore, most of the recruits were unaffiliated with militant organizations. Mohammed Loay Baizid, a 24-year-old Syrian immigrant attending college in Kansas City, claimed that he thought himself assimilated in 1985, but when he read a mimeographed Azzam tract, he wanted to see if there actually were miracles occurring on the battlefield. He planned to go to Pakistan for just three months, but he was caught up in "camaraderie." The departure of these young, impressionable, and perhaps previously socially alienated young men did not always come with familial approval: "Many concerned Saudi fathers went to the training camps to drag their sons home" (Wright, 2006: 109).

Abdullah Ali Mekkawi, an 18-year-old Saudi, learned about the conflict and the role of the mujahidin from magazines such as *Al Jihad* and *Al Bunyan* that provided a contact address in Peshawar for interested parties to seek out upon arrival. Abdullah Annas, who would become Azzam's son-in-law, similarly went to Pakistan after reading MAK publications while in Kuwait (Hafez, 2009: 75–76). Annas, born in Algeria, responded to an article by Azzam warning that the Soviet Union was "going to cancel Islamic life" in Afghanistan, and he approached Azzam during the hajj in Mecca to ask what he should do if he were interested in helping. He recalled that, prior to receiving instructions from Azzam, he did not know where Afghanistan was, what languages were spoken there, or which airline could transport him (Bergen, 2006: 28).

Other participants clearly were involved in prior militant activity, and Afghanistan allowed them the opportunity to escape from factional or government reprisals they faced in their home states. Egypt in particular sent a large number of released political prisoners to Pakistan, from where the government hoped they would never return (Conboy, 2006: 41). Ayman al-Zawahiri, an Egyptian physician who had been imprisoned and tortured for involvement in an attempt to overthrow the regime, first went to Afghanistan to work with refugees in 1980. He determined that the mountainous terrain of Afghanistan was conducive to guerrilla warfare and presented the opportunity to train an army that he could bring home to fulfill his objective of taking power in Cairo. He returned home to recruit insurgents, giving his presentations dressed in Pakistani clothing, before returning full-time to Pakistan in 1986. Once there, he soon formed an ideological partnership with bin Laden, who had grown up in a Western-oriented family before he was apparently introduced to militant Islam by a gym teacher who was a Brother (Wright, 2006: 44, 75).

Experience in the Field

No precise figures are available on the number of transnational militants and charitable aid workers who joined Islamist organizations in Pakistan or continued on to Afghanistan. Former Pakistani ISI chief Hamid Gul claimed that 30,000 foreign mujahidin were in the conflict zone during the war (Crile, 2003: 521). More recent estimates put the figure far lower. Azzam's son-in-law Abdullah Annas stated that the "three to four thousand" foreign recruits were a mere "drop in the ocean" among the mujahidin, and most merely served in Peshawar or elsewhere on the Pakistani side of the border doing humanitarian work (Hafez, 2009: 75). Annas reported that no more than 10 percent of the recruits (approximately 300) actually operated within Afghanistan, and Saudi journalist Jamal Khashoggi, in confirming these figures, added that many volunteers were present only for weeklong "jihad tours" or "jihad vacations" (Bergen, 2006: 41). Wright (2006: 105) contended that there were never more than 3,000 Arab Afghans, and most were killed by the Soviets.

Azzam himself, in mid-1980s sermons compiled as *Martyrs: The Building Blocks of Nations*, reported that of the "involvement of non-Afghans...the number did not exceed a few hundred individuals." Lacey (2008: 82–83) provides the most specific figures, claiming that between 1979 and 1982, no more than 10 foreign volunteers even traveled to Peshawar to aid the Afghans, and only three or four of them actually ventured into Afghanistan. The Arab Afghan jihad began only in 1984, when Azzam left his final university post for recruitment as his full-time job, making speaking tours and publishing magazines through the auspices of his transnational donor network. By the end of 1984, there were 12 foreign mujahidin, 25 in 1985, and 200 in 1986. At this point, bin Laden began working directly with Azzam and financing the transportation and resettlement of recruits, resulting in a "few thousand" foreign fighters present in 1987, mostly from his home countries of Saudi Arabia and Yemen. Many more arrived after the Soviet withdrawal, with as many as 40,000 by 1990.

Like foreign fighters in earlier conflicts who were often socially marginalized in their home polities but active in the institutions of transnational communities, recruits to 1980s Afghanistan were

> Often unwanted renegades in their own countries, and they found the door closed behind them as soon as they left. Other young Muslims, prompted by their own governments to join the jihad, were stigmatized as fanatics when they did so. It would be difficult for many of them to ever return home....As stateless persons they naturally revolted against the very idea of the state. They saw themselves as a borderless posse empowered by God to defend the entire Muslim people. (Wright, 2006: 105)

Jamal al Fadl was originally from Sudan but was living in Brooklyn in 1987 when he was approached by representatives of the community Farouk Mosque, which he later described as a branch of MAK. The information they provided him about the duty to defend fellow Muslims matched what he had already been reading in *Al Jihad*, and he agreed to go. The emir of the Brooklyn community arranged his tickets and visa and provided him with money, and he eventually arrived in Peshawar. "We went to the hotel for two days and somebody come, he gave us a little lecture about jihad. We went after that to the guesthouse and they give you the nickname" (nom de guerre). From there, he proceeded through 45 days of training at different camps that specialized in different weapons (Bergen, 2006: 44–46).

When they arrived in Pakistan, recruits like al Fadl were provided accommodation at MAK hostels (*mada'if*) where foreign volunteers could stay as long as necessary while waiting for the opportunity to go to Afghanistan. Initially, these opportunities were relatively rare, as the local commanders could not easily integrate Arabs into their Pashto- or Dari-speaking local units (Hegghammer, in Kepel and Milelli, 2008: 93). By 1987, when large numbers of Saudis were arriving on the same flights, greeters with buses would meet the recruits on their arrival at the Peshawar airport (Bergen, 2006: 52).

The foreign fighters fell into three broad categories: The first group, mostly from Malaysia, Burma, Indonesia, India, and the Philippines, did not speak Arabic. The second group, Arabs from non-Gulf states such as Algeria, Egypt, and Morocco, generally came from lower socioeconomic backgrounds. The third group was Arabs from the wealthy Gulf states of Kuwait, the United Arab Emirates, and Saudi Arabia. "Most of the mujahidin were Saudi. They had money and sometimes they used good hotels, good restaurants. Some of the Saudis used to come and go as a trip, as a holiday." Eventually, and despite the claims of a global Islamic identity that transcended state boundaries, bin Laden moved to set up all-Saudi training camps (Bergen, 2006: 41–42, 53).

Azzam's initial group of recruits, whom he called the "Brigade of Strangers," had pushed him to let them cross into Afghanistan to join the fight. In 1984, a group of 60 that included bin Laden drove across the border to link up with local mujahidin, but they found that the Soviets had already retreated from the most recent battle and were told "your presence is no longer needed." This initial group returned to Pakistan and soon disbanded. Azzam, hoping to erase national divisions among mujahidin, next dispersed Arabs through various Afghan commands, even though they did not speak any of the local languages or have military training. Predictably, soon "they were cannon fodder." Prince Turki al-Faisal, head of the Saudi General Intelligence Directorate, sought to assert control on the ground and did so by directing bin Laden to fund the Ittihad-i-Islami Afghanistan (Islamic Union of Afghanistan Party) to gain control over its leadership structure (Wright, 2006: 100, 110–116).

Among the Afghan parties, some leaders were at least initially receptive to intermingling their organizations with foreign fighters because of connections through the same transnational channels used in recruitment. The most neofundamentalist of the major parties was Hezb-i-Islami Afghanistan (the Afghan Islamic Party), led by Gulbuddin Hekmatyar, "who has close ties to the Muslim Brotherhood throughout the Middle East and adamantly resists cooperation with other [Afghan] groups" (United States Senate Foreign Relations Committee, 1984: 22). President Zia, a devout Muslim who extended Pakistan's support for the mujahidin, controlled distribution of foreign shipments of arms and money and always ensured that Hekmatyar received supplies before any of the other parties. Other party leaders had studied abroad in Wahhabi madrasas and maintained those connections as well (Westad, 2005: 326, 356).

Initially, foreign volunteers were spread across different insurgent units because Azzam wanted to maximize their presence for propaganda purposes and realized that there were too few of them to make a real difference (Hafez, 2009: 79). Bin Laden differed from this perspective, arguing for the need to create a properly educated and trained Arab force to serve as a vanguard in the wider battle facing the Muslim world, and he sought to open training camps just for the Arab volunteers. Reportedly, Azzam strongly disagreed, marking the beginning of his split with bin Laden, complaining, "We came to serve these people. That is why it is called the Services Bureau" (Coll, 2004: 164).

Bin Laden succeeded in changing the dynamic in late 1984 or early 1985, when Abd-i-Rab Rasoul Sayyaf, whose party he was now funding, gave him the al Sadda training camp within Afghanistan. By the end of year, 25 recruits were training in the camp. One of them, Wael Hamza Jalaidan, a Saudi who had been a Muslim activist and fund-raiser living in Tucson, Arizona, related that the established daily routine in the camp consisted of prayer, study, and only then military operations "if there were any" (Kohlmann, 2004: 6). This insistence on ritual would soon produce conflict between Afghan and foreign insurgents, but it did not prevent the establishment of additional camps inside Afghanistan for the growing legion of transnational volunteers.

The recruitment effort across the global *ummah* yielded recruits not only from the Middle East, Africa, and North America but also from Southeast Asia (or Austronesia). Just as the Arab groups divided by country of origin, the Austronesian Muslims received separate training accommodations and formed their own ethnic insurgent units. The first group of 12 was drawn in 1985 from members of youth branches of Islamist parties in Indonesia and settled in a Sayyaf camp close to Kabul, in the Pakistani town of Sadda, to learn from six "faculties" subjects such as demolitions, cavalry, communications, and artillery. The instructors were a mix of Arab, Afghan, and Pakistani experienced militants, and the curriculum also featured a large amount of conservative religious indoctrination.

Among the 360 other students in the camp, who were mostly Afghan refugees, the Indonesians lived separately and were expected to complete the three-year training course offered to other students in a single year so that they could serve as instructors to other Austronesians. (Of the 12, "four washed out for a variety of reasons and returned home early.") However, the next group of 30 Indonesians arrived in early 1986 before the first cohort could finish their training. For the second wave, while the Indonesians still had to raise their own travel expenses, Sayyaf provided them food using MAK funds. That November, another group of 30 arrived, all with strong prior Islamic educations and most with family connections to the Darul Islam movement responsible for past uprisings at home. Among them was Nurjaman bin Isamuddin (who assumed many noms de guerre before finally settling on Hambali), a 22-year-old whose family strongly objected to his going, but whose community imam granted him the blessing to travel because of his connections with militants in Jakarta. Nonetheless, the future mastermind of the 2002 Bali nightclub bombing still had to pay his own airfare (Conboy, 2006: 44–48, 51).

The Austronesian Muslim component of the mujahidin continued to grow, to the point that, by April 1987, when bin Laden and a group of associates held the "Lion's Den" fortified base for two weeks against a Soviet siege, there was not only an Indonesian contingent serving with him but also a separate Indonesian group formed to relieve them, although it never came close enough to join the battle. Indeed, notwithstanding the boasts of one Indonesian mujahid to the *Singapore Straits Times* in 1988 that he had downed five helicopters with a single round, there is no evidence that Indonesians actually engaged in combat against the Soviets at all, although two dozen were killed in the post-Soviet phase of the conflict against the Communist regime in Kabul. Still, beyond the Indonesians, there were enough Thais and Filipinos to form their own ethnic units as well[15] (Conboy, 2006: 50–51).

Foreign versus Local Insurgents

As the preferred channel for Saudi money and arms, Sayyaf's group quickly grew prominent among the major parties. "The synergy between them made sense: Sayyaf needed funds and combatants; the Arabs needed a conduit for their volunteers." However, aside from Sayyaf, Afghan commanders "generally saw [the foreigners] as nuisances, only slightly less bothersome than the Soviets." Generally they were regarded as "superfluous" and weak by the hardened local mujahidin (Conboy, 2006: 41–42).

Bin Laden noted on his first trip into Afghanistan that the Afghans treated Arabs as "glorified guests" and not fellow warriors, and this was apparently the basis for his insistence on creating all-Arab combat training programs. He could not help but notice that the Afghans did not appear frightened during Soviet attacks, but the Arabs did. Others noticed as well: During one attack, Arab recruits were "thrown into a panic, and they were further humiliated when the Afghan forces asked them to leave because they were so useless." Further incidents of ineffectiveness caused Pakistan to close some Arab guesthouses (Wright, 2006: 101–102, 110–111, 116).

For their part, Arab recruits did not trust the Afghans, who they thought shifted loyalties and would kill foreigners fighting on their own side (Nasiri, 2006: 216–217). Perhaps part of the reason for this perception was that the different Afghan militias would attack each other over private vendettas. Under the Pashtun tribal honor code of Pashtunwali, even jihad did not stop the obligation for vengeance (Yousaf and Adkin, 1992: 34). Additionally, as with Texian rebels a century and a half before, the local fighters "had a much more pragmatic approach to fighting" and would leave the battlefield to tend to their homes and families, leading bin Laden to believe that martyrdom-seeking Arab brigades would ultimately prove more effective in combat (Bergen, 2006: 50).

Kohlmann (2004: 8) noted that many foreign recruits came from upper-middle-class families: "The native Afghan warriors were typically very suspicious of their new Arab allies, regarding these foreigners as 'Gucci' soldiers who were out of touch with the social and religious fabric of the Afghan people." Foreigners and Afghanis "disagreed on almost everything, including politics and religion. The two sides frequently came to armed blows over praying over the body of a fallen comrade or visiting cemeteries and praying and honoring the dead." The transnational Islamist insurgents thought that the Afghans were sacrilegious and followed Azzam's instructions to try to eliminate local cultural customs. The Afghans, fighting first to protect their families, had no interest in providing a training ground for global jihad; they wanted to obtain arms, not more foreigners (Gerges, 2005: 83).

The American anti-Communist volunteer Paul Overby recounted a meeting with a spokesman of the Jamiat-i-Islami (Islamic Society) Party who "griped about foreigners running the resistance." Overby noticed that Arab students sequestered in their training compounds had their own imported diets and referred to them as "rich Muslims." And he noted the problems that ensued when the fundamentalist preachers, whom Azzam had claimed the Afghans "need most of all," actually arrived to serve as chaplains to the rebels.

One "zealous young religious student from Pakistan" arrived and compelled the Afghans to begin practicing Islamic customs such as ritual ablutions and complained to the commander that learning was proceeding too slowly (Overby, 1993: 37, 91, 159, 165). These Islamists appeared more interested in attacking Shia and Hanafi than Russians, and, as one Afghan complained, "They say we are dumb, and we do not know the Koran, and they are more trouble than they are ever going to be worth"[16] (Hafez, 2009: 78).

The Soviet Response

Although there is some debate over the scope and import of foreign mujahidin participation during the war, the Soviet military was aware of outside intervention and apparently developed no protocols distinguishing local from transnational insurgents. Moscow disparaged mujahidin as *basmachi* (bandits), the term used for Central Asian resistance fighters during the 1920s (United States Senate Committee on Foreign Relations, 1984: 20); Soviet troops on the ground similarly referred to them as *dushmani*, a Turkic word for "enemy" (Lebed, 1997: 50). As a recognition that there was no universal Afghan language, perimeter warning signs were written in Russian and English as well as Pashto and Dari (Grau, 1998: 131), and it is likely that the linguistically and culturally diverse native population made it all the more difficult to spot outsiders.

Still, reports by individual Soviet personnel indicated an awareness of the transnational nature of the insurgency or at least the foreign origins of insurgent equipment. One mentioned the capture of mujahidin supplies, which included large amounts of foreign currency "destined to pay their Iranian and Pakistani advisers." Another related the capture of a camp of 150 mujahidin while they were performing calisthenics and combat practice, a description that sounds more akin to the transnational recruits depicted in al Qaeda propaganda videos than hardened local tribesmen. Another, noting that Red Army sleeping bags were water-permeable cotton, declared: "The premier trophy for a Soviet soldier was a mujahidin sleeping bag from the West. They were lightweight, waterproof and warm" (Grau, 1998: 158, 171, 198, 205).

Alexander Lebed (1997: 71–72), the future general and presidential candidate, in early 1982 attempted to figure out "who was fighting against us and why, and I think I got it right. As far as I could see, they fell into six categories:" patriots, people who were fighting to acquire or regain property, religious fanatics, mercenaries, men trying to earn enough money by fighting to afford a bride, and Afghans who were angry at attacks against their innocent villages. Unfortunately, Lebed did not distinguish whether fanatics and mercenaries included foreigners.

Rather than Islamist militants, Soviet soldiers were told that they were preventing American Green Berets from establishing missile launchers on the Soviet border (Heinamaa, Leppanen, and Yurchenko, 1994: 1–2) or that they would be fighting American and Chinese mercenaries (Grau, 1998: 207). "Ideologically, the Soviet leadership was unable to come to grips with war in Afghanistan. Marxist-Leninist dogma did not allow for a 'war of national liberation' where people would fight against a Marxist regime. So, initially the press carried pictures of happy Soviet soldiers building orphanages...." By the end of 1983, the Soviet press had reported only six dead and wounded soldiers, although by that time the number killed exceeded 6,000 (Grau, 1998: 201). Ultimately, the conflict killed more than 13,000 Soviet soldiers, with another 35,000 wounded (Yousaf and Adkin, 1992: 6).

Dark Victory: Soviet Withdrawal and the Failure of Consolidation

The Kremlin and, quietly at first, the Soviet public grew frustrated with their losses in an unexpected occupation that new president Mikhail Gorbachev termed a "bleeding wound." To change the dynamic in Kabul, President Karmal was replaced in May 1986 with the head of the KHAD (the Afghan equivalent of the KGB), Mohammed Najibullah (Westad, 2005: 374). His administration also proved incapable of containing the increasingly well-armed and trained mujahidin, and Moscow began to prepare for a withdrawal of its forces.

The impact of the foreign fighters on this sequence of events was arguably quite limited. Hafez (2009: 79) states that Arab Afghans contingents participated in only a half dozen battles during 1986–1991, and Wright (2006: 110–111) argues that the presence of "several thousand Arabs—and rarely more than a few hundred of them actually on the field of battle—made no real difference in the tide of affairs." By contrast, an al Qaeda report published in 2000 claimed that there had been 2,359 foreign martyrs in Afghanistan: 540 Algerians, 526 Egyptians, 433 Saudis, 284 Libyans, 184 Iraqis, 180 Syrians, 111 Sudanese, and 100 Tunisians (Abou Zahab and Roy, 2004: 15).

Regardless of which participants were responsible for the mujahidin successes, the shifting balance of power prompted CIA Director William Casey to push for expanding insurgent operations north of the Amu Dar'ya into the Soviet Union itself. Casey's strategy was also centered on transnational identity, and he argued that "the ethnic, tribal and religious ties of the people who

lived on both sides of this river should be exploited." Although Pakistan initially balked at complicity in providing weapons to mujahidin for strikes within
Soviet territory, preferring the less provocative distribution of Korans and propaganda books, the ISI eventually facilitated operations 25 kilometers inside the
USSR (Yousaf and Adkin, 1992: 194–195). These included the bombing of three
military and industrial targets in Uzbekistan that prompted the Kremlin to
threaten an invasion of Pakistan unless the raids were halted (Coll, 2004: 161).

Despite this posturing, the continued losses in Afghanistan were weak-
ening Gorbachev's efforts at domestic reform and international reposition-
ing, and he ordered the Red Army withdrawn. On February 15, 1989, Boris
Gromov walked across the Friendship Bridge over the Amu Dar'ya into
Tajikistan, publicly ending the Soviet invasion of Afghanistan. Without the
Soviet presence, the Najibullah regime in Kabul was universally expected to
fall to the rebels within weeks, particularly when Moscow ignored requests for
air strikes as the mujahidin lay siege to Jalalabad. Instead, the PDPA (renamed
the Hizb-i Watan or "Homeland Party" in 1988) held the capital until April
18, 1992, prolonging the war and the expanding the flow of foreign mujahidin
(Westad, 2005: 378).

The extension of the civil war was due largely to Moscow continuing to
send Najibullah $4 billion a year in aid after 1989, with the hope that the
Kabul regime would keep the Afghans too busy to export the jihad to the
Soviet Central Asian Muslim population (Sinno, 2008: 110). Brigadier Yousaf,
the ISI officer responsible for liaison with the mujahidin and who authorized
the attacks inside Uzbekistan, claimed that even after the formal Soviet withdrawal, Moscow also provided "vast quantities of military hardware for the
Afghan Army. In fact, as I know full well, General Gromov was certainly not
the last Soviet soldier in Afghanistan." Yousaf also asserted that the United
States began to withhold critical military aid to the insurgents because both
Washington and Moscow tacitly agreed that an outright victory by the mujahidin was in neither side's strategic interests. The United States instead hoped
to reinstall Zahir Shah and the monarchy and played on the infighting that
began among the various mujahid parties vying for power (Yousaf and Adkin,
1992: 6, 215, 217, 218). The superpower intervention ceased only with the
failed hard-liner coup against Gorbachev, after which Russian President Boris
Yeltsin ended aid to Najibullah and the White House, in turn, cut aid to the
mujahidin. Yeltsin informed Secretary of State James Baker of the new policy
on September 11, 1991 (Gutman, 2008: 33).

The decade between the end of intervention from Washington in
Afghanistan and the occurrence of intervention from Afghanistan in

Washington hardly marked a decline in transnational insurgent activity. In Afghanistan itself, out of an estimated prewar population of 15 million in 1978, only 8 million remained in the country, with 5 million refugees in Pakistan and Iran developing new postnational connections via the neofundamentalist charities and armed groups given reign to run resettlement camps (Yousaf and Adkin, 1992: 31).

Within the country, following a pattern similar to that of postwar Texas a century and a half before, the Soviet withdrawal coincided with a large influx of new foreign fighters. More than 6,000 arrived between 1987 and 1993, more than twice the number that came to fight the Soviets. The new volunteers were different than the earlier mujahidin, "men with large amounts of money and boiling emotions," including many wealthy kids from Gulf states who stayed in air-conditioned luxury guest houses, fired weapons into the air, and returned home claiming that they had been jihadis. Bank robberies increased, as did inter-Arab violence and conflict between foreigners and Afghans. Different parties published attacks on each other, set up rival guest houses for arriving foreigners, and refused to coordinate operations against the Communists (Wright, 2006: 137–138).

"The best hope for mujahidin unity, based on the specifically non-ethnic and non-regional Islamist perspective, failed on the triple dangers of ethnic rivalry, envy and distrust." Schisms also developed between "rural and urban networks" and religious and tribal authority. Although the various parties worked in shifting coalitions to form a stable postconflict government, these efforts were undermined, particularly by Hizb-i Islami, whose leadership had been identified by the U.S. Senate Foreign Relations Committee a decade earlier as being close to the Muslim Brothers and unwilling to work with other local factions. By 1996, the post-Communist civil war had weakened all parties sufficiently for the neofundamentalist Taliban to capture Kabul and begin consolidating power across Afghanistan (Magnus and Naby, 2002: 142).

The fratricidal violence of the post–Red Army civil war gravely damaged ties among the mujahidin remaining in Afghanistan, and the anonymous assassination of Azzam, who had already lost his early influence as spiritual leader of the foreign fighters, reflected the deepening drift of the movement, which appeared to have snatched defeat from the jaws of victory. Egyptian mujahid Abu Hamza al-Masri, later arrested for promoting terrorism as the imam of the Finsbury Park Mosque in London, declared that the recruits "went to Afghanistan to defend their brothers and sisters," not to engage in internecine battles. "They want to struggle against something that is indisputable, which is non-Muslims raping, killing, and maiming Muslims." To maintain a sense of purpose among the recruits, the transnational foreign fighter movement needed to regroup and refocus its message of threat against the *ummah*, now that the Communist Soviets had been defeated. The leadership now looked for another conflict that could be easily framed as a one-dimensional war to protect the faithful from murderous infidels, and it soon located one in Bosnia (Kohlmann, 2004, 27–28).

Al Qaeda and Beyond Afghanistan

In a monograph published in 1991, Olivier Roy, a noted French expert on violent Islamist groups, concluded: "The war in Afghanistan has had no special impact on the spread of Islamic fundamentalism.... It is unlikely that Afghanistan will become a center for the spread of Islamic militancy" because there was "no unified and structured political movement that could turn it into an alternative revolutionary force." The various militant groups were now deeply estranged from each other, so "there has been no Islamist or jihadist Comintern or Islamintern" (Roy, 1991: 44, 69, 117).

In fact, such an organization had already developed and was seeking to prolong its existence rather than declare mission accomplished and fold its tents. With Azzam's death, his vision of a "rapid reaction force" that would defend imperiled Muslim lands as new situations arose was superseded by the offense-based doctrine, espoused by bin Laden and Zawahiri, of worldwide jihad against Westerners and any Muslims deemed to be apostates (Gerges, 2005: 135). Despite this shift of purpose, recruiters for future conflicts would continue to use messages emphasizing threats to the *ummah* and the necessity of mobilizing for defense.

On August 11, 1988, bin Laden announced at a meeting in Peshawar the formation of a group selected from the cream of the Arab Afghans and that he would have a paramilitary force of 314 fighters ready in six months' time, although for what purpose he did not specify. The next meeting on August 20 featured the formal establishment of al Qaeda; bin Laden stated that its military wing would serve Islam and engage in a mission of a limited duration, but he still did not announce specific goals. At the first organizational meeting held in the Afghan town of Khost in early 1989, "new recruits filled out forms in triplicate, signed their oath of loyalty to bin Laden, and swore an oath to secrecy." Single members received $1,000 per month in salary, and married members received $1,500. In keeping with private-sector employment practices in the Middle East, members received a health care plan and an annual month of vacation with paid return airfare. Those who wished to leave would be entitled to severance payments of $2,400 for their continued fealty. Overall, the leadership attempted to present an attractive employment opportunity for those with professional educations[17] (Wright, 2006: 131–133, 141–142).

One evident reason for the continuation of the transnational jihad was that although many Arab Afghans had returned home shortly after the fall of the Communist regime in Kabul, a large number experienced difficulty in obtaining repatriation.

> While their departure for Afghanistan was generally blessed by the regimes in their countries, upon their return the alumni came up against the strong opposition of the authorities because they feared that the "Afghanis" would rapidly turn into a threat against them, due to their military experience and Fundamentalist worldview. Therefore, in the majority of the Maghreb countries, as well as in Egypt and Jordan, the authorities took steps to prevent the return of the volunteers and the joining of the ranks of radical Islamic opposition in their lands. (Schweitzer and Shay, 2003: 25, 56–58)

"Some countries simply refused to let the fighters return. They became a stateless, vagrant mob of religious mercenaries" (Wright, 2006: 163–164).

Bosnia

Compounding the difficulty for the recruits was the announcement by Pakistan in January 1993 that mujahidin offices were to be closed and foreigners without valid visas required to leave the country. While this edict went largely unenforced, it coincided with the availability of just the type of conflict that al Qaeda leadership had been seeking. Bosnia, which presented another Muslim population seeking liberation from a (at least formerly) Communist regime, had already been scouted in April 1992 as a potential resettlement area for displaced foreign fighters.

Sheikh Abu Abdel Aziz Barbaros, a Saudi airline employee of Indian descent who had come to Afghanistan after being recruited at an Azzam lecture in 1984, first went to Bosnia after the fall of Kabul, within weeks of the start of Bosnia-Herzegovina's drive for secession from Yugoslavia. Aziz later related that there had not yet been international media coverage of the conflict and that he previously had no idea where in the world Bosnia was or how many Muslims lived there. Upon experiencing this new civil war, he decided that al Qaeda was uniquely positioned to intervene: "We are not here to bring supplies like food and medicine.... There are a lot of organizations that can do that. We bring men." Shortly thereafter, his new operation was joined by Moataz Billah, an Arab Afghan who had previously been a Muslim student group leader in Egypt, who organized training camps for both Arabs and Bosnians and personally provided paramilitary instruction to almost all of the early foreign fighters in Bosnia.

An estimated 5,000 veterans of Afghanistan and their associates participated in the Bosnian conflict. Kohlmann describes the important formative effect of the Bosnian conflict on the Arab Afghan movement both because it presented the opportunity to disperse agents into Western Europe and recruit "unsophisticated" Westerners and because the insurgents played a far more active role than they had in Afghanistan, although the mujahidin did not directly influence the outcome of the Bosnian conflict either. Foundational myths of al Qaeda, particularly stories of fights to the death with Eastern European "crusaders," are actually products of its second civil conflict rather than its first, and the experience reified "the sacrificial ideology epitomized by Azzam," with the mujahidin viewing themselves as "armed humanitarians" (Kohlmann, 2004: xii–xiii, 16–18, 23).

Recruitment of new volunteers soon began as well, with organs established for Afghanistan quickly engaging in scale shifting to encompass the new civil conflict as one front in a larger war. The enlistment of literate Western Muslims permitted mujahidin groups to translate and publish Arabic sermons into English and French to reach the sons of immigrants who were alienated in their new homelands and estranged from their old ones. In 1993, the Al Kifah Refugee Center, which also began to use the name Care International, issued a flyer offering "A Call to Jihad in Bosnia," which described the human toll of the war, followed by the message "Ask yourself what you are doing for these Muslims.... If you Desire to provide the Emerging Jihad Movement in Bosnia with more than Food and Shelter, Please send your zadaka to Al Kifah." The group's English-language newsletter, *Al Hussam (The Sword)*, which had been publishing stories about Afghan mujahidin, now began running pieces on Bosnia and calls for action. One front-page editorial described an elderly woman who was brutalized and demanded that the reader fight the Serbs for her redemption (Kohlmann, 2004: 12, 39, 41).

The messaging clearly reflects the strategy to present a morally unambiguous reason for continuing the jihad. Abd al-Aziz Awa, later a leader of Palestinian Islamic Jihad, claimed that he went from Afghanistan to Bosnia upon hearing of violations of Muslim women by Christians (Schindler, 2007: 126). A recruitment video titled *The Sword Is the Solution* features an opening shot of an abandoned Soviet tank in Afghanistan that quickly leads to images of Bosnian Serb leader Radovan Karadžić, police confrontations with civilian women, and the mutilation of the body of a young boy. These are followed by readings from the Koran and the narrator insisting in Arabic: "The religion of Allah will not be spread except through Jihad, and the Jihad is through fighting and killing.... Jihad is an activity to be carried out by society as a whole" (Dar al Murabiteen Publications, 2008).

In addition to combatants, recruits were also assigned to al Qaeda–affiliated charitable relief organizations. Bin Laden established the Committee for Islamic Benevolence, known also as the Benevolence International Foundation, which advertised in Arabic-language fund-raising appeals that it was a "trustworthy hand for the support of the mujahidin and refugees." Internal notes to donors informed them that an office in Croatia had been "established for relief operations and support of jihad in Bosnia-Herzegovina.... Contribute with your mujahidin brothers to repel the Zionist-Crusader attack on Muslim lands." The distinction between foreign insurgents and international aid workers was further blurred by the practice of providing mujahidin with identification cards that bore names including the Third World Relief Agency (Kohlmann, 2004: 37, 45–46).

The recruits to Bosnia were a diverse group who appeared to have absorbed the messaging of the civil war as a threat to the *ummah*. A Moroccan jihadi stated in a November 1992 press interview that he had come to fight "Western aggression against the Muslim peoples" and claimed there were already 700 mujahidin in the country. Earlier that fall, small mujahidin units had begun attacking Serb militias, initially with unfavorable results. The first officially claimed action by Muslim foreign fighters in Bosnia occurred in September 1992, when a group of 55 mujahidin that included a Bahraini royal prince attempted to open a supply line to Sarajevo without any heavy weapons and were forced to withdraw with large numbers of casualties. Other recruits included a Kuwaiti former Olympic athlete and son of a governor, a star player on the Qatari national handball team who had been refused permission by his mother to go to Afghanistan years earlier, and a Saudi-born graduate of a Boston prep school who had become involved with Al Kifah while attending college in Tucson (an American center of jihad support). A group of Turkish recruits led by an American commander had separate living quarters, where they received training and sermons via translators (Kohlmann, 2004: 30, 54, 64, 65, 97, 116).

As transnational funds, supplies, and the mix of Afghanistan veterans and fresh recruits continued to flow, the foreign fighters quickly developed into a formidable adversary, one upon which the Sarajevo government came to increasingly rely. "El Mujahidin" was fully integrated into the Bosnian army command structure as Military Unit 5689, and its leaders were recognized and paid as officers (Schindler, 2007: 167). However, as in Afghanistan, neofundamentalist foreign fighters clashed with local insurgents over their culture, as the Arabs complained that the Bosnians were not really Muslims because they drank and danced (Nasiri, 2006: 176). Under pressure by the Clinton administration to expel jihadists as a condition of the Dayton Peace Accords, the foreign battalion officially disbanded in early 1996, with some foreigners joining the national army or marrying locals to escape deportation. Others returned to their Western home countries and formed al Qaeda cells or ventured on to a growing list of civil conflicts entered by Afghan veterans (Kohlmann, 2004: 30, 171, 191).

The mujahidin who served in Bosnia probably played some role in the success of the war of liberation from Serb-dominated Yugoslavia, during which these "armed humanitarians" also engaged in documented atrocities against both Serb and Croatian civilians. These included attacks on Croatian villages and desecration of their churches. Another casualty was certainly the strategy of Abdullah Azzam, in which a trained corps of religious warriors would liberate one occupied Muslim country at a time. Instead, Bosnia provided a springboard for launching smaller groups to numerous foreign states to make attacks simultaneously and ubiquitously. As the father of an American recruit from Detroit who was killed in Bosnia stated, "For Muslims, this is not strange to go and die in other people's homelands" (Kohlmann, 2004: 30, 53, 65).

Abdullah al-Bahri, a bin Laden bodyguard, volunteered for Bosnia and viewed his role as "voluntary work" rather than as a collective religious obligation. However,

> We realized we were a nation [*ummah*] that had a distinguished place among nations. Otherwise, what would make me leave Saudi Arabia— and I am of Yemeni origin—to go and fight in Bosnia? The issues of [secular] nationalism were put out of our minds, and we acquired a wider view than that, namely the issue of the ummah. Although the issue was very simple at the start, yet it was a motive and an incentive for jihad.

Al Qaeda thus successfully performed the frame bridging and scale shift also accomplished by other anti-Western transnational activists during the 1990s, from Chiapas to Seattle. What was at first an apparently local issue was recast as part of a broader, unifying, transnational cause. The appearance of mujahidin in ever more civil conflicts, and their apparent rate of success, legitimated the role of the jihadi as recognized and even accepted. A year after Aziz and his colleagues launched their Balkan operation, not only Bosnia but also the civil conflicts in Somalia and Tajikistan had become jihadist causes (Gerges, 2005: 63).

The Globalization of Jihad

Samuel Huntington (1996: 246) described Afghanistan as the first "civilizational war," and the leadership of al Qaeda intended to polarize those it deemed belonging to the *ummah* of faithful Muslims against apostates and their Western masters (Magnus and Naby, 2002: 27). Its greatest success lay not in the exploitation of community institutions preexisting Afghanistan, but in the social network created between Arab Afghans during the crucible of the war. Affiliates who returned to their home countries to train others or who moved on together between torn conflict states used their solidarity and contacts to share knowledge, transforming al Qaeda from a vanguard to a plan that could be appropriated by new entrepreneurs.

Among the first generation of Arab Afghans, personal connections not only facilitated the establishment of al Qaeda but also increased coordination between militants in local and regional insurgent groups, introducing foreign fighters to a wide array of civil conflicts. In Southeast Asia, Filipino veterans of Afghanistan fighting to secure sovereignty for the local Muslim population invited Indonesian Afghan comrades from the Jemaah Islamiyah group to use the Filipino training facilities of the Moro Islamic Liberation Front, where they would be less likely to face government reprisals. In October 1997, mujahidin from Egypt and Saudi Arabia led suicide attacks against a Filipino army infantry division.

Another insurgent militia fighting for sovereignty for the Muslim southern Philippines founded by Afghan veterans was the Abu Sayyaf Group, named for the Afghan party leader who had first provided training camps to bin Laden, rather than for any indigenous hero of the local population. Ramzi Yousef, a Kuwaiti veteran later convicted of planning the 1993 World Trade Center bombing, also followed Afghan connections back to the Philippines, where his visiting uncle, Khaled Sheikh Mohammed, conceived of a plan to destroy multiple passenger jet aircraft simultaneously that was ultimately passed on to al Qaeda. By September 2001, Indonesian security was aware that its citizens had joined militants in Thailand (Conboy, 2006: 54, 59, 62, 137, 146).

The jihad also spread westward into Central Asia and the Caucasus, where Afghan veterans became separatist leaders in Dagestan and Chechnya, and Arab colleagues arrived as advisors. The nephew of one of these senior mujahidin led the October 2002 attack on a Moscow theater that resulted in hundreds of civilian casualties. Chechnya had been an early post-Afghanistan priority, with bin Laden establishing an office in Baku, Azerbaijan, to process recruits. The Islamic Movement of Uzbekistan reportedly formed after bin Laden met with its leaders and provided seed money and training facilities in Afghanistan (Schweitzer and Shay, 2003: 100, 105, 190). In western China, Muslim Uighurs also went to Afghanistan and Pakistan to train and maintained links to Chechen militants (Rotar, 2004).

Bin Laden had attempted to send his new force to intervene in the Middle East even before the Afghanistan War had ended, offering to lead an Islamic army in defense of Saudi Arabia when invasion by Saddam Hussein's Iraq seemed a possibility in 1990 (Gutman, 2008: 35). Although Riyadh rebuffed this offer, choosing instead the American military and beginning bin Laden's obsession with driving America from the "Land of the Two Holy Places," al Qaeda soon began either to send recruits elsewhere or to provide training in its camps for visiting Muslim insurgents. "In spring 1990, at the peak of the Kashmir crisis, there were reports of Kashmiri insurgents being trained by the ISI in Afghan mujahidin camps" (Roy, 1991: 41).

Harakat ul-Mujahidin, a Pakistani group similar to the Taliban in its neofundamentalism, had been established in the early 1980s during the Pakistani Islamic revival that accompanied the influx of all of the foreign militants and aid groups. It soon began sending recruits to train in bin Laden–financed camps in Afghanistan and enlisted approximately 11,000 recruits, of whom 5,000 were from Pakistani Kashmir and 6,000 were "from other Muslim countries such as Egypt, Algeria, Tunisia, Saudi Arabia, Jordan, Bangladesh, as well as India and the Philippines." It was this group's training facilities that were bombed by the United States on August 8, 1998, in response to the attacks against the American embassies in Kenya and Tanzania (Schweitzer and Shay, 2003: 83–84).

In northern Africa, Afghan veterans also participated in Somalia, where bin Laden claimed he sent 250 mujahidin to fight American forces, although his protectors in the Sudanese government claimed the number was far lower. Apparently, the foreigners provided training to local militias but did not integrate well with the Somalis and reportedly fled after being frightened by the violence of the First Battle of Mogadishu, also attributed as the reason for American withdrawal over the downing of two Black Hawk helicopters. As one jihadi recalled, "The Somalis treated us in a bad way…due to the bad leadership situation there, we decided to withdraw."

In Algeria, returning Afghan veterans split the existing Islamist insurgent groups, strengthening neofundamentalist factions such as the Groupe Islamique Armé, which received financing from bin Laden and attacked not only the state but tens of thousands of supposedly apostate civilians. Bad international publicity caused him to distance himself from the group, but not before the Algerian government appealed to Saudi Arabia, which, tired as well of bin Laden's verbal attacks against the monarchy, stripped him of his citizenship, further radicalizing him (Wright, 2006: 188, 190, 195).

Full Circle: Return to Afghanistan

Bin Laden resided in Sudan under the protection of a sympathetic Islamist regime between 1992 and 1996, but as various governments complained to Khartoum—culminating with Egypt, where a bin Laden–affiliated group had attempted to assassinate President Mubarak—he was finally expelled and rendered stateless. This position was oddly appropriate for an individual promoting extreme transnational political and military activism, but al Qaeda leadership still required a physical residence, and, despite the reservations of the new Taliban regime, they found it through old connections in Afghanistan. With a neofundamentalist regime in place there, seemingly a success of his policies rather than an indication of Islam under threat, bin Laden continued to recruit and organize foreign fighters to strike at enemies of the *ummah*.

Al Qaeda established new training camps that it called Khaldan, a historic name for Central Asia, that provided Arab advisors to the Taliban and also brought in foreign militants to learn paramilitary skills and terrorist tactics and then turned them loose to stage their own operations abroad. These included Ahmed Rassam, an Algerian who formed his own cell in Montreal and who, after receiving no response from Afghanistan concerning the plan he offered, went ahead on his own initiative to attempt the millennium bombing of Los Angeles International Airport (Wright, 2006: 191, 262, 297–298). Another graduate was Nizar Nawar, who drove an oil truck into a Tunisian synagogue in 2002, and who had in his possession the phone numbers of 9/11 hijackers and German cell leaders he had met at Khaldan (Schweitzer and Shay, 2003: 39).

The messaging employed during this period of foreign fighter recruitment varied little from the conflict frames Abullah Azzam had used 20 years earlier.

Mohammed al-'Owhali, a religious Saudi teenager, listened to tapes that glorified martyrdom in sermons and warned of "Kissinger's Promise," a supposed plan to occupy the Arabian Peninsula. "Inflamed by this spurious information, 'Owhali made his way to Afghanistan to join the jihad." There he and the other recruits learned that it was imperative to defend the *ummah* against the four enemies of Islam: heretics, Shiites, America, and Israel. They attended 15 days of boot camp and 45 days of basic training. Graduates could go on to a further 45-day guerrilla warfare school. Also offered were specialty camps in bomb making and espionage, and "Kamikaze Camp," where white-clad members lived isolated and silent. Possibly two members of this last group included 9/11 hijackers Nawaf al-Hamzi and Khaled al-Mihdhar, Saudis who had fought in Bosnia and then with the Taliban against the Northern Alliance (Wright, 2006: 279, 303, 309).

A significant proportion of Taliban forces were transnational in origin, with an estimated 30 percent coming from Pakistan and another 10 percent who were Arabs. The latter were trained to be unit commanders and to fight to the death and were the "most feared by [Northern Alliance] commanders" because of tactics such as blowing themselves up with grenades to avoid capture. By August 2001, the Taliban had come to depend on foreign fighters to defend its territory in the third consecutive civil conflict in Afghanistan since 1978. Bin Laden, on the other hand, told the press that he had invited Muslim youths around the world to "be close to nature" (Gutman, 2008: 189, 190, 243).

The Enduring Legacy of the Afghanistan War

As a result of the September 11 attacks, planned and coordinated by al Qaeda from within Taliban territory, Afghanistan was once again occupied by a foreign superpower and began yet another phase of civil conflict. By this point, the frame of the *ummah* under assault was not merely being peddled by the insurgents against the NATO-backed regime of Hamid Karzai established during Operation: Enduring Freedom; it had become the staple recruitment messaging of Islamists around the world. In Yemen, where in 1994 President Ali Abdullah Saleh had invited thousands of foreign mujahidin to the country to crush a socialist rebellion, instructors stood in classrooms at the Higher Institute for Preaching and Guidance in front of photographs of Hamas suicide bombings and discussed the need for "self-defense," asserting: "Every Muslim who has the ability to defend the Afghans should do so" (Trofimov, 2005: 65, 78).

In the recruitment video *The Sword Is the Solution*, distributed over the Internet to any interested party rather than clandestinely through underground Muslim Brotherhood meetings as messaging had been a generation before, the perpetual jihad and the continuing need to liberate Afghanistan are framed little differently than when the civil conflict there first began:

> This call is not to a simple order, or an exciting journey, for if our goal was near we would not be in need. It is a long road, all of which is treacherous, and which exits this world, but it will lead to the meeting with the results of your work.... It is incumbent upon all Muslims in the world today to stand alongside the Afghanis. It is incumbent upon all Muslims in the world today to carry weapons. If they do not carry them here, then carry them there. If they do not fight here, then fight there. (Dar al Murabiteen Publications, 2008)

Evaluation

The available data from the Afghanistan War supported the two hypotheses. Recruitment during the 1980s centered on existing transnational Islamist institutions such as the Muslim Brotherhood in Arab states and immigrant organizations in the West. This approach appears to have begun to change by the late 1990s as the result of advances in globalized Internet communication, but contact was still made with the likeliest predisposed recruits via Islamist Web sites if not physical sites. (A more detailed discussion of this phenomenon follows in the conclusion.) The hypothesis that recruitment would be framed as a defensive mobilization holds across each civil conflict, regardless of the particular circumstances. Indeed, all contemporary Islamist foreign fighter recruitment appears to share a single continuous narrative initially developed by Azzam a quarter of a century earlier. Azzam himself spoke of ethnic differences between Arabs and Afghans but identified all Muslims as a broader transnational community whose members were obliged to defend each other against a global threat.

A number of authors have noted that the mujahidin recruited to Afghanistan during the 1980s were essentially irrelevant in that particular civil conflict. Roy (1991: 84) wrote of the foreign fighters: "The war would have been won with or without them. Militarily, they represented a tiny and inconsequential factor in the Afghan battle." In this regard, they made little contribution compared with the transnational insurgents who helped secure victory for Israel, prolong the life of Republican Spain, and give Texas martyrs for international legitimacy and sovereignty. However, the legacy established by the network of Arab Afghans in civil conflicts and global terrorism since the defeat of the Soviet Red Army has been unprecedented.

The transition from jihad for Afghanistan to a truly transnational war, ostensibly on behalf of the entire *ummah*, represented a significant reversal in the two-century-long diffusion of the norm that delegitimized fighting for a foreign power as criminal or simply mercenary. As mujahidin proliferated through various conflict zones and violent illicit organizations, they provided their successors with not only field expertise but also reinforcement of their frame that every conflict was one front in a war to save Islam. And they established the jihadi, now synonymous with "foreign fighter," as a role in international politics that was recognized if not accepted.

Unlike previous conflicts in which foreign fighters had returned to their prior lives or settled in their hard-won new communities, the Arab Afghans and the mujahidin who followed them extended their activities out of the conflict zone and established themselves in new ones. In part, they were able to do this because they believed that their efforts had won the war and because they had the resources to continue. It also occurred in part because their host and home states established policies that rendered them stateless and thus truly transnational. With mujahidin and other foreign fighters currently to be found on every populated continent, what began with palace intrigue in the Hindu Kush now affects the security of the entire international community.

Conclusion

Responses to Transnational Insurgency

ON APRIL 27, 2007, the Paktalk online forum hosted a chat session with Abu Adam al Maqdisi, a Palestinian member of the Islamic State of Iraq insurgent organization. Responding in real time, presumably from the conflict zone, to supporters and curious, anonymous potential volunteers, al Maqdisi informed the audience that the insurgency did not need transnational recruits to be foot soldiers; rather, the need was for martyrs. Anyone who came in requesting to serve as a human bomb would need to be evaluated by a militia commander first, and those knowledgeable about sharia might be preserved for leadership roles. Training for jihad did not take place in Iraq but in other states, and anyone interested could get basic information from various jihadi Web sites. However, it would be necessary to plan, train, and make contacts ahead of time because "the whole notion of 'Passionate jihad' and going to Iraq without having someone to contact there is useless" (Kohlmann, 2007: 1–3).

This exchange indicates that, despite the emergence of a plethora of do-it-yourself Internet sites for would-be militants and terrorists and the rise of "self-starter" terrorist groups that use al Qaeda as a template without making direct contact (Kirby, 2007: 425), the fielding of foreign fighters probably remains as much a product of insurgencies developing transnational recruitment mechanisms as it was in the days of Lord Byron and the Friendly Society. Unlike loosely affiliated terrorist networks that permit ad hoc participation, transnational insurgencies require organizations to facilitate the indoctrination, training, and transportation of large numbers of recruits into civil wars in distant conflict states and then their integration into the rebel command structure.

The Significance of the Iraq War (2003–2011)

Although jihadi foreign fighters have been ubiquitous globally since the end of the first Afghanistan War, it was not until evaluations of the deteriorating security conditions in the simmering postwar civil conflict in Iraq in the mid-2000s that they began to be analyzed as a category of actor of import and that the term began to be used in scholarly works and mass media coverage. (See the introduction and appendix A). It is therefore worth asking what happened in Iraq that made such an impression.

With the invasion of Iraq long threatened by the United States, foreign volunteers had already arrived when the regime fell in March 2003 (appendix A). Many of these foreign fighters were veterans of other civil conflicts, and they employed recruitment systems that in some cases had been in place since the early phases of the Afghanistan War. With their conflict framing already digested by their potential audience, whose identities as threatened Muslims had been activated over the past year and a half of the War on Terror, and the apparent efficaciousness of the role of the jihadi validated by numerous conflicts over the past decade and a half, an active recruitment campaign outside Iraq was apparently less vital than efforts to direct interested parties to existing intake operations.

Institutions of Transnational Recruitment

Prominent in the leadership of the transnational insurgents in Iraq was Abu Musab al-Zarqawi, a Jordanian who had followed the advice of his neighborhood Salafist preacher in 1989 and traveled to Peshawar, where he became a reporter for a jihadi newspaper and apparently made the acquaintance of bin Laden (Milelli, in Kepel and Milelli, 2008: 243). After militant activity and imprisonment in Jordan, Zarqawi returned to Afghanistan to establish his own training camp at Herat with bin Laden's approval. His group, Tawid wa'al-Jihad ("Monotheism and Struggle"), relocated to Iraq in 2002 as Washington began announcing plans to topple the Hussein regime. Recruits included Jordanians, Syrians, and members of the Ansar al-Islam, which was based in Kurdish Iraq but had Arab Afghans among its members.[1] It eventually renamed itself al Qaeda in Iraq (Felter and Fishman, 2007: 4).

Martyrdom and Foreign Fighters

The most detailed data on foreign fighters in Iraq available at this time are the result of the U.S. military's discovery in October 2007 of what amounted to an insurgent human resources office for processing foreign fighters in the Iraqi town of Sinjar, close to the Syrian border. Despite the Syrian route into Iraq, the detailed forms (including their home telephone numbers) submitted by 595 recruits indicate that 41 percent were Saudi and 19 percent

Libyan, with Syrians, Yemenis, Algerians, and Moroccans all represented in the high-single-digit percentages. In a number of cases, recruits had traveled together in small groups of acquaintances, with many recruited on university campuses. Most were unmarried young men between the ages of 22 and 24, suggesting that they were first-time recruits and not veteran mujahidin. The records also suggested that most would not be foreign fighters in future conflicts if they had their way; 56 percent stated their preferred duty in Iraq as martyrdom[2] (Felter and Fishman, 2007: 7, 8, 18, 28).

Consistent with prior reports by the Pentagon (see the introduction), in his examination of more than 500 suicide bombings during the occupation of Iraq between March 2003 and August 2006, Mohammed Hafez (2007: 89, 219) observes that "many, if not most" of the perpetrators were foreigners, and a significant number had come from outside the Arabian Peninsula. He thus argues that suicide bombers in the Iraqi insurgency were not fighting for a nationalist cause, but rather that extreme religiosity "appears to hold" as the explanation for why foreigners would incur high costs to sacrifice their lives in a foreign civil conflict and why Shiite civilians and Iraqi state employees were targets.

Although devotion to a particular interpretation of Islam may be what made the conflict salient enough to recruits to sacrifice their own lives and kill others, based on the information that Hafez provides, foreign fighters in Iraq—including suicide bombers—are recruited by the same logic and methods that their non-Muslim foreign counterparts have been recruited by in other civil conflicts for centuries. Even though most foreign fighters in past cases apparently did not set out expressly to die in the field, they often experienced far heavier casualties than did local insurgents because they engaged in essentially suicidal behavior by, for example, refusing to abandon the Alamo when the opportunity presented itself or taking to Spanish battlefields with no training or heavy armament against far superior forces. And prior to the Iraq War, the world suicide bombing capital was previously Sri Lanka, where a civil conflict pitted a predominantly Hindu ethnic minority against a predominantly Buddhist ethnic majority (Pape, 2006).

These recruits may arguably have been the victims of "imperfect information." Some failed suicide bombers also claim that they were deceived (Abawi, 2009) or coerced (Fadel, 2008), and some successful suicide bombings were apparently conducted by mentally incompetent individuals detonated by remote control (Hurst, 2008). The majority of suicide bombers may have been persuaded to become *shahids* through recruitment messaging emphasizing the surety of paradise and the nobility of the cause. However, recruiters in the Spanish Civil War also claimed that it was "of great spiritual benefit in the afterlife to fall in the defense of Christ," and (presumably atheist) Communists held up martyred exemplars, such as one recruit who allegedly died to preserve an airplane for the cause rather than eject safely.

In all of these cases, martyrdom was used by recruiters to entice prospects into combat by mitigating the costs of sacrifice. As the literature on suicide bombers indicates (Bloom, 2005; Pape, 2006; Hafez, 2007), religion plays a role, but so do frames of persecution and duty to the community (similar to the rationale for becoming a foreign fighter) and intergroup competition. Individuals willing to risk their lives to be foreign fighters based on framing of a threatened community would probably be more likely to give their lives in suicide attacks, so it is reasonable to expect overlap between foreign fighters and martyrs.

Jihadis are not unique in this respect, and there are no reliable means for determining that being an Islamist carries greater weight of affect than does the identity of someone willing to be a foreign fighter for Jewish, Catholic, or Communist causes.[3] Amartya Sen (2006) contends that no one has a single level of identity. And this is what makes the work of foreign fighter recruiters so fascinating: that they are able to make one of an individual's identities so salient that he is willing to risk his life for it even when his direct interests are not at stake. The constant casus belli used to recruit foreign fighters, however, is neither death nor glory, but the necessary defense of their transnational identity communities.

Modifications and Consistency in Recruitment Strategies

The strategy of the insurgents to recruit foreign fighters to serve as suicide bombers in Iraq instead of in more conventional roles appears to have been driven by the limited military skills of the most willing volunteers. With the financial constraints that confront most rebel groups, Iraqi transnational insurgent groups preferred to attract recruits with the resources to provide their own transportation costs. Candidates with the wealth to pay their expenses and possibly give cash to other insurgents, and who had connections to Wahhabi institutions that facilitate recruitment, abounded in Saudi Arabia and Kuwait, and one Syrian recruiter reported that Iraqi insurgents requested these nationalities specifically. As there is no military conscription in either state, there were young men available as potential recruits, but none possessed skills that would be helpful in the field, so they were steered toward suicide bombings to maximize their impact (Hafez, 2007: 16, 174).

As with other foreign fighters, the perception of a potentially existential threat to their community made high-cost action preferable to taking none. Persuading volunteers to assume high costs actually solves two organizational problems: overcoming collective action barriers and efficiently employing unskilled recruits. Haganah (later Israel) had sought to recruit only trained military experts and then experienced frustration coordinating all of the unspecialized infantry volunteers. But the Islamic State of Iraq, its affiliates, and other transnational Islamist groups capitalized on the work of Azzam and his successors to define the *shahid* as a legitimate role and sacrificed their unskilled recruits as pawns on the board.

As Hafez (2007: 16, 19, 72, 74, 117) notes, mobilization "consists of more than calling on people to rise up or take to the streets; it involves framing social ills as threats and opportunities for action" and "fashion[ing] shared understandings of the world and selves that legitimate collective action." Both transnational neofundamentalists and local nationalist insurgents view the war as a defensive struggle, with the former also believing in the opportunity to remake the world if the United States is defeated (much as Communists in the 1930s argued that the defeat of fascism would augur a new socialist era). As the establishment of a majority Shiite or secular pro-Western state would also represent significant losses and potential threats, Iraqi police, military, and civilians represented targets as well.

Rather than using theological arguments to justify their cause and tactics, recruiters used mass media to employ the "emotive element" of "highlighting Muslim humiliation and suffering in video clips and audio recordings." These recordings and online publications frame the conflict as a story in three acts: the humiliation, torture, and suffering of Muslims by Westerners, portrayed as constant across the globe; next the impotence or collusion of apostate Arab regimes; finally the inevitable Islamic victory because a righteous few have stepped forward and sacrificed to fight for justice. The montages of footage from different conflicts imply that fighting in Iraq is equivalent to fighting anywhere else in the global theater of conflict and also exploit the perceived legitimacy of suicide bombings in Israel (Hafez, 2007: 118, 141, 144, 168).

The biography of one Kuwaiti suicide bomber claimed that he was moved to jihad in Iraq after watching a video of Palestinians fighting Israeli troops, and the Mujahidin Shura Council insurgent group issued a video of two Saudis who stated that they had traveled to Iraq because "we can't see how our sisters are being dishonored and our brothers in Fallujah are being killed day and night, and no one is helping them, no one is standing beside them." The combatants and martyrs are then used as exemplars in new recruitment material, continuing the cycle. Like Ben Leider, who reportedly "was not content to sit in a ringside seat and watch" the triumph of fascism in Spain, Abu Ahmed al-Kuwaiti left a new marriage because "when he heard the call of God and saw the door of paradise open wide he could not sit around while his brothers were racing to reserve places in the highest paradise" (Hafez, 2007: 141, 143, 151, 177).

More recently, available evidence suggests that the harsh interrogation and imprisonment methods used by the United States against transnational insurgents have become a point of recruitment messaging. "In the case of foreign fighters—recruited mostly from Saudi Arabia, Egypt, Syria, Yemen and North Africa—the reason cited by the great majority for coming to Iraq was what they had heard of the torture in Guantánamo and Abu Ghraib. These abuses, not fundamentalist Islam, had provoked so many of the foreign fighters volunteering to become suicide bombers" (the *Independent*, 2009). Such reports indicate that Iraq is consistent with historical cases of recruitment in that not only were material rewards not emphasized but also the danger posed by participation was not downplayed by recruiters either. As in past cases, recruiters adapted developments in the distant theater of conflict to their message of an advancing threat to the greater community.

Anbar Awakening or History Repeating?

Despite the influx of thousands of foreign fighters during the first three years of the Iraq War and advances in communications strategies, the transnational insurgents still failed to integrate with the local rebels or ingratiate themselves with the public in many communities. As in 1980s and 1990s Afghanistan, while most jihadis were local, their leadership was almost exclusively foreign fighters who antagonized local tribal authority and degraded local culture in favor of strident religious practices (Kilcullen, 2009). The Awakening Council in Anbar Province, a coalition of local tribes and militias that organized in 2006 with the assistance of the United States to fight insurgents, was celebrated as a rare strategic success by the Pentagon and an affirmation that Coalition forces would still be welcomed by the Iraqi populace if they facilitated effective security and governance.

Instead, it seems likelier that the Awakening was simply a manifestation of the usual schism that appeared between transnational and local insurgents in every case examined in this study. Put simply, local combatants typically have at stake their livelihoods as well as their lives—their families and farms matter far more than the constructed community or more abstract threat offered by recruiters to often doctrinaire outsiders. Some degree of dissension with transnational insurgents appears inevitable. Foreign fighters attack the civilian population (Texas and Palestine), engage in battles with local insurgents (Spain and Afghanistan), and find themselves in cultural conflicts that alienate them from those they expect to thank them for their efforts (Israel).

The same held true in Iraq even prior to the Anbar Awakening. When Zarqawi established al Qaeda in Iraq in 2004, he quickly split with bin Laden over the question of whether the "far enemy" (the United States) was the greater threat, instead focusing on the "near enemy" of Iraqi Shiites. His insistence on enforcing strict sharia in areas controlled by his transnational militia "alienated more Iraqis than it attracted" (Felter and Fishman, 2007: 4). In a letter to bin Laden, Zarqawi managed to express frustration with both the local population and what he deemed the limited influx of foreign fighters:

> Their numbers continue to be negligible as compared with the vast magnitude of the battle. Still, we know that there are many brave men, and the army of jihad is already on the move.... Many Iraqis have shown us hospitality and see us as brothers, but when it comes to making their homes a base for launching operations, this is rarer than gold. This is why some brothers are occasionally a burden: we train new recruits while wearing this ball and chain, so to speak. (Milelli, in Kepel and Milelli, 2008: 260–261)[4]

The Continuing Diffusion of Foreign Fighters

Although the foreign fighters of the Iraq War occupied the lion's share of public attention to transnational insurgencies during the first decade of the twenty-first century, Iraq by no means marked a culmination of the trend toward transnationalization that has been increasing since World War II.

The Arab Spring in the Middle East and North Africa

By early 2009, with the Anbar strategy seeming at least temporarily effective in limiting al Qaeda–linked violence in Iraq, all of the respective governments of the Coalition forces announced an end to their active participation in combating the insurgents. However, the United States and, to a lesser extent, the United Kingdom committed to force increases in Afghanistan to defeat the Taliban and al Qaeda–linked insurgencies that persisted there and were bolstered by an influx of foreign fighter veterans of the Iraq conflict. The United

States would not be able to wash its hands of the difficulties of confronting transnational insurgencies by quitting Iraq: Even as it prepared to next leave Afghanistan, it was at the same time hunting foreign fighters belonging to Al Shabaab in Somalia and al Qaeda in the Arabian Peninsula in Yemen, primarily through local proxy forces and drone strikes.

But as jihadis proliferated in other war zones, they failed to participate in the transformational events that swept away the regimes that they hated. In 2011, the largely peaceful civil uprisings that toppled the governments of Tunisia and Egypt were purely domestic affairs led by secular protestors. In the armed confrontation that forced the ouster of President Ali of Yemen, who had invited foreign fighters to defend his regime in 1994, the antagonists against the regime were local tribesmen. In Bahrain, the regime survived with the aid of the Saudi military, and in Libya, it was toppled with the assistance of NATO, but both interventions were by states, not transnational groups. The only recorded instances of non-Libyans who joined the rebels were a handful of non-Muslim Americans.

It was not until 2012, with the international community failing to intervene in the worsening civil war in Syria, that transnational foreign fighters became involved in the Arab Spring, with al Qaeda and its branch in Iraq sending militants and introducing suicide bombings into the conflict. Before them, nonjihadi rebels from neighboring Lebanon joined the fight to topple the Damascus regime they saw as interfering in their own country.

In North Africa, foreign mercenaries, including Tuareg tribesmen, formerly employed by the Gadhafi regime left Libya with its collapse and brought instability with them. Although Tuaregs in different Saharan states had been involved in local rebellions, they had not previously collaborated across national borders. In 2012, they augmented a Tuareg rebellion in Mali, carving out a large region that quickly became a haven for jihadis from al Qaeda in the Islamic Maghreb, based in Algeria, and farther abroad. Transnational jihadis were also reported to be working with the burgeoning Boko Haram insurgency in Nigeria.

No End in Sight in South Asia

Due to the colonial demarcation of Afghanistan, the Pashtun tribesmen who form the backbone of the Taliban have historically moved freely across the border with Pakistan, "about as casually as an American might travel between North and South Carolina" (Yousaf and Adkin, 1992: 37). Such combatants have been classified as foreign fighters, but any efforts to seal the border for security purposes would require establishing a policy on human movement that runs counter to local tradition.

Initially, the post-9/11 Taliban maintained its reliance on Arab leadership, but as the transnationals were gradually killed or lost influence, they were replaced by Afghan commanders. Still, as much as 10 percent of Taliban foot soldiers soon hailed from Pakistan, with the number continuing to rise since 2004. With estimates that more than 20 percent of Taliban casualties were Pakistanis, it became clear that the foreign fighters were once again engaging in deadlier attacks than the locals, being used as cannon fodder, or both (Giustozzi, 2008: 34, 35, 206, 207).

Meanwhile, with the reduction of violence in Iraq, "foreign militants were now flooding into Afghanistan to join Taliban insurgents." In part, foreign fighters may have selected Afghanistan because the greater instability provided a better opportunity to enter the country and make an impact.[5] Another element of the explanation might be that as American forces shifted from Iraq to Afghanistan, insurgents who had been indoctrinated to view themselves in a defensive global war sought to go where they could confront their adversary directly. Insurgent attacks in Afghanistan increased 33 percent in 2008, with military commanders reporting that "in some of these engagements, actually 60 percent of the total force which we have encountered were foreign fighters" (*International Herald Tribune*, 2009).

On the other side of Pakistan, insurgent groups in Jammu and Kashmir were also using foreign fighters to threaten stability on the front lines between two nuclear adversaries. The Lashkar e-Toiba ("Army of the Pure" or LET) was founded in 1980s Afghanistan with the goal of establishing Muslim rule throughout the Indian subcontinent, and its members have reportedly fought in Bosnia, Chechnya, and the Philippines as well. In December 2001, the LET attacked the Indian Parliament in New Delhi, with India blaming Pakistan and both states massing their armies along the Kashmiri border (Schweitzer and Shay, 2003: 76). In November 2008, the group moved farther from its area of operations, launching major terrorist attacks in Mumbai.

What would appear to be the lessons of the Texas Revolution have been implemented by other insurgent groups active in Kashmir, with the presence of foreign fighters an apparent predictor of a preference for violence rather than negotiation. Whereas other groups that rely on Kashmiri fighters have been willing to negotiate with India on the political status of the disputed territory, the Harakat ul-Mujadeen, which has recruited Afghans, Britons, and Arabs, is seen as less willing to compromise on its goal of a sharia state, and its leadership considers foreigners to be more effective insurgents because they are willing to attack civilian Kashmiris (Van Wagenen, 2004: 66).

Developments in Strategic Recruitment

This development, and the increasing use of foreigners as suicide bombers, indicates not only that recruiters are adaptive in their use of conflict framing but also that they learn lessons from their own experiences and those of other transnational insurgents with whom they cross-pollinate between different civil conflicts. One recently observed adaptation to the diverse range of locales and cultures encountered in the global jihad has been to send foreign fighters where they have ethnic ties for operational purposes, such as recruiters in the United Kingdom sending South Asians to Kashmir and Arabs to Iraq (Brandon, 2008: 7, 8). Another has been the use of the Internet for direct recruitment, not only in posting jihadi Web sites and videos of martyrdom operations but also in trolling chat rooms to engage potential recruits in discussions of Islam and obligations to the *ummah* and then directing them to encrypted sites from which they receive recruitment material and social pressure to volunteer. This technique was reportedly used to recruit 16-year-old California native Adam Gadahn, who would join al Qaeda in Pakistan and issue videos as Azzam the American (Weimann, in Ganor, Von Knopr, and Duarte, 2007: 50).

Another development is the decreased reliance on interpersonal networks generated through membership in formal organizations, such as the Communist Party or Zionist groups, exploited by twentieth-century insurgencies. In Arab states, many leaders of Islamist organizations have been imprisoned for their activities, and those who have been tortured and released are often not anxious to resume their activities, leaving a vacuum that has been filled by transnational neofundamentalists (Gerges, 2005: 162). Instead, recruiters now rely on the social networks of the recruits themselves.

In part, this is because of the shift to mass media dissemination of messaging and self-starter militants; however, many recruits in do not live in countries with widespread Internet access. In fact, the Sinjar files indicate that among foreign fighters few transnational volunteers are online and instead are recruited by friends and social acquaintances, rather than through family or religious institutional ties. Most of these connections (an estimated 70 to 80 percent) are veteran foreign fighters who have returned home as respected figures in their communities and who have direct knowledge of the channels necessary for getting recruits to the front lines[6] (Watts, 2008: 1–6).

Preexisting ties to identity groups are therefore still essential components for recruiters. Social networks provide access to the resources that facilitate message dissemination and transportation to the conflict zone, and they also permit application of social pressure to individuals who are accompanying their friends. Trusted acquaintances reinforce the acceptability of insurgent activity and make it more difficult for recruits to abandon their comrades by refusing to travel or fight. For this reason, jihadi groups have also moved to target sports teams for recruitment—being partially successful in the effort to bring an entire soccer squad to Iraq (Hafez, 2007: 22, 23, 177, 202).

Why Are Many Foreign Fighters Now Muslims?

Whether recruiters seek them on football fields or in chat rooms, the identity community used to motivate transnational insurgents in nearly all prominent contemporary cases is the Muslim *ummah*.[7] Although some works (Sageman, 2004; Moore and Tumelty, 2008; Hafez, 2009; Hegghammer, 2010) have equated mujahidin with Spanish Civil War volunteers, these are single-sentence comparisons in the introductory sections of works devoted to particular cases of jihadis. The historical data presented in this project, however, indicate that the recruitment of foreign fighters—from locating potential recruits to conflict framing to their dispatch into battle—is essentially equivalent across cases, regardless of the issue of contention of the conflict. In modern history, transnational insurgencies have been based on various ties of ethnonationalism and ideology, but contemporary foreign fighters in conflicts around the globe now appear to overwhelmingly share the same religious identity.

There is nothing in the data to suggest any intrinsic features of Islam or Muslim communities that should make this so. Rather, the cause appears to be partly the result of a period effect, the coincidence of increasingly globalized communications and transportation technology with a particular identity community whose members have transnational identities that are currently particularly salient. In the first half of the twentieth century, most foreign fighters were members of Communist groups. In the late nineteenth century, the feared perpetrators of transnational violence were anarchists (the *Economist*, 2005). In both of these waves, the militants and insurgents shared a key common trait with mujahidin today: Transnational ideological affiliation was a highly salient identity because immigration and modernization had destroyed other communal ties and produced isolated, embattled individuals ripe for recruitment by movements that spoke to their particular fears.

Omar Nasiri (2006: 2), a former jihadi, describes his old colleagues as "men who had no home. Men reviled in the West because they were not white and Christian, and reviled at home because they no longer dressed and spoke like Muslims." Unprecedented waves of emigration by Muslims to the West deterritorialized the *ummah*, reinventing what it means to be Muslim and what constitutes Muslim lands. Also, Wahhabism and other forms of strict Islam are now offered through the Internet and a global network of madrasas, making national citizenship less consequential as a dividing characteristic of social practices. These same institutions also challenge traditional cultural arrangements as un-Islamic, leaving a transnational Islamic identity as the only alternative between the shunning, alien West and nearly equally closed former home societies. For this reason, many violent neofundamentalists, and an increasing number of foreign fighters, come from Western countries rather than the Middle East. Neofundamentalism has flourished because it has already addressed (and rejected) Westernization and provided a competing alternative—one that recruiters claim is threatened. Roy argues that once founding generations of Muslim immigrants are inevitably assimilated, transnational recruitment, funding, and Web site development will fade (2004: 2, 18, 120–125, 234, 324).

Clifford Geertz (1963) described the ideologization of religion as a response to a *lack* of faith because traditional structures that provide meaning and value are collapsing (Overby, 1993: 190). It is notable that most Islamist foreign fighters, beginning with Abdullah Azzam, do not return to their homelands to fight for Muslims there. They do not hope to reshape their lost societies of origin; rather, they go to the peripheries of the *ummah*, to devastated conflict zones or desolate failed states where cultural and governmental institutions are weak and they stand a greater chance of building a theologically correct society when they have defeated the oppressor: "Radical militant jihadists fight at the frontier to protect a center where they have no place. They fight not to protect a territory but to recreate a community.... Contemporary mujahidin are pessimistic because they know that there is no longer a fortress to protect, that the enemy is in the fortress" (Roy, 2004: 289, 305, 313).

What Can We Learn from the Historical Cases?

It is evident that little is novel about the recruitment of foreign fighters in contemporary civil conflicts, except perhaps that the use of the Internet has shifted the importance of social organizations from recruitment venues to means of facilitating mobilization. The four historical case studies demonstrated strikingly consistent patterns of target audience selection, framing and messaging, mobilization mechanisms, and relative disharmony in the field between local and transnational insurgents. Similar patterns should be observable in other historical cases, and these consistencies would be hallmarks of modern and future instances of transnational insurgency as well.

The observation set data presented in chapter 2 indicate that transnational insurgencies are disproportionately successful, winning nearly as many wars as they lose, as compared with insurgencies overall, which lose by more than a 2:1 ratio. The population of cases is too small to establish meaningful statistical significance, and the evidence is likewise insufficient to argue causation rather than correlation. It may simply be the case that insurgencies that are sufficiently organized to recruit transnationally are better positioned to win regardless.

The foreign fighters in the four historical cases all made impacts, some in more direct ways than others. The intransigence of the foreign fighters in Texas was a major reason that the rebel forces succeeded in capturing San Antonio de Béxar at the end of 1835, and their defeats and subsequent summary executions at the Alamo and Goliad turned international public opinion in favor of Texan sovereignty. Similarly, the International Brigades suffered heavy casualties in their ultimately futile effort to prevent the ascension of the Axis powers, but their efforts likely prolonged the Spanish Civil War by more than two years and forced the depleted Franco regime to remain neutral during World War II. The foreign recruits on the winning Nationalist side made far less meaningful contributions, with the largest contingent withdrawing after engaging in just one battle (against their own side). Israel eventually credited its transnationally recruited volunteers, particularly the pilots, with a vital role in winning independence, while the defeated Arab Liberation Army still proved a more effective opposition than local militias. It is widely believed that the Arab Afghans made little direct military contribution to the outcome of their initial war, but they became an effective fighting force in Bosnia, considered valuable by the Sarajevo government, and alumni continue to play significant roles in conflicts elsewhere. Foreign fighters are consequential factors in civil conflicts, and the fact that they are responsible for higher levels of violence in Iraq (as described in the introduction) is not surprising in the broader historical context of transnationals who view themselves as fighting desperate defensive struggles.

In each case, recruiters exploited the structures of existing social networks and organizations that tied pools of potential recruits to each other and to the local insurgents. These ranged from leadership figures in local communities (in the cases of Texas and both 1940s and contemporary Arab recruits) to religious institutions (Afghanistan) to ideological organizations such as Communist Party chapters (Spain) to ethnic community clubs (Israel). The social ties fostered through these structures provided both the rationale and the means of recruitment: Membership in these communities generally provided a highly salient source of identity to targeted recruits, who otherwise tended to be members of oppressed minority groups or economically marginalized and therefore not active as citizens within their broader national polities.

It seems surprising that few foreign fighter insurgencies have been connected to ethnic diasporas when kinship presents the strongest set of ties, encompassing family as well as community institutions. And yet from Kurds to Tamils, in most ethnic conflicts, diaspora communities send financial assistance rather than foreign fighters—guns but not sons. The phenomenon reinforces the necessity of recruiters employing the frame of existential threat, with ethnic conflicts involving at least the credible threat of genocide being those where foreign fighters appear.

Regardless of the nature of the identity shared (or constructed, in the case of the antifascists of the 1930s), recruiters consistently frame the distant civil conflict as an eventual threat to the entire transnational community group, and they inform recruits that their own government is blind to the threat; it is therefore both their duty and in their self-interest to fight now while there is still time. This message of defensive mobilization is a constant across cases. What varies is how recruiters frame their relation to the target audience. If their initial approach is unsuccessful because it generates too few recruits (Texas) or the recruiters want to avoid sacrificing existing community members (the 1930s Comintern), the insurgents reframe the conflict as having a different central issue of contention that affects a broader potential audience.

The messaging of the need for defense frequently emphasizes the protection of women in the community (present in all cases) utilizing norms of social obligation within the groups. Women usually feature in atrocity propaganda that graphically portrays the necessity of intervention and the consequences in store for the transnational population if the threat is not checked and spreads. The arrest and prevention of other such attacks makes assuming the high risks and costs of participation a highly rational strategy that overcomes barriers to collective action without the need for large amounts of material compensation.

Even in cases when victorious recruits were entitled to land (Texas) or assistance with business opportunities (Israel), significant percentages or even large majorities of the volunteers passed on the opportunities and simply returned home. In part, this may have been because their difficult experiences in the field and conflict with local insurgents disenchanted a number of foreign fighters (all cases), but it may also have been because the main objective communicated by recruiters was the necessity of stopping atrocities against their own kind. The spread of private, global communications through the Internet has made it easier to broadcast atrocity imagery to self-selecting audiences: Instead of sneaking close-ups of corpses into theatrically released propaganda films (such as Ivens and Hemingway's 1937 *The Spanish Earth*), far more graphic portrayals of threat are disseminated via various projihadi Web sites.

Managing the Transnational Future

There is another reason that the vast majority of foreign fighters today are Islamists: As noted in the previous chapter, after the conclusion of the 1980s round of civil war in Afghanistan, mujahidin were refused entry or persecuted by home governments that feared they would continue their jihadist activities rather than settle down to normal daily lives. The fact that virtually all foreign fighters in Texas, Spain, and Israel-Palestine, even those who had previously been involved in contentious politics, reintegrated into civilian life in their home countries is an indication that this policy actually perpetuated the jihad and contributed to its global diffusion. Both Muslim Brothers and Communist revolutionaries in prior decades were perceived as legitimate revolutionary threats by their home governments, and yet they were reclaimed rather than left to further organize transnationally. A similar comparison may be drawn with the nineteenth-century anarchists who were also exiled by their governments and traveled between different underground groups, becoming "connectors" who passed along best practices to violent activists in other countries (Aydinli, 2008: 909).

Current Approaches

As indicated by the debate over the closure of the detention facility at Guantánamo Bay, which houses a number of transnational insurgents that few states seem willing to accept upon release, mitigating levels of transnational violence is not a simple matter of amnesty. Even the jihadi rehabilitation programs attempted by Saudi Arabia, Yemen, and other states have yielded decidedly mixed results both at home and abroad, where three graduates of the

Yemeni program were killed fighting in Somalia (Johnsen and Boucek, 2008: 1–4).

The United States attempted to limit foreign fighter entry to Iraq by controlling key crossing points. In some areas, bulldozers were used to build berms of sand to serve as physical barriers. Another strategy was targeting the Syrian smugglers who brought transnational recruits across the border. Unlike the Comintern and Haganah, al Qaeda in Iraq and other insurgent groups left foreign volunteers to provide their own transportation and outsourced the final stage to experienced border runners. There is some evidence of distrust between the two parties to the transaction: Al Qaeda asked foreign recruits to rate the service provided by the smugglers and report just how much money they were ultimately charged (Felter and Fishman, 2007: 25–27). While such weak supply chains do present obvious counterinsurgency (COIN) possibilities for co-opting paid smugglers, the U.S. record in interdicting drugs and immigrants entering its own borders (and preventing recruits from leaving for past foreign wars) does not bode well for a policing approach to other conflicts, especially where border conditions are even less manageable.

Other states have taken different approaches to limiting the supply of foreign fighters with varying degrees of success. Russia has targeted key Arab Chechens for assassination to disrupt leadership and recruitment networks, with some reported success (Moore and Tumelty, 2008: 427). With China and several Central Asian republics, Russia also formed the Shanghai Cooperation Organization in 2001, in part to coordinate efforts directed against transnational insurgency and terrorism (Rashid, 2002: 202). The Netherlands adopted a different tack, providing counseling and employment to dislocated Muslim immigrants to better integrate them into Dutch society and reduce the influence of militant groups that also offer social services (Ministerie van BZK, 2002: 14–15). But the subsequent suicide bombing attack in Iraq by a Dutch-born woman who converted to Islam demonstrates that, like transnational violence in the Caucasus, no approach will stop every determined insurgent (Rotella, 2006).

Policy Recommendations: Lessons of History

In the case of foreign fighters, the genie is out of the bottle: They fill a recognized political role, their effective practices serve as models for emulators and are self-consciously replicated, and the data indicate that they are relatively successful and that their numbers are on the increase. State and international laws have not prevented them, and norms of national citizenship grow weaker as the number and proportion of insurgencies that go transnational rise. Given that both historic and contemporary foreign fighters have been responsible for greater levels of violence and for prolonging conflicts—whether for good or bad causes—states that engage in COIN operations have understandable motives for preventing the transnationalization of civil conflicts.

The first lesson from the historical record is that insurgencies use the same type of messaging for all types of foreign fighters, regardless of whether they are coethnic with the local insurgents or share some other affiliation, and regardless of the issue of contention in the civil conflict. The shared identity communities—whether religious, ideological, or nationalist—through which recruits identify with distant insurgents provide the social structures that enable dissemination of recruitment messages and permit the mobilization of foreign fighters. Most recruits are already highly active members of these institutions but are marginalized within their broader polities. These shared transnational identities and the duties that come with roles as members of the community are therefore highly salient to the recruits, more so than ties of national citizenship.

This consistent pattern of foreign fighter recruitment messaging and mobilization across all types of cases carries useful implications for COIN planning. If insurgencies recruit foreign fighters by persuading them that they face a potentially existential threat as a member of a particular group, then threatening them still further with punitive measures or force is unlikely to deter them from mobilizing. On the contrary, doing so would support the frame of threat and might make high-risk, high-cost behavior seem even more necessary to forestall greater losses.

Likewise, maintaining a high force profile in conflict zones as a deterrent against insurgents is also likely to provide fodder for recruitment propaganda. Although there are valid strategic reasons for establishing forward military bases and force projection, and large numbers of personnel are necessary on the ground in successful COIN operations, efforts to use these practices to discourage foreign fighter interest in particular conflict zones are likely to fail.

A more effective approach would be to shift emphasis to preventing recruitment in the first place, and the historical data suggest two avenues for attempting to do so. The first possibility, and the second lesson of history for policy makers, concerns the enhancement of law enforcement efforts in disrupting the recruitment and mobilization process. Targeting particular identity groups for surveillance and infiltration invites charges of prejudice, whether they are Muslims today or the Jewish Americans of the 1940s who were refused passports to limit the possibility that they would join the fight for Israel's independence.

Nonetheless, homeland security requirements and COIN efforts require identification of targets for intelligence gathering. The data from the historical cases indicate relatively consistent demographic information that can be used to establish a profile of likely recruits that does not distinguish between the particulars of different identity groups and offers some antidiscrimination protection. Recruiters find foreign fighters among men who are in their early 20s and are first- or second-generation immigrants. Typically, they come from lower socioeconomic status backgrounds, and available information suggests broken homes feature prominently, perhaps indicating why membership in community groups is so salient to them. Older recruits are targeted because of their prior military experience; younger recruits are enthusiastic members of the organizations that tie them to the distant insurgents and through which they are contacted by recruiters. Most recruits do not see themselves as mercenaries; instead, they genuinely believe that they are fighting in a defensive war rather than an elective war.

Recruiters strategically employ frames and emotive imagery designed to stimulate outrage and fear. They offer appeals to defend transnational communities because they believe that they can make obligations to these groups more salient to the recruits than their duties as citizens, which in most countries include a proscription against foreign military service. Usually this is not a difficult pitch to make because recruiters have selected potential targets among groups that serve as alternatives to civic participation for the disaffected poor or minorities.

Therefore, the third policy implication that can be drawn from historical cases is that the ultimate solution to foreign fighter recruitment is to diminish the salience of the transnational groups through which recruitment is conducted. Identities are built through the structures of social transactions that provide roles in relation to other members of the group. Roles generate expected norms of behavior that influence decision making, including duty to the group. More contact through these social channels strengthens the salience of particular identities and connections with other members. Foreign fighter recruits tend to be active in subcultures and are willing to fight for them because they identify more closely with other members abroad than they do with fellow citizens of the country in which they reside.

Preventing recruitment would therefore be a question of reducing the centrality of transnational groups as social structures in the lives of the recruits and replacing them with institutions of citizenship instead. Rather than attempting to suppress any group, a misguided approach that would surely backfire and generate recognition of threat, the alternative is to build the appeal of national civil and military institutions to facilitate greater identification with the state and fellow citizens.

Although some view nationalism as a threatening phenomenon, it presents an alternative to transnationalism, and it is not necessary to fight fire with fire. The Arab Spring of 2011—reminiscent of the cascading democratic and nationalist revolutions of the nineteenth century—and the absence of a jihadi presence within it during the first year of upheavals illustrates that the perception of the possibility of efficacy through national civil society obviates the appeal of transnational civil society groups that claim that they alone are capable of bringing justice.

Likewise, the U.S. military is held up as a benign and effective social leveler, muting divisions in ethnicity and class among members of the armed forces even after their service has concluded; COIN planners should consider efforts to build effective government agencies and professionalize the militaries in targeted states that produce significant numbers of foreign fighters. This form of soft power cooperation might even be viewed as beneficence by some otherwise potential recruits.

The Future of Foreign Fighters

This study has presented the potential for increased levels of international violence posed by the growing propensity for insurgencies to recruit transnationally. It has also demonstrated that foreign fighters are not a new phenomenon and that most recruits are neither mercenaries nor fanatics bent on domination. Rather than for greed, most mobilize in response to perceived threat. Recruits may have their own motives of adventure, vindication of the group, or simply lack of a better alternative opportunity, but recruiters across highly varied conflicts in time and space consistently use the same frame of defensive mobilization.

Globalization and the success of past foreign fighter–driven rebel groups are increasing the probability that insurgencies will transnationalize their violence in an effort to tip the balance of forces enough to win their civil conflicts. These efforts are desperation ploys attempted when the insurgencies are not strong enough to win on their own and are unable to obtain sufficient assistance from a friendly foreign state. Foreign fighters in these instances are responsible for higher levels of violence because they believe that their people are fighting a losing struggle for survival and because they do not have their own assets and families in the area to protect. Rather than confronting them in the field or attempting to disrupt their mobilization, establishing alternate identities for them as citizens would best remove the rationale for their participation.

Increasing numbers of foreign fighters are a cause for concern, not alarm. Indeed, a number of transnational volunteers fought what would widely be considered "the good fight" against even greater evils, and their members are acclaimed as heroes. In either case, transnational insurgencies have been with us for a long time and appear likely to be factors in civil conflicts for the foreseeable future. When examined as a broad phenomenon, the consistent logic behind recruitment is apparent and suggests counterstrategies. It is to the benefit of the recruits, the states they fight, and the civilians caught in between to understand why they really fight and to use this information to identify the routes to peace.

APPENDIX A

Development of the Term Foreign Fighter

ALTHOUGH TRANSNATIONAL INSURGENCIES have existed for centuries, the fact that they have not been perceived as a singular type of phenomenon by political scientists is evident from the lack of any existing term in the discipline used to describe the concept. As the survey of theoretical literature in chapter 1 demonstrates, there has been no recognition of this particular type of actor in civil conflicts, despite successive generations of transnational insurgents attempting to legitimize their activities by directly comparing their actions to those taken by other foreigner rebels in other wars.[1] The term *foreign fighter* is used here because it is widely employed in popular media reports, primarily concerning jihadis, and appears to generate greater recognition of the concept it describes than does any more jargon-laden term attempted in its stead.

But if the term carries currency in relation to current events, it should be possible to map its diffusion as a constitutive tool for understanding the actors it describes. The adoption of the concept of the foreign fighter carries two significant implications. The first is that the very act of recognition indicates that there is something unexpected or extraordinary in the presence of a foreigner in a conflict. Egyptians, Algerians, or Pakistanis fighting as insurgents in Iraq are not presumed to be the same as Iraqi insurgents fighting in Iraq. The second is that the term is generalizable, carrying the same meaning for Saudi insurgents in Afghanistan as for Moroccan insurgents in Iraq because the type of actors and their functions are presumed to be similar enough to warrant categorization. But where and when did our concept of the foreign fighter emerge?

A Lexis-Nexis database search for the origin of the term in media use yields not answers, but interesting patterns. Prior to 1988, and continuing through the 2001 invasion of Afghanistan, a reference to a foreign fighter in a news article was more likely to concern a professional boxer or military aircraft. In fact, the first relevant appearance of the term, in a 1983 broadcast by the state Iraqi News Agency, was an announcement that the growing ranks of the Popular Army domestic militia needed "no foreign fighters or volunteers," presumably in contrast to the anti-Baathist SCIRI then operating in southern Iraq with the assistance of Iranian fellow Shiites.

However, the first use of the term to describe a foreign insurgent appeared in a headline published on March 21, 1988, by the *Times* of London covering a story about a victory by Afghan mujahidin "aided by Saudi, Egyptian and Pakistani fighters" against pro-Soviet government forces: "Khost Outpost Falls to Mujahidin Led by Foreign Fighters" (Gorman, 1988). An article the following year in the *Independent* reported on South Africa's 32 Battalion, which had formed around the nucleus of Angolan FNLA rebels in exile (Dowden, 1989).

Subsequent mentions of rebel foreign fighters through 1992 all appeared in British newspaper articles concerning "the growing number of foreign fighters" with Croatian separatist forces against the Yugoslav central government. A 1991 report noted the rise of "Black Legions" that included more than 100 Europeans of various nationalities. The British adventure seekers and Iberian former newspaper correspondents were reported to earn 59 pounds a month, as compared with the former French Foreign Legionnaires, "who received serious money to train Croat forces" (Tanner, 1991).

Comparisons with a prior transnational insurgency emerged the following year. One report claimed that "the Yugoslavian civil war has more foreign fighters involved than any conflict since the Spanish Civil War. Unlike the International Brigade…the English fighting in Yugoslavia are not there to preserve liberty," but were "mercenaries" escaping dead-end lives to earn "100 pounds per month and an inspiration" (*Evening Standard*, 1992). Ted Skinner, a British volunteer, told a reporter before he was killed by Serb paramilitaries that the situation was analogous to German expansionism during the Spanish Civil War, arguing, "If they get away with it in Bosnia, who's to say they won't in Kosovo?" (LeBor, 1993).

In 1993, the *New York Times* quoted an Indian security official as estimating that "the total figure [of foreign fighters in Kashmir] is about 400," including 200 Afghans (Hazarika, 1993). That same year, the *Toronto Star* covered the conflict in Bosnia, noting that "military units on all sides of the barricades have eagerly recruited foreign fighters"[2] (Bugjaski, 1993).

Although the concept had clearly come to represent the same thing regardless of the particular conflict, location, or issue of contention, there were only nine uses of the term in this context in media reports between 1988 and 1993. Although the appellation began to be employed by reporters covering Chechnya as well (Deutsche Presse-Agentur, 1994) and received more mentions due to American insistence that mujahidin leave Bosnia as part of the 1995 Dayton Peace Accords, the term appeared only another 39 times in the global media between the beginning of 1994 and September 10, 2001.

The first post-9/11 mention appears in the Lexis-Nexis database on September 15,

2001, noting the dilemma faced by Taliban officials contemplating turning over Osama bin Laden to the United States and risking the wrath of "thousands of foreign fighters indispensable in their war against the Northern Alliance" (Associated Press, September 15, 2001). By October 15, 2001, there had still been only five more appearances of the term, despite the preparations of the international community to confront al Qaeda forces in Afghanistan.

But by the end of the year, the term *foreign fighter* had appeared at least 313 times. What brought it into popular currency was the aftermath of the Battle of Kunduz on November 27, 2001, in which "thousands of Afghan Taliban fighters who gave up were allowed safe passage out," while "under the terms of the Kunduz surrender, foreign fighters were to be imprisoned in the town's jail pending an investigation of their links with bin Laden" (Associated Press, November 27, 2001). Therefore, although American military operations had not created the identity and role of the foreign fighter, by publicly distinguishing transnational from local combatants, they did highlight it and give it a context particular to current geopolitics. Following the end of hostilities at Kunduz, the term appeared 102 times in major world newspapers during 2002, all references to foreign Muslim insurgents in locations from Kashmir to Georgia.

The invasion of Iraq was even more significant in entrenching this concept in the public consciousness than the routing of the Taliban and al Qaeda in Afghanistan. In early 2003, prior to the launch of the assault by Coalition forces on March 19, the term appeared 17 times; by the end of the year, it appeared another 660 times. It appeared more than 1,000 times in each subsequent year. The explosion of coverage in major world newspapers both creates and reinforces awareness of the role of the foreign fighter as one to be assumed in any manner of insurgency, and the anecdotal evidence indicates that foreign fighters indeed conceptualize themselves as carrying on the activities of prior transnational insurgents.

APPENDIX B

Observation Set Coding

THE DATA CONSIST of several items of relevant information about each recorded civil conflict and insurgency. I use this information to establish the population of foreign fighter insurgencies, as well as a typology of foreign fighters that permits the formation of hypotheses on the effects of key variables and the causal paths by which message dissemination and recruitment occurred (George and Bennett, 2004: 69, 235). Collier, Brady, and Seawright (in Brady and Collier, 2004: 250–255) describe this collection of "all the numbers for one case" as an "observation" and note that "dataset observations" may be combined with additional information found in "causal process observations." I therefore term the universe of potential cases with sets of observations on recorded civil conflicts as the *observation set*, and it forms the basis of case selection for stage 2, which analyzes recruitment messages.

By using existing data sets to build the observation set, I avoid selecting on the dependent variable and demonstrate the prevalence of foreign fighters among all civil conflicts and under which conditions they appear most likely to occur. To obtain the largest and most accurate number of observations, I combined the Correlates of War (COW) Intrastate War 1816–1997 and the Uppsala-PRIO Intrastate Conflict 1946–2005 data sets to create an inclusive list of civil conflicts since the entrenchment of the modern international system with the establishment of the Concert of Europe.

Still, the two data sets proved limiting as well. The earliest data points are contained in the Correlates of War Intrastate War set, which begins in 1816. This juncture does not limit the findings significantly because, as noted, prior to the Napoleonic Wars, norms of citizenship and military service were not comparable to those of the modern period. But a number of other conflicts for which evidence is available (for example, the wars of liberation in South America in which thousands of British fought for Simón Bolívar during the 1810s and 1820s) are not in either set and must therefore be excluded. The periodically updated data set is available at www.foreignfighter.com and, as COW and PRIO also regularly update their data sets, fresh appearances of foreign fighters will be available for addition to the observation set.

Both COW and PRIO have thresholds of 1,000 battle deaths for inclusion. Although COW is restricted to battlefield fatalities, PRIO's criteria for inclusion include civilian deaths. I have eliminated redundant reporting between the two sets so that particular conflicts are not counted twice. This step proved to be more difficult than I expected because both data sets included multiple entries for a number of conflicts by different stages, such as fresh outbreaks of violence after several months of peace or the introduction of a new faction of combatants. Retaining these existing distinctions proved significant to coding efforts because different phases of civil conflicts had different issues of contention. Afghanistan, for example, went from a war of national liberation against the Soviet Red Army and its puppet government to a battle between local factions without an overarching ethnic component.

Coding Rules

I defined a *foreign fighter* as a member of an insurgency who is not a citizen of the state in which a civil conflict occurs, has traveled for the purpose of becoming an armed belligerent in an intrastate conflict, and is not in the employ of a regular state military force. This definition includes foreign volunteers in irregular militias but excludes both state foreign legions and private security companies that have either been hired directly by states or by state-sanctioned private firms operating in conflict zones.

I coded conflicts singly rather than by year but list them in different iterations when the factions change. For example, Afghanistan has been in a state of civil war involving Islamist insurgents since the 1970s but has had three completely different incumbent regimes during this time (Soviet-backed Communists, an attempted indigenous national government, and the U.S.-backed Karzai administration), so it was logical to list each phase of the conflict separately.

Coding conflicts as ethnic or nonethnic is also potentially contentious. I relied on Kalyvas's (2006: 365) observation that, while the process is often far more complicated: "Civil wars are typically described, classified, and understood on the basis of what is perceived to be their overarching cleavage dimensions." The particulars of each case in which foreign fighters could be observed determined whether a conflict was coded as ethnic. For example, 1980s Afghanistan was an ethnic conflict based on records indicating that repelling the Soviet invasion was the primary objective of the insurgents (Yousaf and Adkin, 1992: 2), whereas in 2000s Iraq, the primary targets of attacks were not Coalition forces, but rather local security forces and Shia civilians (Hafez, 2007: 5). But ultimately no nominalist categorizations will be incontrovertible.

I conducted background research on each of the 331 civil conflicts in the combined observation set, using Internet search engines and online newspaper archives, including Keesing's and LexisNexis, for evidence of foreign fighters among the insurgents. Limitations on the available data no doubt mean that there were conflicts in which transnational recruits appeared that I was unable to capture and that there is an even larger population of transnational insurgencies than recorded.

Even in the best documented cases, such as the Spanish Civil War, there is wide and active disagreement about the number of foreign fighters who participated, and I therefore coded the presence of foreign fighters in each civil conflict in a binary fashion, with a 0 representing no available evidence of any foreign fighters in that conflict and a 1 representing documented evidence of their presence. Although the best available estimate of the number of foreign fighters present in each observation is recorded, the unreliability of the figures in most circumstances mitigates against attempting accurate inferences. Part of the reason for the dearth of reliable data is the lack of transparent or verifiable record keeping by the insurgencies themselves.

Another is the incentives for both sides in the conflict to lie about the appeal or strength of the insurgents. For example, estimates of the number of mujahidin in 1980s Afghanistan varied by an order of magnitude from 50,000 to more than half a million. More recent histories claim numbers only in the hundreds or low thousands. The conflicts are therefore simply coded by whether foreign fighters are known to have been present, whether there were 20 or 20,000. Similarly, because of the difficulty in gathering reliable data, I have made no attempts to code transnational insurgents in this broad study by whether they participated in combat operations or some other form of support.

Categories Coded

I include a number of variables from the existing data sets that relate directly to the two hypotheses tested, while others control for potential extraneous factors and provide additional data about trends in transnational insurgencies. The variables imported from the existing sets include the date range of the conflict, geographical region, and outcome. I combine the original data sets' categories coding issue of contention to classify each conflict as either ethnic or nonethnic and also code whether foreign fighters were present and, if so, whether they were predominantly of the same ethnic group as the local insurgents and whether they appear to have been mainly cross-border participants or if they had to travel from other states more distant to the conflict.

I have also listed the approximate numbers or ranges of the numbers of foreign fighters reported present in each observation, with a notation where no information is currently available. These data, along with any correlation between presence of foreign fighters and the length of the conflict, are not directly relevant to my research question but are included in the observation set because they may be of use in future studies. To this end, I have standardized the data between the two sets. For example, COW provides the variable "Winner," with seven different possible outcomes of a civil conflict, which I have reduced to four, using the same criteria, and applied to the PRIO observations as well. The COW conflicts that were settled after the 1998 cutoff of the data set have also been updated.

Evidentiary Standards

As there is currently no other available comparative list of instances of foreign fighters beyond jihadi Islamists, this study draws on an extremely wide array of source material to examine and document the hundreds of civil conflicts contained in the combined data set. As noted, because the participants in civil conflicts might actually be the parties least likely to keep accurate records, there is no premium on original sources to establish either the presence or numbers of foreign fighters in a conflict. All instances where foreign fighters are reported to be present in a civil conflict are checked against available sources, primarily to establish presence but also to determine ranges of numbers, states of origin, casualties, and other data that might be recorded.

Typology

To test the hypothesis that foreign fighters are more likely to appear in nonethnic than ethnic civil conflicts, each conflict is coded as ethnic or nonethnic (1 or 0). While there is no formal consensus on the criteria for an ethnic civil war, Sambanis's (2001) definition of *ethnic conflict* as one for self-determination rights for a nation or ethnic group is employed here. This distinction is relevant because of observations in which foreigners who were not coethnics intervened in ethnonationalist rebellions, for instance, Islamists in Chechnya.

Notes

INTRODUCTION

1. Although his father told the press that Elomar had been "brainwashed" by a radical cleric, he was released the following month for lack of evidence. In October 2009, his uncle and four codefendants were convicted of plotting the largest terrorist attack in Australian history.

2. Examples include Paz (2005), Krueger (2007), Hafez (2007), Felter and Fishman (2007), Watts (2008), and Hewitt and Kelly-Moore (2009). Moore and Tumelty (2008) examine the fielding of foreign fighters in Chechnya. Hegghammer (2010) provides an overview of jihadi foreign fighters but examines them as a single movement rather than differentiating between mobilization processes in the various individual conflicts.

3. My gratitude to Robert Stoker for succinctly expressing this parallel when I described this project to him.

4. That is, Machalniks in 1948 Israel compared themselves with the International Brigades in the Spanish Civil War, whose members had compared themselves with the English and French who fought in the Greek and American wars of independence, respectively. Contemporary jihadis refer openly to mujahidin in 1980s Afghanistan, and so on.

5. Staniland (2005) and Salehyan (2009) use the term *transnational insurgency* to describe locally based insurgencies that obtained cross-border resources or safe havens, such as the Vietcong, or groups such as the Tamil Tigers and IRA that received funding from diasporas abroad.

CHAPTER 1

1. Byron, the link between "radical reformers at home and the romantic crusaders in the field," led efforts in Great Britain to recruit volunteers and raise funds for the transnational Philiki Etaireia faction in the Greek War of Independence (1821–1829). While other notables, including political philosopher Jeremy Bentham, aided

Philhellene publicity, Byron actually fought and died in the siege of Messolonghi in 1824 (Woodhouse, 1971: 71, 90, 114–118).

2. Emperor Henry IV, for example, had a number of peasants who rallied to his cause during an invasion castrated afterward to reinforce this division.

3. Elsewhere, converts to Islam have also joined violent groups affiliated with their religious identity that operate at the expense of their state. In 2005, in the Netherlands, former police officer Martine van der Oeven was arrested in conjunction with assassination plots against prominent Dutch political and media figures. The same year, a Belgian woman named Muriel Degauque became the first suicide bomber in Iraq who was a female convert of Western origins when she drove a vehicle loaded with explosives into an American military convoy (Rotella, 2006).

4. For example, members of Hmong and other Southeast Asian expatriate communities in California have been implicated in a number of terrorist and paramilitary plots directed against the Communist governments of their homelands, including running training camps in the United States for forces preparing for infiltration. In June 2007, an elderly Laotian community activist was indicted for attempting to procure Stinger missiles and heavy armaments for a planned squad of foreign fighters (Powers, 2007).

5. Moore and Tumlety (2008: 23) contend that foreign fighters did not *become* jihadis in Chechnya, but rather they went to Chechnya because they already saw themselves as jihadis and fulfilled their own expectations for the role.

6. Modern state laws against foreign military service originated with the U.S. Neutrality Act in 1794, but it was not until the twentieth century that the cascading norm of binding sovereignty resulted in legal measures in the majority of countries in the international system (Thomson, 1994).

CHAPTER 2

1. The current Order of the Knights Templar is a transnational Masonic fraternity that claims no direct continuity with its historical forebear, which existed 1119–1307. Another Templar-inspired group, the Sovereign Military Order of the Temple of Jerusalem, was founded as a transnational charitable organization in 1804 and accredited as a nongovernmental organization (NGO) by the UN in 2001. The Order of Saint John, chartered in 1113, controlled Rhodes, Tripoli, and Smyrna at various times during the Middle Ages. From 1530 to 1798, it held sovereignty over Malta before being ejected by Napoleon and the superior forces of the French state. The order continues today as a transnational charitable organization with a stated membership of 11,000 across 37 countries.

2. In addition to well-known names like Lafayette and L'Enfant, there were more than 100 such French officers in the rebel American forces. A number of other nobility heeded the call as well, although apparently not all were qualified and a number could not speak English. Congress accepted some recruits but sent the others back, paying their fare both ways.

3. The U.S. Department of State: "Although the United States opposes service by U.S. citizens in foreign armed forces, there is little we can do to prevent it since each sovereign country has the right to make its own laws on military service.... The current laws are set forth in Section 958–960 of Title 18 of the United States Code...." Loss of citizenship may occur if an individual serves "in the armed forces of any foreign country as a commissioned or non-commissioned officer" or "voluntarily and with the intention of relinquishing U.S. citizenship enters or serves in foreign armed forces engaged in hostilities against the United States."

4. Interestingly, the other side was presumed to be bringing in more formidable help: "The growing numbers of foreign fighters in Croatia has led to tales in the Belgrade press of German ex-Nazis emerging from hideouts in South America to settle scores with their old Serbian foes" (Tanner, 1991).

5. In the years leading up to World War II, fliers seemed to enjoy a special license in public acceptance to serve in distant conflicts, perhaps because of romanticism surrounding those treated as new knights of the air. The cases mentioned here were probably among those inspiring numerous comic book multinational pilot squadrons. *Military Comics* #1 (August 1941) alone featured the Polish-led Blackhawks, with separate stories of volunteer American fliers fighting evildoers in China and Ethiopia. Disney's 2001 film *Pearl Harbor* likewise depicts an American volunteer in the British Royal Air Force as heroic, not disloyal.

6. Civil wars, in which insurgencies are the rebels, are typically defined as conflicts in which at least 1,000 deaths occurred. See appendix B for detailed information on case selection and coding.

7. There are obvious pitfalls to labeling a wide panoply of transnational groups as coethnic or coreligionists. Sociologists recognize the potential pitfalls of determining the influence of identity groups as nominalists, that is, imposing labels on them to meet the researcher's analytic requirements regardless of their independent ontological status. Alternatively, the realist approach is to determine the meaningfulness of a network to its members by just how much identity it produces. In this sense, the boundaries of membership in a group are positional, meaning members share some attribute such as all attending the same school or participating in some activity. Indeed, it is interaction that is measured as defining the boundaries of a network, with the frequency of activity determining the strength of the tie. Pfeffer and Salancik (1978: 32) argued that the boundary of membership is where the decision-making discretion of an organization supersedes that of the individual or another organization on a given activity (Laumann, Marsden, and Prensky in Burt and Minor, 1983: 20–23). While self-conscious outsiders joined foreign fighter groups (e.g., gentiles with MACHAL in Israel as described in chapter 5), the records indicate that recruitment of nonnationals of the conflict state by various insurgencies were nonetheless organized in the name of either particular ethnicities or nonethnic identities such as ideological or religious cohort. Given the records of messaging still extant, the use of group institutions centered on the relevant

identity to foster recruitment, and the responses of volunteers indicating that these identities were salient to them, I am sufficiently confident in the relevance of the particular identity divisions to employ them in classifying foreign fighters by type.

8. For a description of an apparently failed recruitment attempt, see the Ethiopia section of chapter 4.

9. Other studies, including Lyall (2010), indicate an operational value to employing coethnics in insurgency and counterinsurgency.

10. My gratitude to the anonymous reviewer for Oxford University Press who pointed out this alternative.

CHAPTER 3

1. Although the colonization laws had required an equal balance of Americans and Europeans to forestall efforts to annex Texas to the United States, these had not been enforced (Resendez, 2005: 37).

2. "The business of volunteering for New Spain has become a perfect mania," argued Madison administration agent William Shaler, and would "open Mexico to the political influence of the U.S. and to the talents and enterprise of our citizens" (Brands, 2004: 39).

3. "Against the advocates of independence were the conservative defenders of the status quo. These included, as always, those early settlers who had grown comfortable under Mexican rule and who now became alarmed at the ascendancy of late arrivals." Those who had benefited from Mexican rule feared that they would lose their special exception to conduct slavery if Texas joined the United States (Roberts and Olson, 2001: 279).

4. The attack on Anahuac was led by South Carolina native William Barrett Travis, who would later serve as commander during the Battle of the Alamo.

5. Yucatán represents an interesting case in that its government tried unsuccessfully to obtain American assistance, but when the rebels attempted to form an expressly Mayan state, they apparently did not seek support from Maya in neighboring Guatemala or British Honduras (now Belize).

6. As problems mounted with the foreign fighters, "later, as an inducement to join the regular army rather than the volunteers, the land bounty was raised by an additional 160 acres and $24 in cash" (Hardin, 1994: 59).

7. For example, Sterne sold land in Nagadoches, Texas, for 50 cents an acre, whereas comparable land was selling for $1.25 in the United States. By ending Mexican rule and limits on immigration, Sterne stood to make a fortune from his holdings (Miller, 2004: 53).

8. A Masonic plaque in Alamo Plaza honors Alamo defenders and Masons William Barrett Travis, Jim Bowie, Davy Crockett, and Jim Bonham. Travis and Bowie were Texians, having immigrated from the United States prior to the revolution. Crockett famously arrived in Texas only shortly before the Battle of the Alamo, and Bonham organized the Mobile Greys foreign fighter group.

9. Resendez describes liberalism as a worldwide movement in the 1820s that swept aside existing religious and political institutions in favor of individual political and economic liberties. References to such a movement, particularly in the Greek War of Independence, were employed by recruiters, as will become evident later in this chapter.

10. Mobile Grey leader James Butler Bonham wrote to Houston, stating: "I shall receive nothing, either in the form of service or pay, or lands, or rations" (Hardin, 2007: 21).

11. Roberts and Olson (2001: 524) argue: "[Not] even most of the latecomers who arrived in response to the bounties promised to the volunteers in the Texan army were merely opportunists. They believed in liberty, as they understood the term."

12. Although a number of foreign fighters had colorful pasts, historians note that the Texian leadership were hardly models of social responsibility. Houston was nicknamed "Big Drunk" by the Cherokee, who adopted him when he ran away from home; Travis and Bowie, among others, shared some combination of financial scandals and arrests for violence.

13. Recruiters also held drives for the militias at Tammany Hall. Antebellum New York was a major cotton exporter, and support for extending slave territory was stronger in the city than anywhere else in the north.

14. Electing officers was in keeping with the view of most Americans in the 1830s, who had a low opinion of trained officers corps and did not believe that soldiers needed professional training to fight (Winders, 2004: 35). The same practice was also reported by foreign recruits in the Israeli War of Independence.

15. Another account relates that the uniforms, sewn while Shackleford drilled recruits in the public park, were based on the American flag and that the dress versions had white trousers with a blue sash (Simpson, 1978: 3).

16. Lack (1992: 143) notes that, unlike the American volunteers, the settlers also had to go home to protect their own property.

17. One officer in the expedition was Hungarian George Fisher, who had also fought in the Serbian uprising against the Ottoman Empire in 1813 as part of the Slavonic League, an Austrian-sponsored effort "to relieve their country of Serb revolutionaries during the latter days of the Napoleonic Wars" (Miller, 2004: 88). This reported case of transnational insurgency is not in the Correlates of War data and is therefore not included in the observation set.

18. The flag remains on display in a museum in Mexico City, despite the active efforts of a number of American officials, including George W. Bush, to have it returned to the United States (Scott, 1995).

CHAPTER 4

1. The International Brigade Memorial Trust Web site links to the various national group Web sites. The Anglophone contingent sites tend to list extensive bibliographies of works throughout the past 70 years, whereas the French, Mexican, and Italian sites provide scattered individual interviews conducted recently.

2. Once the IB had been established at Albacete on October 14, 1936, the existing *centuria* were incorporated as battalions. Johnston (1967: 82) adds that the Republic paid militia men 10 pesetas ($1.20) per day until the end of 1936, but after that it paid only members of the IB or regular army.

3. "The formation of the Brigades came to be launched through the Comintern. This was partly because it already had a strong disciplined organization and partly because the Labour-Socialist International being directed by the strongest members—the British and the Scandinavian parties—would not encourage or accept joint cooperation with the Comintern to organize volunteers" (Mangilli-Climpson, 1985: 38; Southworth Collection, UCSD).

4. Joe Dallet, the commissar of the Abraham Lincoln Battalion, wrote a letter to his mother shortly before he was killed, asking that she not be angry with the party because "they twice refused me permission to go and only gave in finally after I pestered the hell out of them and repeatedly insisted" (Joe Dallet Box 1, File 11, ALBA, Tamiment Library, New York University).

5. According to Luis Bolin (1967: 212), Franco's wartime press secretary, each of these brigades had three or four battalions, and there was also an 86th Brigade, which was the only one that had truly mixed nationalities. The others, he claimed, had to be separated "to put an end to the brawls which frequently broke out between them."

6. One of its mixed companies had no commissar because none could be found who spoke enough Serbo-Croatian or Magyar to be effective with the Yugoslav and Hungarian recruits. It is not reported here if one was found for the Bulgarians in the company.

7. The U.S. Socialist Party claimed to have raised 500 men for a Eugene Debs Column but could not raise the required $50,000 to send them to Spain. Debs recruits therefore had to join other units in the XV Brigade (Rosenstone, 1969: 95).

8. A 1941 FBI memorandum notes: "Thus it appears that the ALB and the VALB were virtually the same organization" (FBI File 8, ALBA, Tamiment Library, New York University).

9. Notably, Esmond Romilly, the nephew of Winston Churchill, who eventually made his own way to Spain.

10. The only unit in the IB with an expressly Jewish membership and identity was the Botwin Company, a Yiddish-speaking outfit that served within the mostly Polish Dombrowski XIII Brigade. It was created in Spain during a reorganization of existing battalions (Zaagsma, 2001: 1, 6, 13).

11. A memorial service for Leider held at Carnegie Hall brought an audience of more than 3,000 to hear speeches by Hollywood celebrities, elected officials, including one member of Congress, and the prominent Rabbi Stephen S. Weiss (Edwards. 1997: 108).

12. Slaughter (1972: 47; Southworth Collection, UCSD), however, argues that leading Communists, like Emil Kleber, the first commander of the IB, would not seem to be motivated be personal glory because they employed aliases.

13. Edwards (1997: xi, 6) states that some pilots in Spain had also "flown for Pancho Villa's pathetic air force" during the Mexican Revolution of 1913–1914, and other

pilots are mentioned as having flown on the government side. Other examples of early mercenary pilots referenced here were in "Paraguay's Civil War," "the Greco-Turkey Balkan Conflict of 1922," and "the White Russian and Polish armies against the Bolsheviks." The Russian Civil War is included in the observation set; the Russo-Polish War was not a civil conflict and is not included, despite the presence of the Kosciusko Flying Squadron.

14. Author Salaria Kee would later recount, "[I] didn't even know what a Communist was. I thought it was for white people only, like the mafia" (Justin Byrne, in Carroll and Fernandez, 2007: 79).

15. The messaging was not always obscured. The *New York Herald Tribune* reported on December 10, 1937, that Earl Browder, executive secretary of the U.S. Communist Party, spoke to an audience of 3,500 at the Hippodrome the night before to ask for volunteer "replacements for dead and wounded veterans of the Abraham Lincoln Battalion" (FBI File 13, ALBA, Tamiment Library, New York University).

16. An example is found in the correspondence of Kenneth Hollister of Newark, New Jersey, who wrote to both the Communist Party and to the FALB front organization "The North American Committee to Aid Spanish Democracy." Hollister and his wife offered to pay their own way to Spain to assist with the effort but were dismissed instead with the explanation that "Spanish officials discourage the sending to Spain of general foreigners" (ALBA, Tamiment Library, New York University).

17. After this meeting, Fisher gave a speech to the Young Communist League, the substance of which he does not recount. It is probably safe to assume that Fisher was held up as a role model for Young Communists, in which case his speech might be considered a forerunner to the *shahid* martyrdom videos recorded by Islamists.

18. Seaman Jack Reid had slightly different categories to describe his fellow Britons in Spain. Aside from "idealists," he encountered "adventurers," drawn by the excitement of conflict, and "holiday boozers," who expected recreation and were sorely disappointed when they could not easily return home. It is understandable that there would be far fewer of these weekend warriors coming on the long passage from North America (Howard and Reynolds, 1986: 20–21).

19. Krivitsky (1939: 95), who was in a position to know, reported that passports were rarely returned but went instead to the uses of OGPU. American passports in particular were apparently prized.

CHAPTER 5

1. Joe Woolf, a MACHAL veteran and historian, argues that only non-Jewish volunteers should be considered "foreign fighters" because Jews were entitled to Israeli citizenship (Correspondence, December 13, 2007). Both he and Smoky Simon, President of World MACHAL, also stressed the publicly stated goal of various Arab leaders at the time to complete the extermination of the Jewish people as an argument that the 1948 war was one of survival, not merely a civil conflict

(Correspondence, February 3, 2008). I rely on the official Israeli government designation of MACHAL as volunteers who intended to return to their countries of origin, and the fact that recruitment and fielding of volunteers began during the British Mandate period before Israeli statehood and invasion by foreign Arab armies, to include MACHAL among transnational insurgencies.

2. The alacrity of Haganah in developing proficient paramilitary operations is attributable to the numerous European Jewish underground resistance fighters who joined at the end of World War II. Some of these began to train DPs in Cyprus in 1946, and others were among the first sailors and pilots recruited. Thus there was already a precedent for Haganah as a transnational entity (Milstein, vol. 4, 1998: 222–224).

3. Henry Montor, head of the United Jewish Agency, aided Ben-Gurion by inviting 17 top donors from the United States and Canada to Sonneborn's New York residence (Milstein, vol. 1, 1996: 357). Although established philanthropists, not all were active Zionists. One asked at the first meeting, "What is a Palestinian Jew like?" Ben-Gurion's response: "Like an Iowa farmer" (Slater, 1994: 329–330).

4. The Sonneborn Institute met for nearly two and a half years before chartering Materials for Palestine in mid-1947 (Bercusson, 1984: 42). Ben-Gurion told Haim Slavin, the agent in charge of munitions procurement, to use Zionist channels but to find engineers, "not good Jews." Despite this advice, Slavin ultimately recruited the Bronx Zionist Boys Club to crate his weapons shipments (Heckelman, 1974: 31–32, 60).

5. The landlords of the famous Copacabana nightclub in Manhattan were Haganah agents who lent out the hotel building above as office space to run the American mobilization efforts (Hochstein and Greenfield, 1987: 35).

6. The Egyptians also hired foreign pilots, offering $2,000 per trip, with active recruitment in New York, where they "hired a half-dozen American pilots" (Livingston, 1994: 183–197).

7. In early 1948, Toronto synagogues displayed posters insisting, "Stand up and be counted!" The Jewish Agency initially asked for 1,000 Canadian volunteers but ultimately limited the goal to a more realistic 300. Ben Dunkelman, charged with overseeing recruitment, estimated that he would need to raise $1,000 per recruit from the Canadian Jewish community to pay for training and transport (Bercusson, 1984: 60, 62).

8. Gillette had attempted to serve as a foreign fighter himself in the Second Boer War, but his offer to volunteer against the British was rejected by the Afrikaner insurgents (United States Senate, 1984: 16).

9. Dunkelman, 1976: 160. Meetings were mostly held in private homes with groups of 10 to 15 potential recruits.

10. When Leonard Weissman was questioned by the FBI for violating the United Nations arms embargo on Palestine, he attempted to justify his actions by comparing himself to France's Lafayette aiding the American colonies and American citizen Éamon de Valera's role in Irish independence (Slater, 1970: 167).

11. Sister Benedict, a South African volunteer nurse, later converted to Judaism (Correspondence, Ute Ben Yosef, October 11, 2007).

12. Livingston (1994: 15–17, 88), who recounted that as a pilot he was offered $25 per week plus $7 per day to cover meals, claimed that the two gentile pilots he knew were paid the lowest wages and that they must therefore have been "particularly idealistic."

13. Although the accounts of most recruits are consistent that interviewees were warned of the consequences of participation, one radar technician claimed to have believed LLP that he was genuinely going to relieve Palestinian Jews of their farming duties while they fought and was shocked to have been pressed into the military (Heckelman, 1974: 178). The weight of the medical exam is challenged by the enlistment of one volunteer with a wooden leg and others with serious vision problems (Weiss and Weiss, 1998: 202).

14. Raab continued his career in transnational insurgency after the conclusion of the war, "flying munitions to Biafran rebels" in 1960s Nigeria (Slater, 1970: 232).

15. Haganah had also established a small flight training school at Cream Ridge, New Jersey, in the 1930s, the opening of which featured Albert Einstein as guest speaker (Weiss and Weiss, 1998: 81).

16. Machalnik Emanuel Zev Suffot noted that some of his acquaintances in England considered going but ultimately did not because of parental intervention (Questionnaire response, May 4, 2008).

17. Susman (2004: chapter 5, p. 1) recalled Machalniks were told that the ALA was a force of 6,000 mercenaries whose pay was to come from what they could loot.

18. A reference to past transnational armies, Yarmuk units were named for a key battle in which Salah al-Din (Saladin) defeated the forces of the Crusaders (Lorch, 1961: 80).

19. The contacts with whom Qawuqji treated included future Israeli Prime Minister Golda Meir.

20. In his 1949 memoir, Eitan recounted an instance in which "about 20" North African Jews disobeyed his order to stop looting after a battle (Shachar, 2002: 4).

21. Annapolis graduate Paul Shulman became the first commander of Israel's Navy, while U.S. Air Force veteran Nat Cohen became the first head of Air Force intelligence (Weiss and Weiss, 1998: 20).

CHAPTER 6

1. Conversation with Thomas Hegghammer, March 5, 2009.

2. In all cases in which I have cited material from an audio or video recording, I have provided a URL in the bibliography for some version of that recording or a transcription. Exact translations may vary.

3. President Nur Mohammed Taraki, who imprisoned Parcham members of his government and pleaded for a Soviet invasion of Iran after the revolution, was no

favorite of Moscow. The situation grew even worse in October 1979, when his assassination attempt against his deputy backfired. Moscow feared the new president, Hafizullah Amin, was emotionally unstable and that he would "do a Sadat on us" and ally with the United States. With détente perceived to be dead and SALT II negotiations bottled in the U.S. Senate, any plausible reaction by Washington was less a concern than potential Iranian efforts to topple Afghanistan and move on to the Soviet Muslim population (Westad, 2005: 310–318).

4. By 1984, when transnational recruitment began, an estimated 3 million Afghan refugees were in Pakistan, a figure representing 20 percent of the prewar population (United States Senate Committee on Foreign Relations, 1984: iii).

5. It is impossible to avoid speculating about the provenance of some of the source material I encountered while researching this chapter. This material includes several memoirs ostensibly published by freelance journalists who spent time with the mujahidin and painted them in decidedly sympathetic terms. Some recount strikingly similar stories, such as bravery demonstrated by arms thrust into campfires to the point of third-degree burns.

6. *Political Islam* is defined as an ideology for state governance designed to address issues of modernity, whereas neofundamentalism shuns modernity and looks back to an idealized golden age of the seventh century (Harpkiven, 1997: 276). The Iranian revolution was political Islam; Afghanistan under the Taliban was neofundamentalism.

7. The Grand Mosque uprising was an early transnational Islamist affair, featuring "four or five hundred insurgents... Yemenis, Kuwaitis, Egyptians, and even some Black American Muslims" (Wright, 2006: 90).

8. In fact, the editor of the English translation noted that Azzam was not exhorting recruits to join a caravan to Afghanistan, but a caravan of martyrs on their way to the afterlife.

9. This prioritization reflects not only the difficulty in penetrating the Israeli security perimeter but also Azzam's discomfort with the secular Palestine Liberation Organization.

10. Zawahiri also "wrote about the Afghan people with barely disguised condescension" (Coll, 2004: 103).

11. Senyor, a 20-year-old from Jeddah who died in September 1985, was reportedly the first Saudi killed in Afghanistan (Burke, 2004: 74).

12. Al Kifah remained active beyond the end of the Afghanistan War, marshaling mujahidin in Bosnia. Although it formally disbanded in 1993, the organization apparently simply continued its old work under new names.

13. Elsewhere, Médecins sans Frontières and other French NGOs provided mujahidin with combat medical training.

14. Westad (2005: 355) noted that CIA funds went to Islamic charities that recruited primarily in North Africa. It is possible to infer that the U.S. intelligence community was also complicit in recruitment within the United States, in violation of

federal law. In the case of Afghanistan, no reports of enforcement of these laws are extant, and it is a matter of speculation as to what level of official support Azzam and his colleagues may have enjoyed on their recruitment trips.

15. Southeast Asian, mostly Filipino, volunteers began to arrive in Pakistan as early as 1982 (Conboy, 2006: 42).

16. Overby (1993: 40–41) reported that, among all foreign volunteers, the Afghans were interested in allowing only Germans to fight with them or otherwise aid them, because they had heard that Germans were fellow Aryans.

17. Although thousands of al Qaeda–linked militants received training or material aid of some sort, intelligence agencies consider subjects to be members of al Qaeda only if they swore an oath of loyalty to bin Laden (Wright, 2006: 270). After bin Laden's death, al Qaeda affiliates swore loyalty to Zawahiri as his successor (Roggio, 2011).

CONCLUSION

1. The Turkish Foreign Ministry claimed in 2004 that 1,500 Kurdish PKK militants were operating in Iraq.

2. A U.S. Army interrogator (name withheld, conversation December 9, 2008) reported that foreign insurgents that he encountered in Baquba were better educated than the mostly illiterate local population and that he could pick them out on the street during security sweeps because of their dialects.

3. There have been individuals who have been foreign fighters for different causes in different conflicts but no record that any have been asked which cause meant more to them.

4. The same dynamic played out in Afghanistan as well, where the local "Good Guys" of Gizab rose up against the Taliban (Chandrasekaran, 2010).

5. Which is precisely the reason Abdullah Azzam advised mujahidin to think of Afghanistan first a quarter of a century before.

6. The remaining 20 percent are recruited by an even split between formal organizations and self-direction via the Internet.

7. There are, of course, less prominent cases of foreign fighters who are not Muslim. The World Bank spent $500 million during 2002–2009 to demobilize and reintegrate foreign fighters in western and central Africa who otherwise drifted between zones of conflict as an "insurgent diaspora" (IBRD, 2010).

APPENDIX A

1. For example, Machalniks in 1948 Israel compared themselves with the International Brigades in the Spanish Civil War, whose members had compared themselves with the English and French who fought in the Greek and American wars of independence, respectively. Contemporary jihadis refer openly to mujahidin in 1980s Afghanistan, and so on. Contemporary sources from the Spanish Civil War employed the term to describe the IB.

2. The total number of "mercenaries" in Bosnia in April 1993 was estimated at between 5,000 and 20,000. In addition to the soldiers of fortune described in previous articles were also a number of diaspora Croatians "fighting a Christian crusade against both Serbian Communism and Islamic extremism." By contrast, Serbs were reported to have received volunteers from Orthodox states "to defend the allegedly endangered Serbs from 'Catholic fascists' and 'Islamic militants.'" Russians were said to make up the largest group, with at least 500 on three-month contracts at $25 per month. "Muslim mercenaries" were estimated at 4,000, including one Afghan company of more than 400.

Bibliography

Abawi, Atia. (January 2, 2009) "Teen trained to be suicide bomber feels tricked." www.cnn.com/2009/WORLD/asiapcf/01/02/afghan.suicide.recruit/index.html.

Abou Zahab, Mariam, and Olivier Roy. (2004) *Islamist Networks: The Afghan-Pakistan Connection*. New York, Columbia University Press.

Abraham Lincoln Brigade Archives (ALBA). All materials by permission of the Tamiment Library and Robert F. Wagner Labor Archives, Eleanor Holmes Bobst Library, 10th Floor, New York University, 70 Washington Square South, New York.

Ahrne, Goran. (1994) *Social Organizations*. London, SAGE.

Altom, Bennie Lou Hook. (1997) *Elizabeth Barnhill and the Texian Wolf Hunt: Tennessee Volunteers in the Republic of Texas 1842*. Dallas, Texas, self-published.

Anderson, Benedict. (1998) *Spectres of Comparison: Nationalism, Southeast Asia and the World*. New York, Verso.

Associated Press. (September 15, 2001) "Afghans Vow Revenge if U.S. Strikes."

———. (November 27, 2001) "Prisoners Continue Revolt."

Austin, Stephen F. (1836) *An Address delivered by S.F. Austin of Texas to A Very Large Audience of Ladies and Gentlemen in the Second Presbyterian Church, Louisville, Kentucky on the 7th of March, 1836*. Lexington, Kentucky, J. Clark.

Australian Associated Press. (March 6, 2007) "'Nine' Plotted Violent Sydney Jihad." *Sydney Morning Herald*.

Avant, Deborah D. (2005) *The Market for Force*. New York, Cambridge University Press.

Aydinli, Ersel. (October 2008) "Before Jihadists There Were Anarchists: A Failed Case of Transnational Violence." *Studies in Conflict and Terrorism*, 31(10): 903–923.

Azzam, Abdullah. (1985) *Martyrs: The Building Blocks of Nations*. www.religioscope. com/info/doc/jihad/azzam_martyrs.htm.

———. (1987) *Join the Caravan*. www.hoor-al-ayn.com/Books/Join%20the%20Caravan.pdf.

———. (1988) *The Lofty Mountain*. www.hoor-al-ayn.com/Books/lofty.pdf.

Balch-Linday, Dylan, Andrew Enterline, and Kyle Joyce. (2008) "Third Party Intervention and the Civil War Process." *Journal of Peace Research*, 45(3): 345–363.

Barker, Eugene C. (1904) *The Finances of the Texas Revolution*. Boston, Ginn.

Barnard, J. H. (1883) *Dr. J. H. Barnard's Journal*. Goliad, Texas, The *Goliad Advance* (reprinted 1965).

Basch, Linda, Nina Glick-Schiller, and Cristina Szanton-Blanc. (1994) *Nations Unbound*. New York, Routledge.

BBC News. (January 13, 2005) "Q&A: Equatorial Guinea Coup Plot." http://news.bbc.co.uk/1/hi/world/africa/3597450.stm.

Bercusson, David J. (1984) *The Secret Army*. New York, Stein and Day.

Berdal, Mats R., and David M. Malone. (2000) *Greed and Grievance: Economic Agendas in Civil Wars*. Boulder, Colorado, Lynne Rienner.

Bergen, Peter L. (2006) *The Osama bin Laden I Know*. New York, Free Press.

Bessie, Alvah, and Albert Prago, eds. (1987) *Our Fight: Writings of the Veterans of the Abraham Lincoln Battalion*. New York, Monthly Review Press.

Bloom, Mia. (2005) *Dying to Kill: The Allure of Suicide Terror*. New York, Columbia University Press.

Bolin, Luis. (1967) *Spain: The Vital Years*. Philadelphia, J. B. Lippincott.

Brady, Henry, Kay Lehman Schlozman, and Sidney Verba. (1999) "Prospecting for Participants: Rational Expectations and the Recruitment of Political Activists." *American Political Science Review*, 93(1): 153–168.

Brady, Henry E., and David Collier. (2004) *Rethinking Social Inquiry*. Lanham, Maryland, Rowan and Littlefield.

Brandon, James. (October 2008) "British Muslims Providing Foot Soldiers for Global Jihad." *CTC Sentinel*, 1(11): 7–10.

Brands, H. W. (2004) *Lone Star Nation*. New York, Doubleday.

Branigin, William. (February 28, 2006) "Report Offers Gloomy View of Insurgencies." *Washington Post*.

Brinkerhoff, Jennifer. (2009) *Digital Diasporas: Identity and Transnational Engagement*. New York, Cambridge University Press.

Brinkley, William C. (1952) *The Texas Revolution*. Baton Rouge, Louisiana State University Press.

Brome, Vincent. (1966) *The International Brigades: Spain 1936–1939*. New York,. William Morrow.

Bronner, Ethan. (October 10, 2010) "Transcripts on '73 War, Now Public, Grip Israel." *New York Times*.

Brown, Gary. (1999) *Volunteers in the Texas Revolution: The New Orleans Greys*. Lanham, Maryland, Republic of Texas Press.

_____. (2000) *Hesitant Martyr in the Texas Revolution: James Walker Fannin*. Lanham, Maryland, Republic of Texas Press.

Bugajski, Janusz. (April 10, 1993) "Yugoslav Wars a Godsend for Hired Guns." *Toronto Star*.

Bull, Hedley. (2002) *The Anarchical Society*, 3rd ed. New York, Columbia University Press.

Burt, Ronald S., and Michael J. Minor. (1983) *Applied Network Analysis: A Methodological Introduction*. Beverly Hills, California, SAGE.

Buzan, Barry, Ole Waever, and Jaap de Wilde. (1998) *Security: A New Framework for Analysis*. Boulder, Colorado, Lynne Rienner.

Cailingold, Asher. (2000) *An Unlikely Heroine: Esther Cailingold's Fight for Jerusalem*. Edgware, Great Britain, Valentine Mitchell.

Call, Vaughn R. A. (1999) "Giving Time, Money, and Blood: Similarities and Differences." *Social Psychology Quarterly*, 62(2): 276–290.

Canadian Broadcasting Company. (November 15, 2004) "'We Will Kill Them': Russia on Foreign Fighters in Chechnya." *CBC News*. www.cbc.ca/world/story/2004/11/14/chehnya041114.html.

Carr, E. H. (1984) *The Comintern in the Spanish Civil War*. London, Macmillan.

Carroll, Peter N. (1994) *The Odyssey of the Abraham Lincoln Brigade: Americans in the Spanish Civil War*. Stanford, California, Stanford University Press.

Carroll, Peter N., and James D. Fernandez, eds. (2007) *Facing Fascism: New York and the Spanish Civil War*. New York, Puffin Foundation.

Carroll, Peter N., Michael Nash, and Melvin Small, eds. (2006) *The Good Fight Continues: World War II Letters from the Abraham Lincoln Brigade*. New York, New York University Press.

Castañeda, Carlos E., translator. (1928) *The Mexican Side of the Texas Revolution*. Dallas, Texas, P. L. Turner.

Chaliand, Gerard, translated by Tamar Jacoby. (1981) *Report from Afghanistan*. New York, Viking.

Chandrasekaran, Rajiv. (June 21, 2010) "U.S. Eager to Replicate Afghan Villagers' Successful Revolt against the Taliban." *Washington Post*.

Clapham, Christopher, ed. (1998) *African Guerillas*. Kampala, Uganda, Fountain.

Cohen, Eliot A. (1985) *Citizens and Soldiers: The Dilemmas of Military Service*. Ithaca, New York, Cornell University Press.

Coll, Steve. (2004) *Ghost Wars: The Secret History of the CIA, Afghanistan, and Bin Laden, from the Soviet Invasion to September 10, 2001*. New York, Penguin.

Collier, Paul, and Anke Hoeffler. (2004) "Greed and Grievance in Civil War." *Oxford Economic Papers*, 56(4): 563–595.

Collins, Larry, and Dominique Lapierre. (1972) *O Jerusalem!* New York, Simon and Schuster.

Collum, Danny Duncan. (1992) *"This Ain't Ethiopia, But It'll Do"—African-Americans in the Spanish Civil War*. New York, G. K. Hall.

Conboy, Ken. (2006) *The Second Front: Inside Asia's Most Dangerous Terrorist Network*. Jakarta, Indonesia, Equinox.

Connor, Walker. (1994) *Ethno-Nationalism: The Quest for Understanding*. Princeton, New Jersey, Princeton University Press.

Cook, Robert, translator. (2001) *Njal's Saga*. London, Penguin.

Cooley, John. (1999) *Unholy Wars: Afghanistan, America and International Terrorism.* London, Pluto.

Cooper, Dillard. (1895) *Fannin's Massacre: A True and Correct Account by One of the Survivors.* Llano, Texas, Times Job Print.

Crile, George. (2003) *Charlie Wilson's War.* New York, Atlantic Monthly Press.

Crisp, James E. (2005) *Sleuthing the Alamo.* New York, Oxford University Press.

Dahlem, F. (May 1938) "The Military Work of the Eleventh International Brigade." *Communist International,* 15(5): 445–454.

Dar al Murabiteen Publications. (2008) *The Sword Is the Solution.* www.metacafe.com/watch/4787876/the_sword_is_the_solution_by_abdullah_azzam_rahimahullah.

Daughters of the Republic of Texas Library (DRTL), 300 Alamo Plaza, San Antonio, Texas.

Davis, Graham. (2002) *Land! Irish Pioneers in Mexican and Revolutionary Texas.* College Station, Texas A&M University Press.

Davis, William C. (2003) *Lone Star Rising: The Revolutionary Birth of the Texas Republic.* New York, Free Press.

Deckel, Ephraim. (1959) *SHAI: The Exploits of Hagana Intelligence.* New York, Thomas Yoseloff.

Degenne, Alain, and Michel Forsé. (1999) *Introducing Social Networks.* London, SAGE.

Deutsche Presse-Agentur. (December 20, 1994) "Russian Forces Approach Grozny in Heavy Fighting." Deutsche Presse-Agentur.

Diani, Mario, and Doug McAdam, eds. (2003) *Social Movements and Networks: Relational Approaches to Contentious Actions.* Oxford, Oxford University Press.

Dorronsoro, Gilles. (2005) *Revolution Unending: Afghanistan 1979 to the Present.* New York, Columbia University Press.

Dunkelman, Ben. (1976) *Dual Allegiance.* New York, Crown.

Duval, John C. (1892) *Early Times in Texas.* Austin, Texas, HPN Gammel.

The *Economist.* (August 18, 2005) "For Jihadist, Read Anarchist."

Edwards, John Carver. (1997) *Airmen without Portfolios: U.S. Mercenaries in Civil War Spain.* Westport, Connecticut, Praeger.

Ehrenberg, Herman, translated by Charlotte Churchill. (1968) *With Milam and Fannin: Adventures of a German Boy in Texas' Revolution.* Austin, Texas, Pemberton.

Eisenwein, George, and Adrian Shubert. (1995) *Spain at War: The Spanish Civil War in Context 1931–1939.* London, Longman.

Elliot, Andrea. (July 12, 2009) "A Call to Jihad from Somalia, Answered in the U.S." *New York Times.*

———. (January 27, 2010) "The Jihadist Next Door." *New York Times.*

Elliott, Claude. (December 1944) "Georgia and the Texas Revolution." *Georgia Historical Quarterly,* 28(4): 1–18.

———. (1947) *Alabama and the Texas Revolution.* Denton, Texas State Historical Association.

Elpeleg, Zvi. (1993) *The Grand Mufti: Haj Amin al-Hussaini.* London, Frank Cass.

Fadel, Leila. (August 25, 2008) "Dazed Iraqi Teen Suicide Bomber Says She Didn't Want to Die." McClatchy Newspapers.

Fearon, James D., and David F. Laitin. (2003) "Ethnicity, Insurgency, and Civil War." *American Political Science Review*, 97: 75–90.

Felter, Joseph, and Brian Fishman. (2007) *Al Qaida's Foreign Fighters in Iraq: A First Look at the Sinjar Records*. West Point, New York, Combating Terrorism Center.

Ferguson, Yale, and R. J. Barry Jones, eds. (2002) *Political Space: Frontiers of Change in a Globalizing World*. Albany, State University of New York Press.

Finer, Jonathan. (November 17, 2005) "Among Insurgents in Iraq, Few Foreigners Are Found." *Washington Post*.

Finnemore, Martha. (2003) *The Purpose of Intervention: Changing Beliefs about the Use of Force*. Ithaca, New York, Cornell University Press.

Fisher, Harry. (1998) *Comrades: Tales of a Brigadista in the Spanish Civil War*. Lincoln, University of Nebraska Press.

Florini, Ann M. (2000) *The Third Force: The Rise of Transnational Society*. Washington, DC, Carnegie Endowment for International Peace.

Fowler, Kenneth. (2001) *Medieval Mercenaries*, Vol. 1. Oxford, Blackwell.

Fowler, Michael C. (2005) *Amateur Soldiers, Global Wars*. Santa Barbara, California, Praeger Security International.

Fraser, Ronald. (1979) *Blood of Spain: An Oral History of the Spanish Civil War*. New York, Pantheon.

Fuller, Graham E. (2002) "The Future of Political Islam," *Foreign Affairs*, 81(2): 48–60.

Gamson, William A. (1992) "The Social Psychology of Collective Action." In Aldon Morris and Carol Mueller, eds. *Frontiers in Social Movement Theory*. New Haven, Connecticut, Yale University Press, pp. 53–76.

Ganor, Boaz, Katharina Von Knop, and Carlos Duarte, eds. (2007) *Hypermedia Seduction for Terrorist Recruiting*. Amsterdam, Netherlands, IOS.

Gates, Scott. (2002) Recruitment and Allegiance: "The Micro-Foundations of Rebellion." *Journal of Conflict Resolution*, 46(1): 111–130.

Geertz, Clifford, ed. (1963) *Old Societies and New States*. New York, Free Press.

George, Alexander L., and Andrew Bennett. (2004) *Case Studies and Theory Development in the Social Sciences*. Cambridge, Massachusetts, MIT Press.

Gerassi, John. (1986) *The Premature Anti-Fascists*. New York, Praeger.

Gerges, Fawaz A. (2005) *The Far Enemy: How Jihad Went Global*. New York, Cambridge University Press.

Giustozzi, Antonio. (2008) *Koran, Kalashnikov, and Laptop: The Neo-Taliban Insurgency in Afghanistan*. New York, Columbia University Press.

The *Globe and Mail* (Toronto) (December 14, 1998) "A Mercenary Tale."

Goffman, Erving. (1974) *Frame Analysis: An Essay on the Organization of Experience*. London, Harper and Row.

Gorman, Edward. (March 21, 1988) "Khost Outpost Falls to Mujahidin Led by Foreign Fighters." The *Times* (London).

Grau, Lester. (1998) *The Bear Went over the Mountain: Soviet Combat Tactics in Afghanistan*. Portland, Oregon, Frank Cass.

Grau, Lester, and Michael Gress, eds. (2002) *The Soviet-Afghan War: How a Superpower Fought and Lost*. Lawrence, University of Kansas Press.

Greenspun, Hank. (1966) *Where I Stand*. New York, David McKay.

Gurr, Ted Robert. (1993) "Why Minorities Rebel: A Global Analysis of Communal Mobilization and Conflict since 1945." *International Political Science Review*, 14(2): 161–201.

Gutman, Roy. (2008) *How We Missed the Story: Osama bin Laden, the Taliban, and the Hijacking of Afghanistan*. Washington, DC, United States Institute of Peace.

Hafez, Mohammed M. (2007) *Suicide Bombers in Iraq: The Strategy and Ideology of Martyrdom*. Washington, DC, United States Institute of Peace.

———. (2009) "Jihad after Iraq: Lessons from the Arab Afghans." *Studies in Conflict and Terrorism*, 32(2): 73–94.

Hansen, John Mark. (1985) "The Political Economy of Group Membership." *American Political Science Review*, 79(1): 79–96.

Hardin, Stephen L. (1994) *Texian Illiad*. Austin, University of Texas Press.

———. (2007) *Texian Macabre: The Melancholy Tale of a Hanging in Early Houston*. Abilene, Texas, State House Press.

Harpkiven, Kristian Berg. (August 1997) "Transcending Traditionalism: The Emergence of Non-State Military Formations in Afghanistan." *Journal of Peace Research*, 34(3): 271–287.

Hazarika, Sanjoy. (August 24, 1993) "Afghans Joining Rebels in Kashmir." *New York Times*.

Heckelman, A. Joseph. (1974) *American Volunteers and Israel's War of Independence*. New York, KTAV.

Hegghammer, Thomas. (2010–11) "The Rise of Muslim Foreign Fighters." *International Security*, 35(3): 53–94.

Heinamaa, Anna, Maija Leppanen, and Yuri Yurchenko, eds. (1994) *The Soldiers' Story: Soviet Veterans Remember the Afghan War*. International and Area Studies, Research Series Number 90, Regents of the University of California.

Hersman, R. K. (2000) *Friends and Foes: How Congress and the President Really Make Foreign Policy*. Washington, DC, Brookings Institution.

Hewitt, Christopher, and Jessica Kelley-Moore. (2009) "Foreign Fighters in Iraq: A Cross-National Analysis of Jihadism." *Terrorism and Political Violence*, 21: 211–220.

Hochstein, Joseph M., and Murray S. Greenfield. (1987) *The Jews' Secret Fleet*. Jerusalem, Israel, Gefen.

Hockenos, Paul. (2003) *Homeland Calling: Exile, Patriotism, and the Balkan Wars*. Ithaca, New York, Cornell University Press.

Hoffer, Eric (1951) *The True Believer*. New York, Harper & Row.

House of Commons. (2006) *Report of the Official Account of the Bombings in London on 7th July 2005*. London, The Stationery Office.

Howard, Russell, and Reid Sawyer, eds. (2004) *Terrorism and Counter-Terrorism.* New York, McGraw-Hill.

Howard, Victor, and Mac Reynolds. (1986) *The MacKenzie-Papineau Battalion: The Canadian Contingent in the Spanish Civil War.* Ottawa, Canada, Carleton University Press.

Huntington, Samuel P. (1964) *The Soldier and the State.* New York, Vintage.

———. (1996) *The Clash of Civilizations and the Remaking of the World Order.* New York, Simon and Schuster.

Hurst, Stephen R. (February 1, 2008) "Mentally Retarded Bombers Kill Scores in Baghdad." Associated Press.

The *Independent.* (April 26, 2009) "Torture? It Probably Killed More Americans Than 9/11." www.independent.co.uk/news/world/middle-east/torture-it-probably-kille d-more-americans-than-911-1674396.html.

The International Bank for Reconstruction and Development/World Bank. (2010) *Multi-Country Disarmament and Reintegration Program Final Report.* Washington, DC. www.mdrp.org/PDFs/MDRP_Final_Report.pdf.

International Herald Tribune. (February 4, 2009) "Afghanistan Says Foreign Fighters Coming from Iraq."

Iraqi News Agency. (February 6, 1983) "Ramadan on Iraq's Popular Army." *BBC Summary of World Broadcasts,* February 8, 1983.

Israel Ministry of Foreign Affairs. (May 1, 1999) "Focus on Israel: Machal—Overseas Volunteers." www.mfa.gov.il/mfa/mfaarchive/1990_1999/1999/5/focus%20on%20 israel-%20machal%20-%20overseas%20volunteers.

Jackson, Jack, ed. (2003) *Almonte's Texas.* Austin, Texas State Historical Association.

Jenkins, William H. (April 1965) "The Red Rovers of Alabama." *Alabama Review,* 18(2): 106–112 (Red Rovers Vertical File, DRTL).

Jervis, Robert. (1976) *Perception and Misperception in International Politics.* Princeton, New Jersey: Princeton University Press.

Jesse, Neal, and Kristen Williams. (2005) *Identity and Institutions: Conflict Reduction in Divided Societies.* Albany, State University of New York Press.

Johnsen, Gregory, and Christopher Boucek. (November 2008) "The Dilemma of the Yemeni Detainees at Guantanamo Bay." *CTC Sentinel,* 1(12): 1–4.

Johnston, Verle B. (1967) *Legions of Babel: The International Brigades in the Spanish Civil War.* University Park, Pennsylvania State University Press.

Jordan, Jonathan W. (2006) *Lone Star Navy.* Washington, DC, Potomac.

Kafka, Zacharia. (2002) "Machal Finland." *American Veterans of Israel,* Fall: 5–6.

Kalyvas, Stathis. (2006) *The Logic of Violence in Civil War.* New York, Cambridge University Press.

Kalyvas, Stathis, and Nicholas Sambanis. (2005) "Bosnia's Civil War: Origins and Violence Dynamics." In Paul Collier and Nicholas Sambanis, eds. *Understanding Civil War: Evidence and Analysis,* Vol. 2. Washington, DC, World Bank, pp. 191–228.

Katz, Leslie. (June 5, 1998) "U.S. Veterans of '48 War Recall Their Zionist Passion." *Jewish Bulletin*, San Francisco. www.jewishsf.com/content/2-0-/module/display-story/story_id/8843/format/html/edition_id/168/displaystory.html.

Katzew, Henry. (2003) *South Africa's 800: The Story of South African Volunteers in Israel's War of Independence*. Tel-Aviv, Israel, Telfed.

Kaufman, Stuart J. (2001) *Modern Hatreds: The Symbolic Politics of Ethnic War*. Ithaca, New York, Cornell University Press.

Keck, Margaret E., and Kathryn Sikkink. (1998) *Activists beyond Borders: Advocacy Networks in International Politics*. Ithaca, New York, Cornell University Press.

Keene, Judith. (2001) *Fighting for Franco: International Volunteers in Nationalist Spain during the Spanish Civil War*. London, Leceister University Press.

Kegley, Charles, and Gregory Raymond. (1987) "Long Cycles and Internationalized Civil War." *Journal of Politics*, 49(2): 481–499.

Kelley, G. A., and L. B. Miller. (1969) "Internal War and International Systems: Perspectives on Method." *Occasional Paper 21*, Harvard University Center for International Affairs.

Kepel, Gilles, and Jean-Pierre Milelli, eds. (2008) *Al Qaeda in Its Own Words*. Cambridge, Massachusetts, Belknap Press of Harvard University Press.

Kilcullen, David. (2009) *The Accidental Guerilla*. New York, Oxford University Press.

Kinsey, Christopher. (2006) *Corporate Soldiers and International Security: The Rise of Private Military Companies*. Oxon, England, Routledge.

Kirby, Aidan. (2007) "The London Bombers as 'Self-Starters': A Case Study in Indigenous Radicalization and the Emergence of Autonomous Cliques." *Studies in Conflict and Terrorism*, 30(5): 415–428.

Kohlmann, Evan F. (2004) *Al-Qaida's Jihad in Europe: The Afghan-Bosnian Network*. New York, Berg.

———. (April 27, 2007) "Interview with Foreign Fighter for the Islamist State of Iraq." *Global Terror Alert*, https://flashpoint-intel.com/inteldocument/isimaqdisi0507.pdf.

Kontominas, Bellinda. (June 25, 2007) "Australian Killed, Three Arrested in Lebanon Unrest." *Sydney Morning Herald*.

Krivitsky, W .G. (1939) *In Stalin's Secret Service*. New York, Harper and Brothers.

Krueger, Alan B. (2007) *What Makes a Terrorist: Economics and the Root of Terror*. Princeton, New Jersey, Princeton University Press.

Kurzman, Dan. (1970) *Genesis 1948*. Cleveland, Ohio, World.

Lacey, Jim, ed. (2008) *A Terrorist's Call to Global Jihad: Deciphering Abu Musab Al-Suri's Islamic Jihad Manifesto*. Annapolis, Maryland, Naval Institute Press.

Lack, Paul D. (1992) *The Texas Revolutionary Experience: A Political and Social History*. College Station, Texas A&M University Press.

Laraña, Enrique, Hank Johnston, and Joseph Gusfield, eds. (1994) *New Social Movements: From Ideology to Identity*. Philadelphia, University of Pennsylvania Press.

Lavendera, Ed. (October 8, 2007) "Soldier's Dad Faces Ouster." CNN News. www.cnn.com/video/#/video/us/2007/10/08/lavandera.kia.deport.cnn.

Lebed, Alexander. (1997) *My Life and My Country*. Washington, DC, Regnery.

LeBor, Adam. (February 10, 1993) "Network of Hatred Traps Mercenaries." The *Times*.

Levenberg, Haim. (1993) *Military Preparations of the Arab Community of Palestine, 1945–1948*. Portland, Oregon, Frank Cass.

Levy, Jack S. (1996) "Loss Aversion, Framing, and Bargaining: The Implications of Prospect Theory for International Conflict." *International Political Science Review*, 17(1): 179–195.

Lia, Brynjar. (1998) *The Society of the Muslim Brothers in Egypt*. Reading, United Kingdom, Ithaca.

Lichbach, Mark. (1994) "What Makes Rational Peasants Revolutionary? Dilemma, Paradox, and Irony in Peasant Collective Action." *World Politics*, 46(3): 383–418.

Liukonnen, Petri. (2007) *The Author's Calendar*. Finland, Kuusankosken kaupunginkirjasto. www.kirjasto.sci.fi/malraux.htm.

Livingston, Harold. (1994) *No Trophy, No Sword: An American Volunteer in the Israeli Air Force during the 1948 War of Independence*. Chicago, edition q.

Lorch, Netanel. (1961) *The Edge of the Sword: Israel's War of Independence 1947–49*. New York, G. P. Putnam's Sons.

Lovin, Hugh Taylor. (1963) *The American Communist Party and the Spanish Civil War 1936–1939*. University of Washington dissertation, University Microfilms, Ltd., Ann Arbor, Michigan (1978).

Lowenstein, Ralph. (2006) *Machal Museum*, American Veterans of Israel, American Jewish University.

Lyall, Jason. (2010) "Are Coethnics More Effective Counterinsurgents? Evidence from the Second Chechen War." *American Political Science Review*, 104(1): 1–20.

MacIntyre, Ben. (2004) *The Man Who Would Be King: The First American in Afghanistan*. New York, Farrar, Straus and Giroux.

MacKinley, John. (2002) *Globalization and Insurgency*. Oxford, International Institute for Strategic Studies.

Magnus, Ralph, and Eden Naby. (2002) *Afghanistan: Mullah, Marx, and Mujahid*. New York, Basic Books.

Malet, David. (2007) *The Foreign Fighter Project*. www.foreignfighter.com.

Mandel, Robert. (2002) *Armies without States and the Privatization of Security*. Boulder, Colorado, Lynne Rienner.

Mangilli-Climpson, Massimo. (1985) *Men of Heart of Red, White and Green: Italian Antifascists in the Spanish Civil War*. New York, Vantage.

Mardor, Munya. (1959) *Haganah*. New York, New American Library.

Markovitzky, Yaacov. (2007) *Machal, Overseas Volunteers in Israel's War of Independence*. Tel Aviv, Israel, World Machal.

McDonough, Kevin. (November 22, 2005) "I'm King Cooper." United Features Syndicate, *Washington Post Express*: 22.

Merrill, Austin. (September 10, 2007) "Letter from Timbuktu." *Vanity Fair Web Exclusive*. www.vanityfair.com/politics/features/2007/09/sahara200709.

Michaels, Jim. (May 9, 2007) "Study: Insurgencies Like Iraq's Usually Fail in 10 Years." *USA Today*. www.usatoday.com/news/world/iraq/2007-05-08-insurgency-report_N.htm.

Miller, Edward L. (2004) *New Orleans and the Texas Revolution*. College Station, Texas A&M University Press.

Miller, Thomas Lloyd. (1971) *The Public Lands of Texas 1519–1970*. Norman, University of Oklahoma Press.

Milstein, Uri. (1996–98) *History of Israel's War of Independence* (vols. 1–4). Lanham, Maryland, University Press of America.

Ministerie van BZK. (December, 2002). www.aivd.nl.

Ministry of Justice. (1946) *The Red Domination in Spain*. Madrid, Spain, Tribunal Supremo, Ministrio Fiscal.

Monteath, Peter. (1994) *Writing the Good Fight: Political Commitment in the International Literature of the Spanish Civil War*. Westport, Connecticut, Greenwood.

Moore, Cerwyn, and Paul Tumelty. (2008) "Foreign Fighters and the Case of Chechnya: A Critical Assessment." *Studies in Conflict and Terrorism*, 31(5): 412–433.

Moore, Molly. (May 13, 2007) "Legendary Force Updates Its Image." *Washington Post*.

Murray, Edmundo. (January 2007) *Ireland and Latin America*. www.irlandeses.org/murrayintro.htm.

Myers, Lisa. (June 20, 2005) "Who Are the Foreign Fighters in Iraq?" *NBC Nightly News*, www.msnbc.msn.com/id/8293410/.

Nasiri, Omar. (2006) *Inside the Jihad*. New York, Basic Books.

Nelson, Cary, and Jefferson Hendricks, eds. (1996) *Madrid 1937: Letters of the Abraham Lincoln Battalion from the Spanish Civil War*. New York, Routeledge.

The *New York Times*. (December 21, 1919) "Brooklyn Boys Aid Poland."

News Agencies. (December 23, 2008) "Bush Pardons Man Who Gave Israel Arms in 1948 War." *Ha'aretz*.

Niou, Emerson, and G. Tan, (2005). "External Threat and Collective Action." *Economic Inquiry*, 43 (3): 519–530.

O'Donnell, Peader. (1937) *Salud: An Irishman in Spain*. London, Methuen.

Olesen, Thomas. (2005) *International Zapatismo: The Construction of Solidarity in the Age of Globalization*. London, Zed.

Overby, Paul. (1993) *Holy Blood: An Inside View of the Afghan War*. Westport, Connecticut, Praeger.

Pandaram, Jamie, and Ed O'Laughlin. (June 27, 2007) "Boxer among Australians Held." *Sydney Morning Herald*.

Pape, Robert. (2006) *Dying to Win*. New York, Random House.

Parker, Ned. (July 15, 2007) "Saudi's Role in Iraq Insurgency Outlined." *Los Angeles Times*.

Parsons, Talcott. (1937) *The Structure of Social Action*. New York, McGraw-Hill.

Paz, Reuven. (March 2005) "Arab Volunteers Killed in Iraq: An Analysis," Project for the Research of Islamist Movements, PRISM, *Series of Global Jihad*, No. 1/3.

Pearson, Frederic. (1974) "Foreign Military Interventions and Domestic Disputes." *International Studies Quarterly*, 18(3): 259–290.

Pfeffer, J., and G. R. Salancik. (1978) *The External Control of Organizations: A Resource Dependence Perspective*. New York, Harper and Row.

Porrath, Ziporah. (2004) "Mahal2000—Today's Overseas Volunteers in the IDF." *American Veterans of Israel*, Fall: 5.

Powell, Walter W., and Paul DiMaggio. (1991) *The New Institutionalism in Organizational Analysis*. Chicago, University of Chicago Press.

Powers, Ashley. (June 7, 2007) "Battle's Not Over When They Enter U.S." *Los Angeles Times*.

Preston, Julia. (February 14, 2009) "U.S. Military Will Offer Path to Citizenship." *New York Times*.

Quinn, Patrick, and Katherine Shrader. (June 30, 2005) "Foreigners Responsible for Most Suicide Attacks in Iraq." Associated Press.

Rabasa, Angel, et al. (2007) *Money in the Bank: Lessons Learned from Past Counterinsurgency (COIN) Operations*. Santa Monica, California, RAND.

Radu, Michael, ed. (1990) *The New Insurgencies: Anti-Communist Guerillas in the Third World*. London, Transaction.

Rashid, Ahmed. (2002) *Jihad: The Rise of Militant Islam in Central Asia*. New York, Penguin.

Reid, Stuart. (2007) *The Secret War for Texas*. College Station, Texas A&M University Press.

Rennie, John. (2006) *London History: 100 Faces of the East End*. United Kingdom, Lulu. http://eastlondonhistory.com/2011/06/16/vidal-sassoons-cockney-roots/.

Resendez, Andres. (2005) *Changing National Identities at the Frontier: Texas and New Mexico 1800–1850*. Cambridge, Cambridge University Press.

Richardson, B. Dan. (1982) *The Comintern Army*. Lexington, University Press of Kentucky.

Riotte, Jean. (1936) *Arriba Espana!...Espagne, éveille-toi!* Tarbes, France, Orphelins-Apprentis.

Roberts, Randy, and James S. Olson. (2001) *A Line in the Sand: The Alamo in Blood and Memory*. New York, Free Press.

Rogan, Eugene C., and Avi Shlaim, eds. (2001) *The War for Palestine: Rewriting the History of 1948*. Cambridge, Cambridge University Press.

Roggio, Bill. (July 26, 2011) "AQAP Leader Pledges Oath of Allegiance to Ayman al Zawahiri." *The Long War Journal*.

Romeiser, John Beals, ed. (1982) *Red Flags, Black Flags: Critical Essays of the Spanish Civil War*. Potomac, Maryland, Studia Humanitatis.

Rosenau, James N. (1964) *International Aspects of Civil Strife*. Princeton, New Jersey, Princeton University Press.

Rosenstone, Robert A. (1969) *Crusade of the Left: The Lincoln Battalion in the Spanish Civil War*. New York, Pegasus.

Rotar, Igor. (April 2004) "The Growing Problem of Uighur Separatism." *China Brief*, 4(8).

Rotella, Sebastian. (January 10, 2006) "European Women Join Ranks of Jihadis." *Los Angeles Times*.

Roy, Olivier. (1991) *The Lessons of the Soviet/Afghan War*. Adelphi Papers 259, Brassey's for IISS.

———. (2004) *Globalized Islam: The Search for a New Ummah*. New York, Columbia University Press.

Rubin, Barry, and Judith Culp Rubin, eds. (2002) *Anti-American Terrorism and the Middle East*. Oxford, Oxford University Press.

Rust, William. (1939) *Britons in Spain*. London, Lawrence and Wishart.

Sageman, Marc. (2004) *Understanding Terror Networks*. Philadelphia, University of Pennsylvania Press.

Saideman, Steven. (1997) "Explaining the International Relations of Secessionist Conflicts: Vulnerability versus Ethnic Ties." *International Organization* 51: 721–753.

———. (2001) *The Ties That Divide: Ethnic Politics, Foreign Policy, and International Conflict*. New York, Columbia University Press.

Salehyan, Idean. (2009) *Rebels without Borders: Transnational Insurgencies in World Politics*. Ithaca, New York, Cornell University Press.

Sambanis, Nicholas. (2001) "Do Ethnic and Non-Ethnic Civil Wars Have the Same Causes?" *Journal of Conflict Resolution*, 45(3): 259–280.

Schattschneider, E. E. (1960) *The Semi-Sovereign People: A Realist's View of Democracy in America*. Hinsdale, Illinois, Dryden.

Schechtman, Joseph B. (1965) *The Mufti and the Fuehrer*. New York, Thomas Yoseloff.

Schindler, John R. (2007) *Unholy Terror: Bosnia, Al-Qa'ida, and the Rise of Global Jihad*. St. Paul, Minnesota, Zenith.

Schweitzer, Yoram, and Shaul Shay. (2003) *The Globalization of Terror*. Piscataway, New Jersey, Transaction.

Scott, John. (1991) *Social Network Analysis: A Handbook*. London, SAGE.

Scott, Stefanie. (June 15, 1995) "Bush OKs Alamo Banner Retrieval." *San Antonio Express*.

Sen, Amartya. (2006) *Identity and Violence: The Illusion of Destiny*. New York, W. W. Norton.

Shachar, David. (2002) "With French Machal in a Negev Brigade." *American Veterans of Israel*, Fall: 2–4.

Shain, Yossi. (2007) *Kinship and Diasporas in International Politics*. Ann Arbor, University of Michigan Press.

Sheffer, Gabriel. (2003) *Diaspora Politics: At Home Abroad*. Cambridge, Cambridge University Press.

Simpson, Virginia Gray. (1978) "The Red Rovers of Courtland, Alabama." *The Journal of Muscle Shoals History*, Vol. 6. Sheffield, Alabama, Tennessee Valley Historical Society, pp. 3–12 (Red Rovers Vertical File, DRTL).

Sinno, Abdulkader H. (2008) *Organizations at War: In Afghanistan and Beyond*. London, Cornell University Press.

Slaughter, Margaret Jane. (1972) *Italian Anti-Fascists: Italian Volunteers in the Spanish Civil War*. University of New Mexico dissertation, University Microfilms, Ann Arbor, Michigan (1978).

Slater, Leonard. (1970) *The Pledge*. New York, Simon and Schuster.

Smith, Scott S. (1999) "Simon Bolivar: Liberator of Latin America." www.militaryheritage.com/bolivar.htm.

Snow, David, Louis Zurcher, and Sheldon Ekland-Olson. (1980) "Social Networks and Social Movements: A Micro-Structural Approach to Differential Recruitment." *American Sociological Review*, 45(4): 787–801.

Snow, David, et al. (1986) "Frame Alignment Processes, Micromobilization, and Movement Participation." *American Sociological Review*, 51(4): 464–481.

Snow, Robert. (2003) *Deadly Cults: The Crimes of True Believers*. Westport, Connecticut, Praeger.

Southworth Collection. All materials by permission of the Mandeville Special Collections Library, Geisel Library, University of California at San Diego, 9500 Gilman Drive, La Jolla, California.

Spicehandler, Daniel. (1950) *Let My Right Hand Wither*. New York, Beechhurst.

Staniland, Paul. (2005) "Defeating Transnational Insurgencies." *Washington Quarterly*, 29(1): 21–40.

Stets, Jan E., and Peter J. Burke. (2000) "Identity Theory and Social Identity Theory." *Social Psychology Quarterly*, 63(3): 224–237.

Stiff, Edward. (1840) *The Texan Emigrant*. Cincinnati, Ohio, George Conclin.

Stoker, Donald. (January 15, 2007) "Insurgencies Rarely Win—And Iraq Won't Be Any Different (Maybe)." *Foreign Policy*.

Stout, Jay A. (2008) *Slaughter at Goliad*. Annapolis, Maryland, Naval Institute Press.

Stradling, Robert. (2003) *History and Legend: Writing the International Brigade*. Cardiff, Wales, University of Wales Press.

Sullivan, J. D. (1969) "International Consequences of Domestic Violence: Cross-National Assessment." Presented to the annual meeting of the American Political Science Association, New York, September.

Susman, David. (2004) *An African Shopkeeper*. Simon's Town, South Africa, Fernwood.

Swidler, Ann. (1986) "Culture in Action." *American Sociological Review*, 51(2): 273–286.

Tanner, Marcus. (October 31, 1991) "Foreigners Rally to Croatian Flag." The *Independent*.

Tapp, Hambleton. (January, 1973) "Kentuckians at the Alamo." *Register of the Kentucky Historical Society*, 71(1): 1–29.

Tarrow, Sidney. (2005) *The New Transnational Activism*. New York, Cambridge University Press.

Thomas, Hugh. (2001) *The Spanish Civil War*. New York, Modern Library.

Thomson, Janice. (1994) *Mercenaries, Pirates, and Sovereigns: State-Building and Extraterritorial Violence in Early Modern Europe*. Princeton, New Jersey, Princeton University Press.

Tilly, Charles. (1978) *From Mobilization to Revolution*. Boston, Addison-Wesley.

———. (2002) *Stories, Identities, and Political Change*. Lanham, Maryland, Rowan and Littlefield.

Trofimov, Yaroslav. (2005) *Faith at War: A Journey on the Frontlines of Islam, from Baghdad to Timbuktu*. New York, Henry Holt.

Turnbull, Patrick. (1964) *The Foreign Legion*. London, Heinemann.

United Nations Regional Integrated Information Networks. (September 8, 2005) "DRC: Army to Start Expelling Foreign Fighters on 30 September." All Africa Global Media (AllAfrica.com).

United States Department of State (July 1998) *Possible Loss of U.S. Citizenship and Foreign Military Service*. http://travel.state.gov/law/citizenship/citizenship_780.html.

United States Senate. (1982) *Oral History of Stewart McClure, Part I*. www.senate.gov/artandhistory/history/resources/pdf/McClure1.pdf.

United States Senate Committee on Foreign Relations. (1984) *Hidden War: The Struggle for Afghanistan*. Staff Report 98–181. Washington, DC, U.S. Government Printing Office.

Urry, John. (2003) *Global Complexity*. Cambridge, United Kingdom, Polity.

Vagts, Alfred. (1959) *A History of Militarism*. New York, Meridian.

Valaik, John David. (1964) *American Catholics and the Spanish Civil War 1931–1939*. University of Rochester dissertation, University Microfilms, Ann Arbor, Michigan (1978).

Van Wagenen, Matthew. (2004) *An Analysis of the Indian Government's Counterinsurgency Campaign in Jammu and Kashmir*. U.S. Army General Command and Staff College. www.dtic.mil/cgi-bin/GetTRDoc?AD=ada428962.

Vatikiotis, P. J. (1967) *Politics and the Military in Jordan*. London, Frank Cass.

Vertovec, Steven, and Robin Cohen, eds. (2002) *Conceiving Cosmopolitanism*. Oxford, Oxford University Press.

Walt, Stephen M. (1985) "Alliance Formation and the Balance of World Power." *International Security* 9(4): 3–43.

Ward, Henry F., and A. A. MacLeod. (1936) *Spain's Democracy Talks to America*. New York, American League against War and Fascism.

Wasserman, Stanley, and Katherine Faust. (1994) *Social Network Analysis*. New York, Cambridge University Press.

Watson, Adam. (June 5, 2002) "International Relations and the Practice of Hegemony." Encounter with Adam Watson Lecture, University of Westminster, England. http://www.polis.leeds.ac.uk/assets/files/research/english-school/watson-hegemony02.pdf.

Watts, Clinton. (2008) *How Are Foreign Fighters Recruited?* New York, P J Sage.

Weiss, Jeffrey, and Craig Weiss. (1998) *I Am My Brother's Keeper: American Volunteers in Israel's War of Independence 1947–1949*. Atglen, Pennsylvania, Schiffer Military History.

Westad, Odd Arne. (2005) *The Global Cold War*. New York, Cambridge University Press.

Whitlock, Craig. (June 10, 2006) "Death Could Shake Al Qaeda in Iraq and around the World." *Washington Post.*

———. (February 20, 2007) "Terrorist Networks Lure Young Moroccans to War in Far-Off Iraq." *Washington Post.*

———. (October 19, 2009) "Flow of Terrorist Recruits Increasing." *Washington Post.*

Williams, Rhys H. (1996) "Religion as a Political Resource: Culture or Identity?" *Journal for the Scientific Study of Religion*, 35(4): 368–378.

Winders, Richard Bruce. (2004) *Sacrificed at the Alamo: Tragedy and Triumph in the Texas Revolution.* Abilene, Texas, State House Press.

Witte, Griff, and Shariq Hussain. (December 12, 2009) "Pakistani Officials Unraveling Plot to Send Men to Afghanistan." *Washington Post.*

Wong, Cindy. (June 2002) "Statues to Honor Haitian Soldiers." *Miami Herald.* http://www2.webster.edu/~corbetre/haiti-archive-new/msg12232.html.

Woodhouse, C. M. (1971) *The Philhellenes.* Rutherford, New Jersey, Fairleigh Dickinson University Press.

Woolf, Joe. (2002) "Machal South Africa." *American Veterans of Israel*, Fall: 6–7.

Worthington, Andy. (2007) *The Guantánamo Files.* London, Pluto.

Wright, Lawrence. (2006) *The Looming Tower.* New York, Alfred A. Knopf.

Xenophon Group. (August 14, 2005) *French Volunteers and Supporters of the American Revolution.* http://xenophongroup.com/mcjoynt/volunt.htm.

Young, Kevin R. (1986) *Texas' Forgotten Heroes.* Goliad County Historical Commission (DRTL).

Yousaf, Mohammad, and Mark Adkin. (1992) *The Bear Trap: Afghanistan's Untold Story.* London, Leo Cooper.

Zaagsma, Gerben. (2001) *Jewish Volunteers in the Spanish Civil War: A Case of the Botwin Company.* University of London. http://www.academia.edu/164402/Jewish_volunteers_in_the_Spanish_civil_war._A_case_study_of_the_Botwin_company.

Zaidan, Ahmad Muaffaq. (1999) *The "Afghan Arabs" Media at Jihad.* Islamabad, Pakistan, Pakistan Futuristics Foundation and Institute.

Zeidan, David. (2001) "The Islamist View of Life as a Perennial Battle." *Middle East Review of International Affairs*, 5(4): 26–53.

Index

Printed in the USA/Agawam, MA
July 9, 2014

592785.016